STORM KIN
ART CENTE
SCULPTURE
GUIDE

MW01615478

WWW.STORMKING.ORG

Published by
STORM KING ART CENTER
1 Museum Road
New Windsor, NY 12553
+1 (845) 534-3115
info@stormkingartcenter.org

www.stormking.org

ISBN: 978-0-9991183-0-6
Library of Congress Control Number: 2017945657

Printed in Iceland
Designed by Omnivore

This project is supported in part by an award from the
National Endowment for the Arts. Additional support
is provided by the Charina Endowment Fund and
Sidney E. Frank Foundation.

Contributors:
Theresa Choi
Ellen Grenley
Nora R. Lawrence
Victoria Lichtendorf

Some entries are based in part on past writing and research
for Storm King Art Center by Marie Busco, Ursula Lee,
Maureen Megarian, Joan Pachner, and Susan Fisher Sterling.

Many thanks to Mary Ann Carter and Anthony Davidowitz
for their work on this project. Additional thanks to Rachel
Coker, Elizabeth Harmon, and Colleen Zlock.

Edited by Jennifer Liese.

COVER: Alexander Calder, *The Arch*, 1975
INSIDE FRONT COVER: Alexander Liberman, *Adam*, 1970
INSIDE BACK COVER, FROM LEFT: Menashe Kadishman, *Suspended*, 1977;
Alice Aycock, *Three-fold Manifestation II*, 1987 (refabricated 2006)

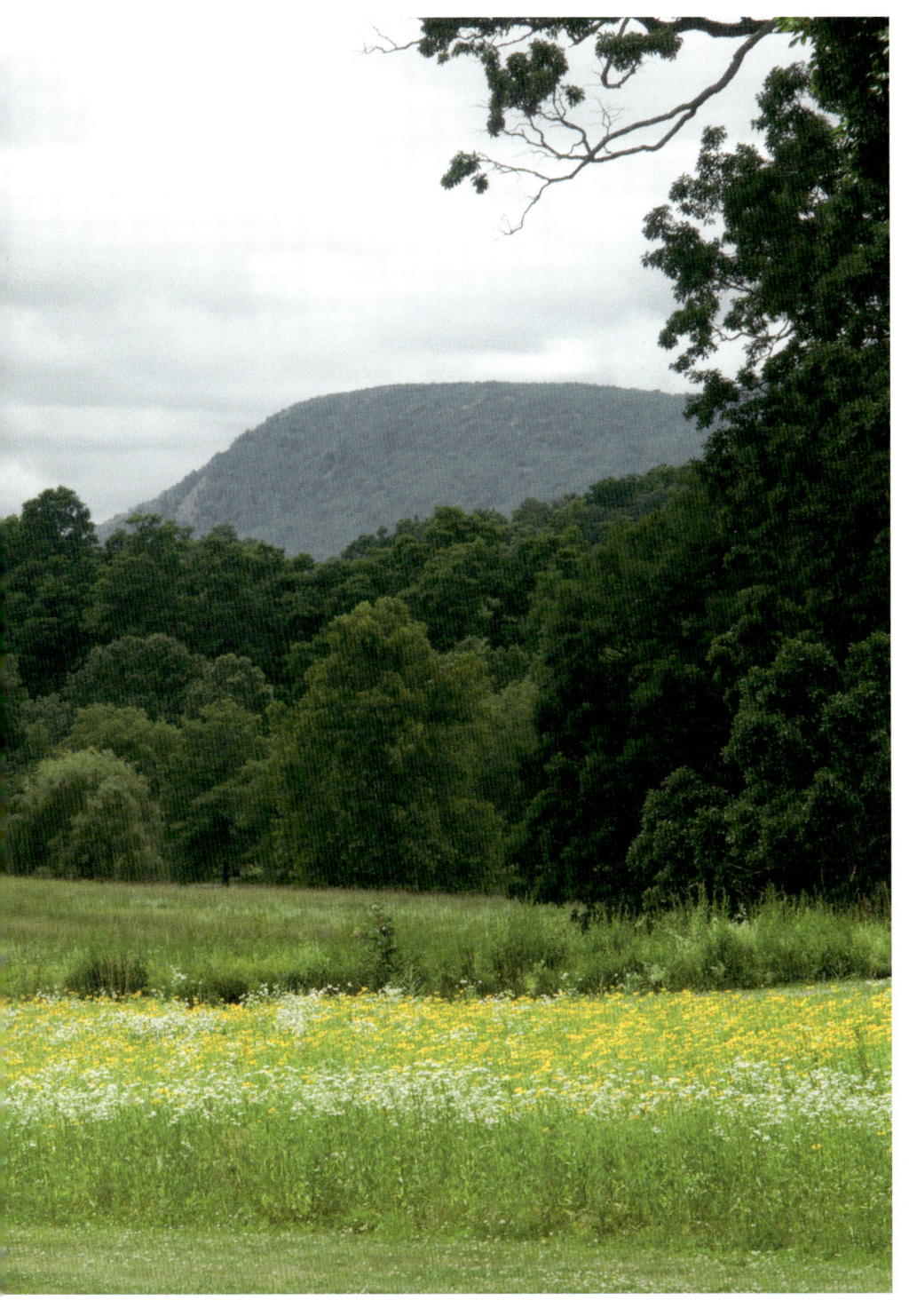

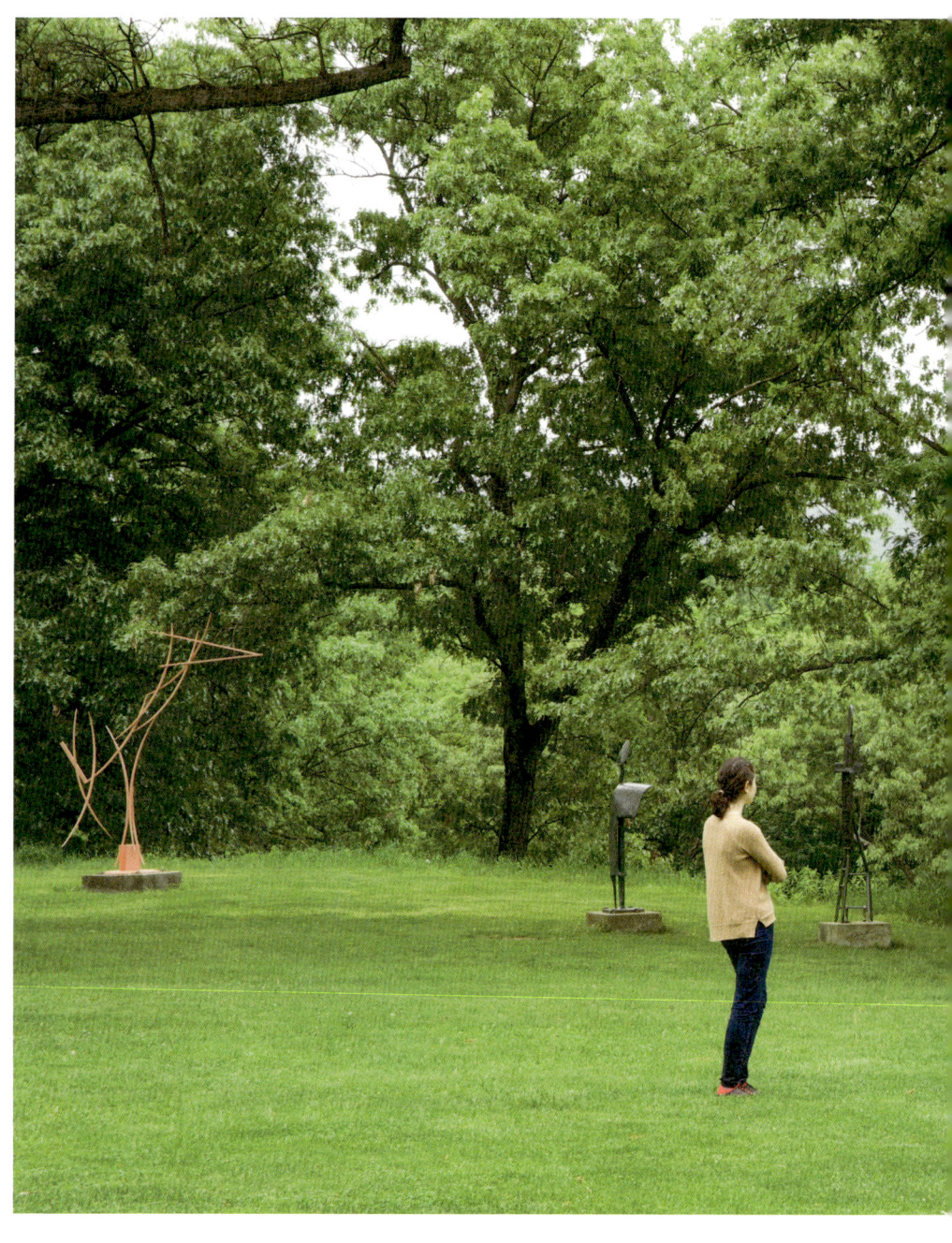

Partial view of the David Smith Collection. FROM LEFT: *Study in Arcs*, 1957; *Personage of May*, 1957; *The Sitting Printer*, 1954-55; *Becca*, 1964, and *XI Books III Apples*, 1959

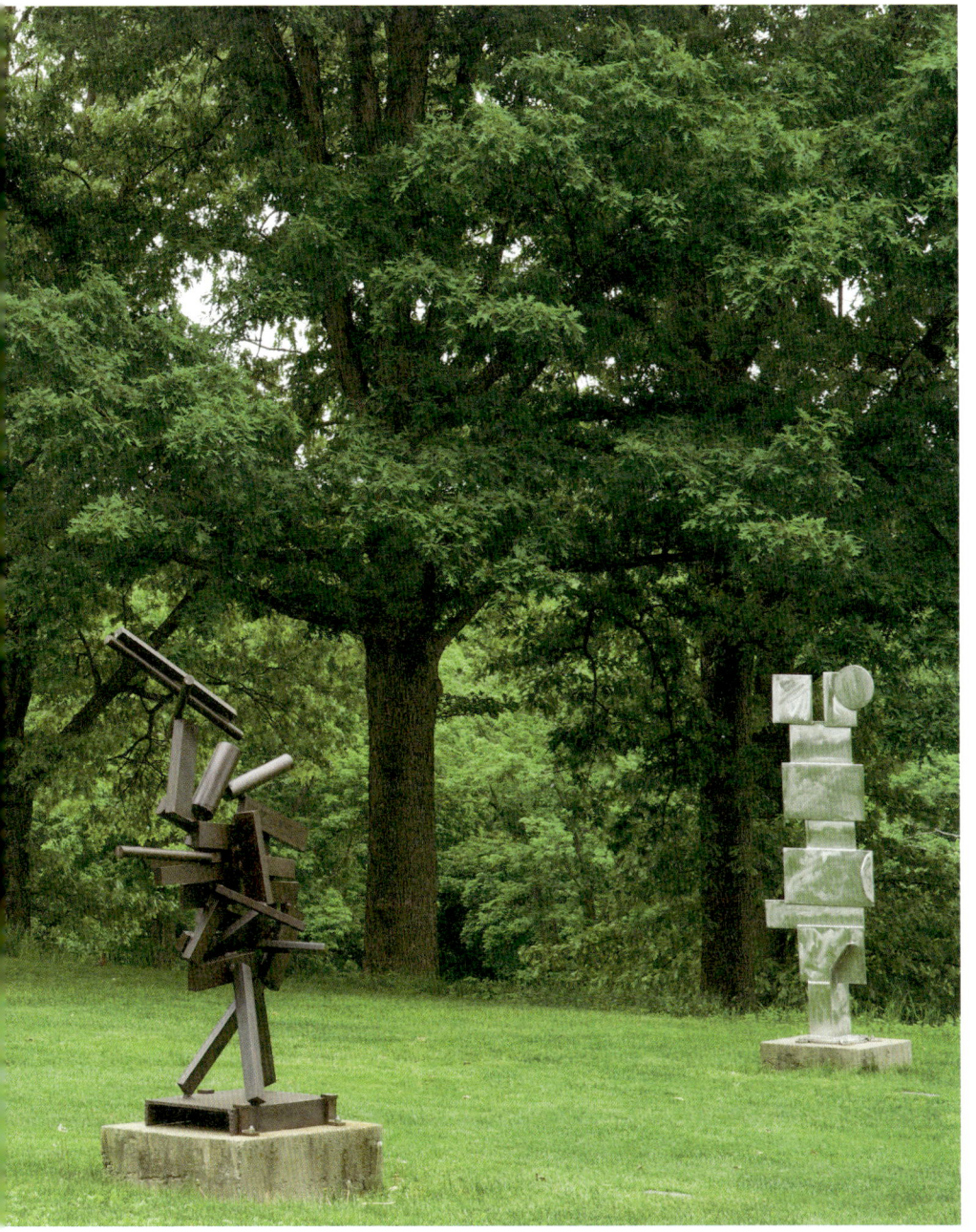

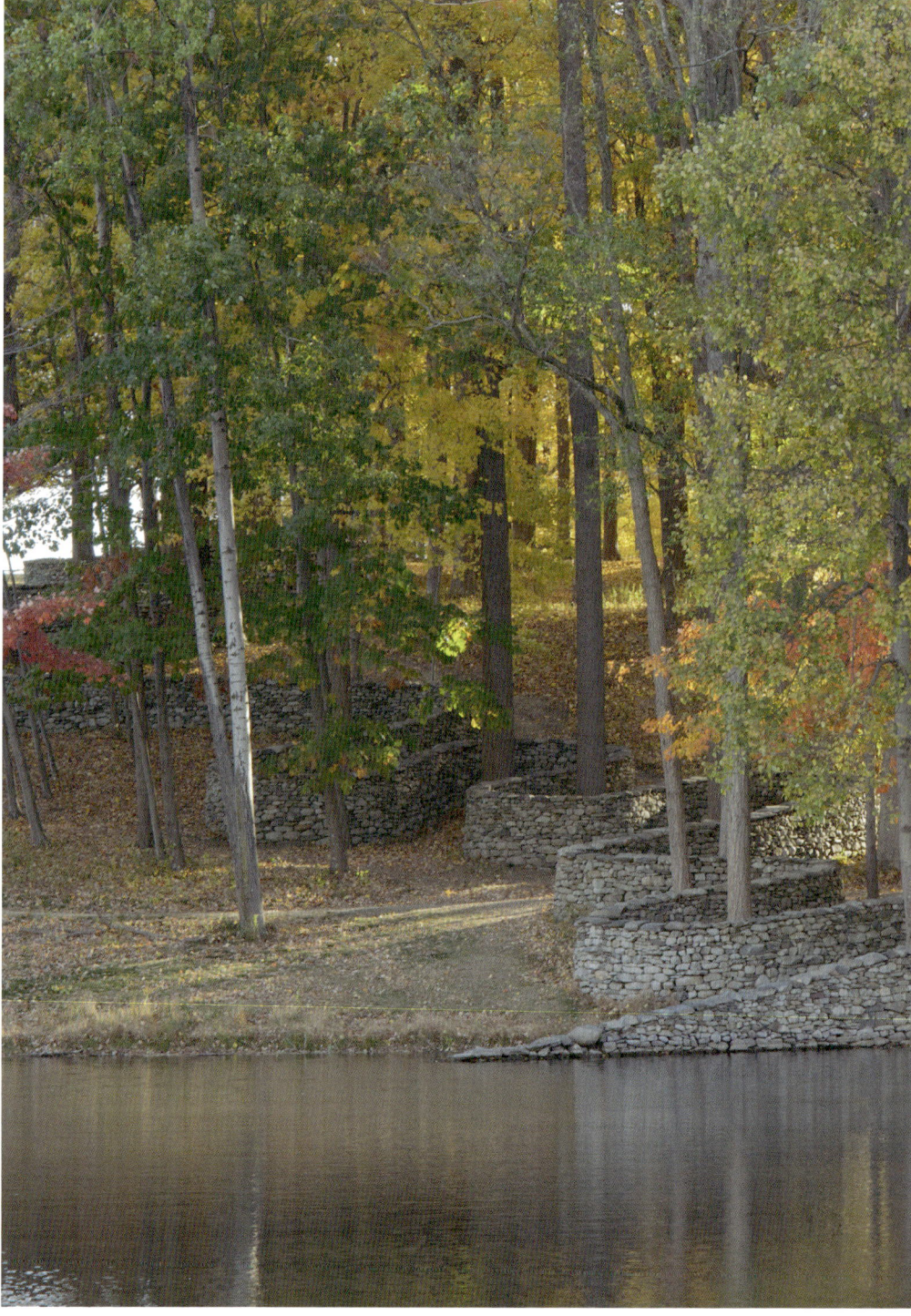

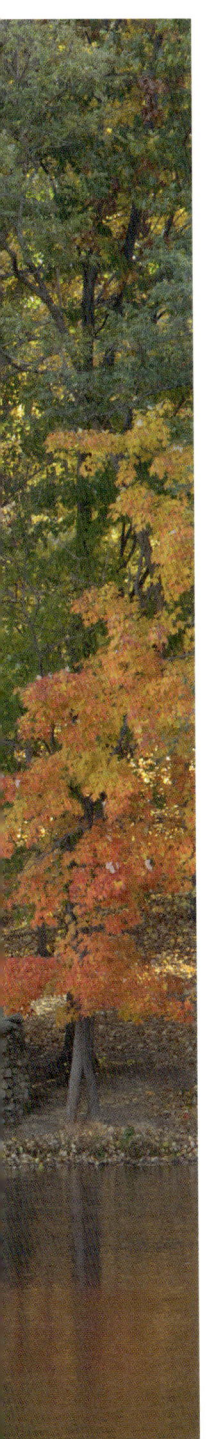

INTRODUCTION

Taking its name from nearby Storm King Mountain, a majestic peak overlooking the Hudson River, Storm King Art Center was founded by Ralph E. Ogden in 1960 with the ambition of establishing an innovative center for visual art and music. From the start, Ogden sought the assistance of his son-in-law, Storm King's Founding Chair and President, H. Peter Stern—who had also been recruited by Ogden to run the family manufacturing business, Star Expansion Company. Ogden and Stern would go on to lead the development of one of the world's preeminent sculpture parks.

The Art Center began with indoor exhibitions in the Museum Building—a Normandy-style chateau designed by Maxwell Kimball and built in 1935 by Ogden's friend, Vermont Hatch, as a weekend house. After Hatch's death in 1959, Ogden purchased the house and some twenty-three acres of the Hatch Estate (the area now known as Museum Hill) for Storm King through the Ralph E. Ogden Foundation. Ogden did not have a significant art collection, but he wanted to learn more about art and to pursue his interests in preserving open space, farming, and landscape.

In 1961 Ogden traveled to Austria, where he purchased five sculptures that he subsequently sited on Storm King's grounds. In 1966 he visited the home and studio of the late sculptor David Smith in Bolton Landing, New York, in the Adirondack Mountains. As an engineer and farmer, Ogden was intrigued by Smith's use of industrial techniques and found materials, and he especially admired how the artist had sited more than eighty

Andy Goldsworthy, *Storm King Wall*, 1997–98

sculptures outdoors in the fields—Smith had referred to his property in Bolton Landing as a "sculpture farm"—with spectacular mountain views. In early 1967 Ogden acquired thirteen of Smith's sculptures for Storm King, still the largest purchase of the artist's sculptures at one time, and these works became the core of the collection. The historic acquisition marked a turning point for Storm King, with Ogden deciding to focus on large-scale outdoor sculpture. His vision was carried forward by Stern and David R. Collens, Storm King's Director and Chief Curator, who joined Storm King in 1974.

In the winter of 1975–76, after Ogden's death, Stern met Mark di Suvero. The artist was exhibiting his large-scale sculptures outdoors across the five boroughs of New York City in conjunction with a retrospective of the artist's work at the Whitney Museum of American Art. Stern invited di Suvero to bring some of these works to Storm King, forging what would become a decades-long connection between the museum and the artist. The pioneering placement of di Suvero's work in former farm fields led to the consideration of new sites by other artists and Collens. In the past three decades, three artists have chosen to locate large site-specific commissions around the property: Richard Serra in a southern farm field; Andy Goldsworthy at the forest's edge; and Maya Lin in a former gravel pit.

Since its founding, major landscaping projects have been central to Storm King's trajectory, fostering a close dialogue between art and nature. The five-hundred-acre grounds were acquired over time in order to exhibit an expanding outdoor sculpture collection, as well as for the preservation of views and open space. In the mid-1950s many of the neighboring farms and estates had been severely impacted by the construction of the New York State Thruway, directly west of the Art Center. Large open gravel pits remained in the ravaged landscape. Ogden, joined by William A. Rutherford, Storm King's talented landscape architect, set out to reclaim and transform the land in what Rutherford described as a visionary art and environmental project. Rutherford worked with Ogden, Stern, and Collens to design future sites for sculpture installation, prioritizing long views of the Hudson Highlands, Black Rock Forest, and Storm King Mountain (all located east and south of Storm King), as well as of Schunnemunk State Park (to the west). One of the most ambitious projects was the creation, over a five-year period in the 1980s, of a grand hillside and walking path from Museum Hill to the South Fields. Gravel was shaped into the gentle slope on which four sculptures by Alexander Calder are located today. This building and the transformation of the landscape have been accompanied by an ongoing dedication to maintenance and conservation of Storm King's flora and fauna. Storm King has planted tall native grasses and conducts controlled burns to reinvigorate the soil and reduce invasive species. The native grasses have been joined in recent years by native wildflowers, which attract and sustain insects, honeybees, butterflies, and birds.

Decades of vision have created this unique place to experience art and nature. Today, Storm King remains committed to supporting artists, presenting ambitious exhibition and public programming, pursuing thoughtful landscape design and preservation, and creating educational opportunities and moments of discovery for all visitors.

FOLLOWING SPREAD: View of the South Fields; all works by Mark di Suvero, FROM LEFT: *Pyramidian*, 1987/1998; *Beethoven's Quartet*, 2003; *Mon Père, Mon Père*, 1973-75; *Mother Peace*, 1969-70

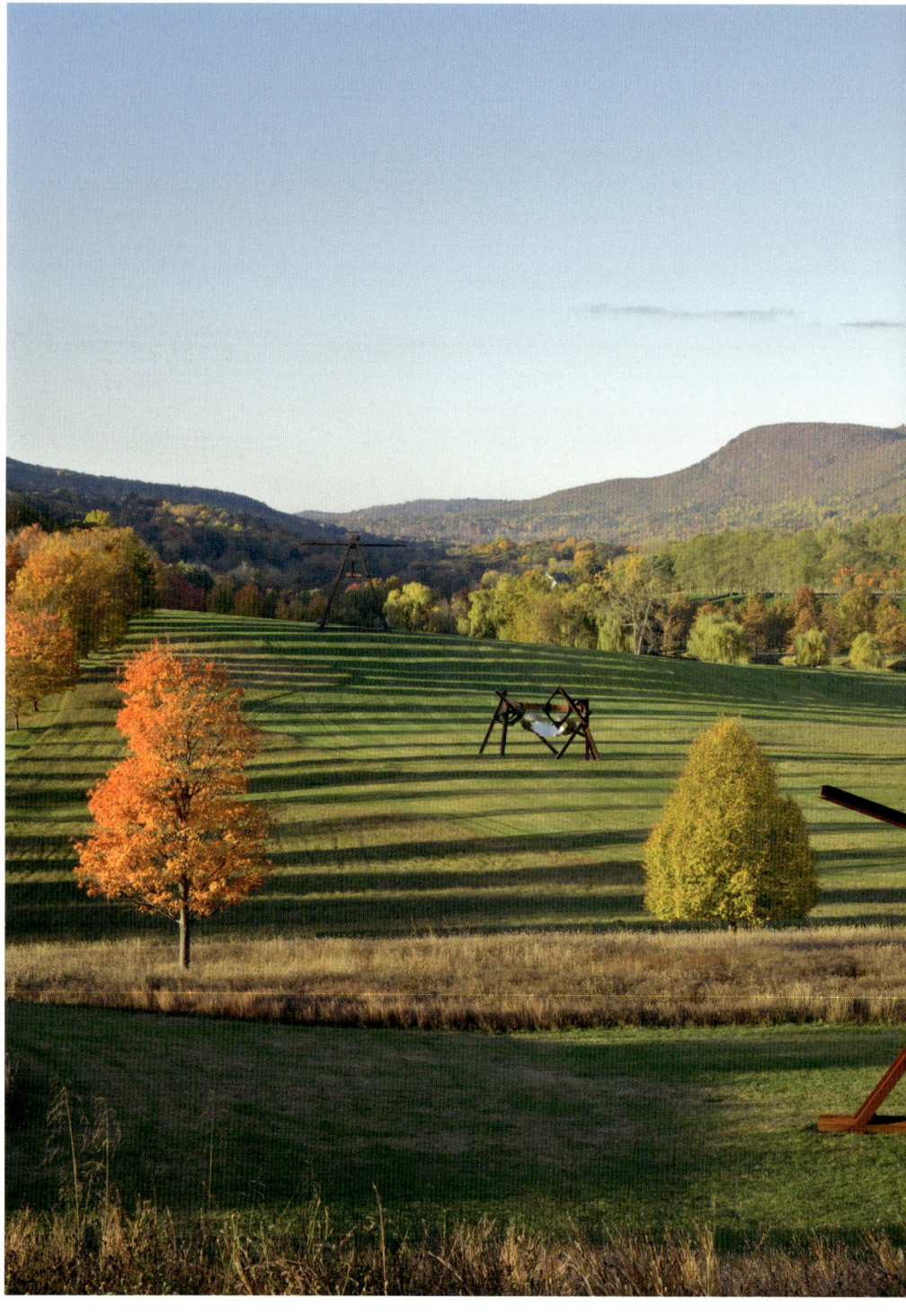

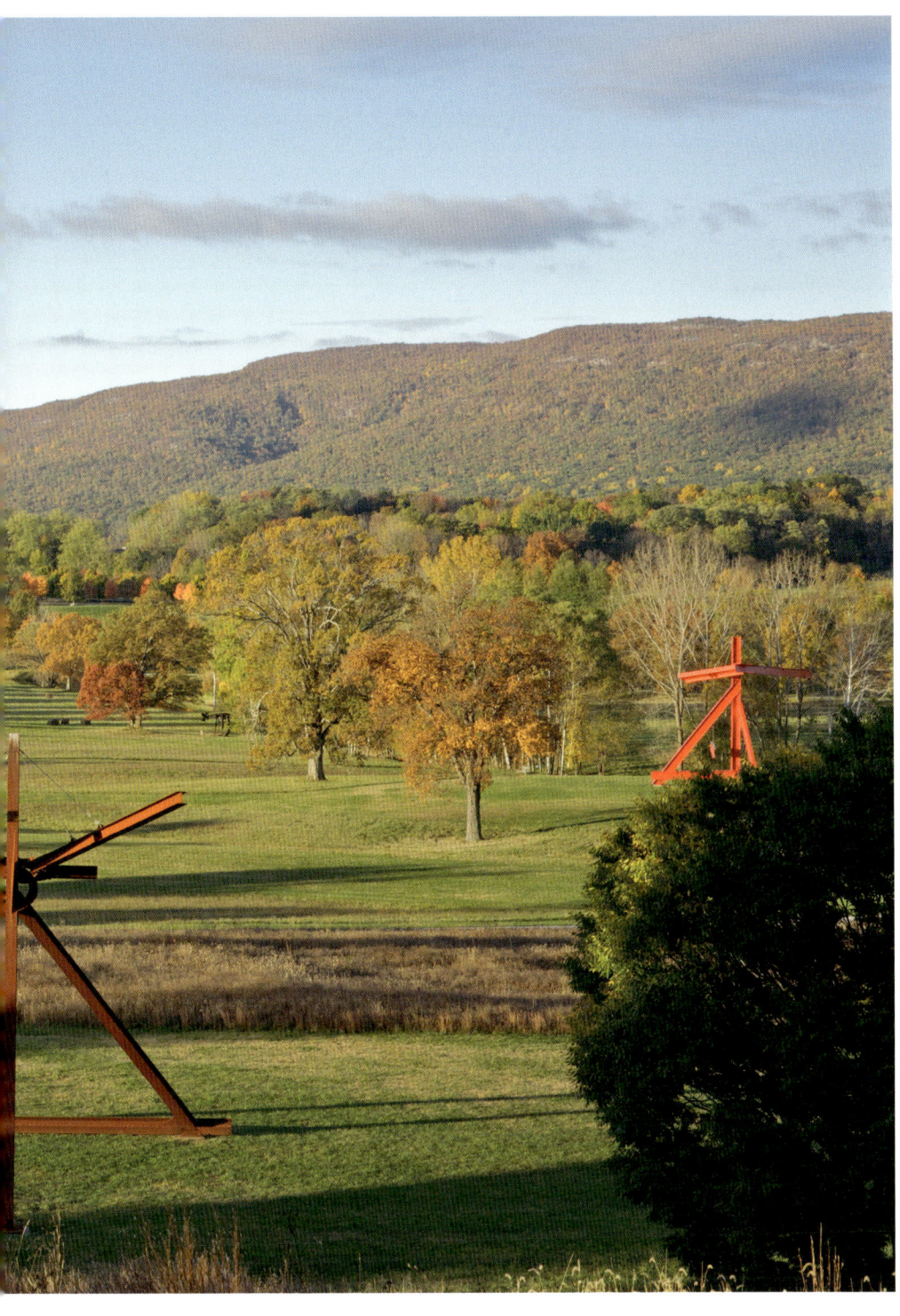

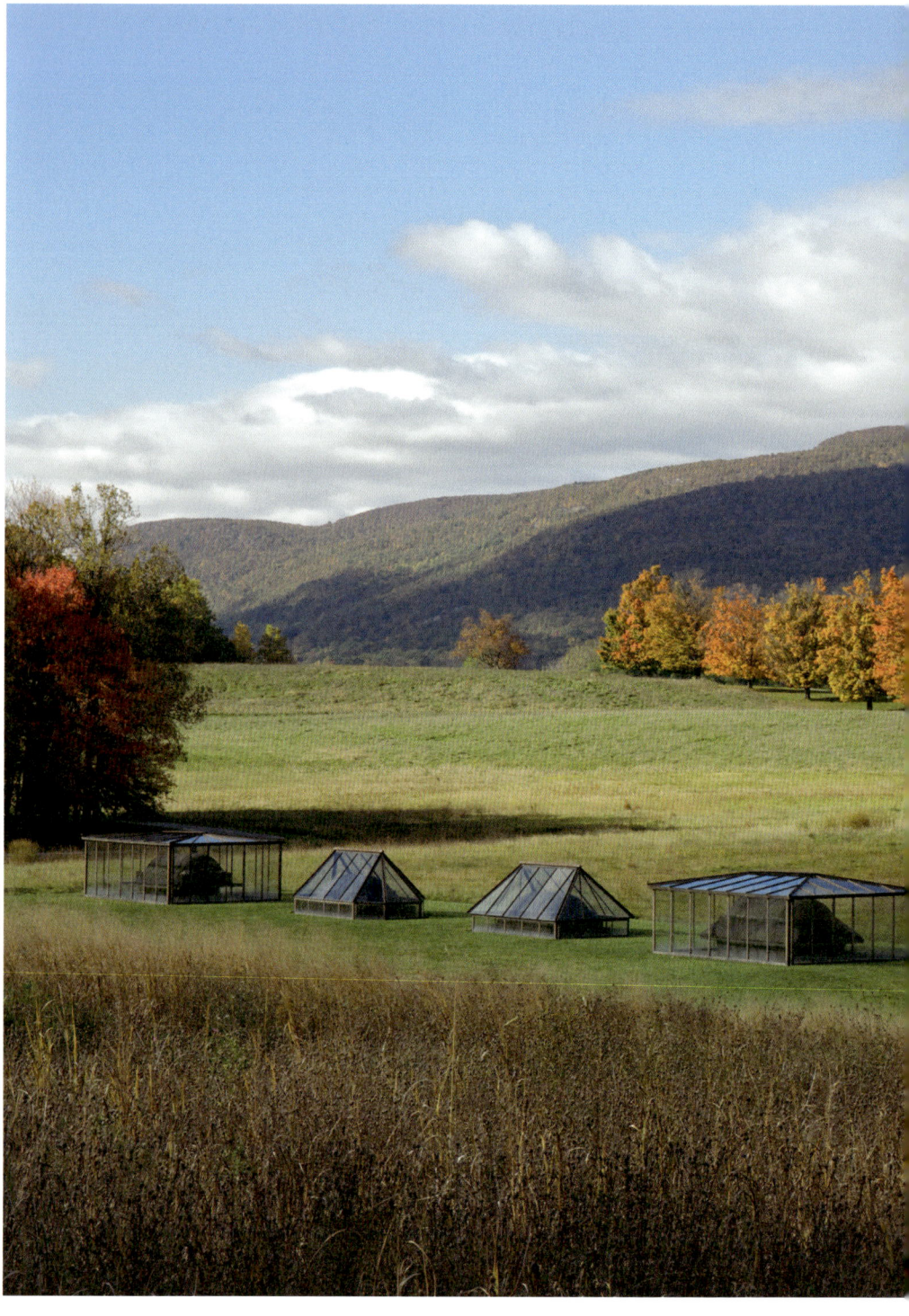

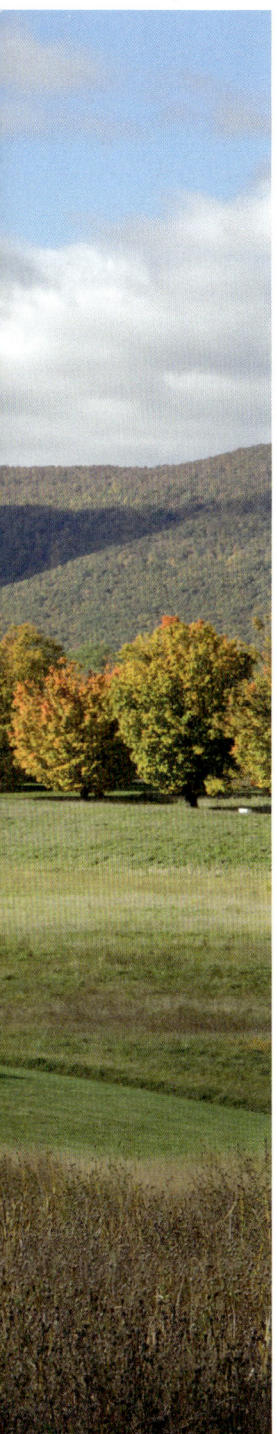

MAGDALENA ABAKANOWICZ

POLISH, 1930–2017

SARCOPHAGI IN GLASS HOUSES, 1989
WOOD, GLASS, AND IRON
8' 6½" x 17' 2½" x 143' 3" OVERALL

GIFT OF THE ARTIST; ADDITIONAL SUPPORT PROVIDED BY ERNEST
AND PATRICIA OHNELL, THE RALPH E. OGDEN FOUNDATION,
CYNTHIA HAZEN POLSKY, THE HORACE W. GOLDSMITH FOUNDATION,
JIM AND MARY OTTAWAY, THE MARGARET T. MORRIS FOUNDATION,
THE JOSEPH H. HAZEN FOUNDATION PURCHASE FUND, VERA G.
LIST, AND SHERRY AND JOEL MALLIN

The central elements of this sculpture, the sarcophagi, were originally parts from models used for casting engines by arms manufacturer Schneider-Creusot, in Le Creusot, near Lyon, in the nineteenth and twentieth centuries. In 1982 Magdalena Abakanowicz was invited by the French cultural ministry to visit the industrial district of Le Creusot. There, she found a selection of monumental casting models—engines for ships, submarines, canons, turbines, and other machinery. Cutting away parts to focus on the essential form of each model, Abakanowicz revealed inner swelling shapes that suggested human bellies. She saw an analogy between the energy generated by the turbine engine and that created by the belly. The oak forms were installed on new bases and enclosed in glass and steel structures, both to protect them and to contain the potential energy they represented.

Abakanowicz, born to aristocratic parents on a family estate near Warsaw, grew up a lonely, introspective child. The horrors and trauma of World War II she experienced as an adolescent and later restrictions under the Communist regime indelibly stamped the character of her art. Abakanowicz's mysterious sculptures allude to violence, loss, decay, and mourning.

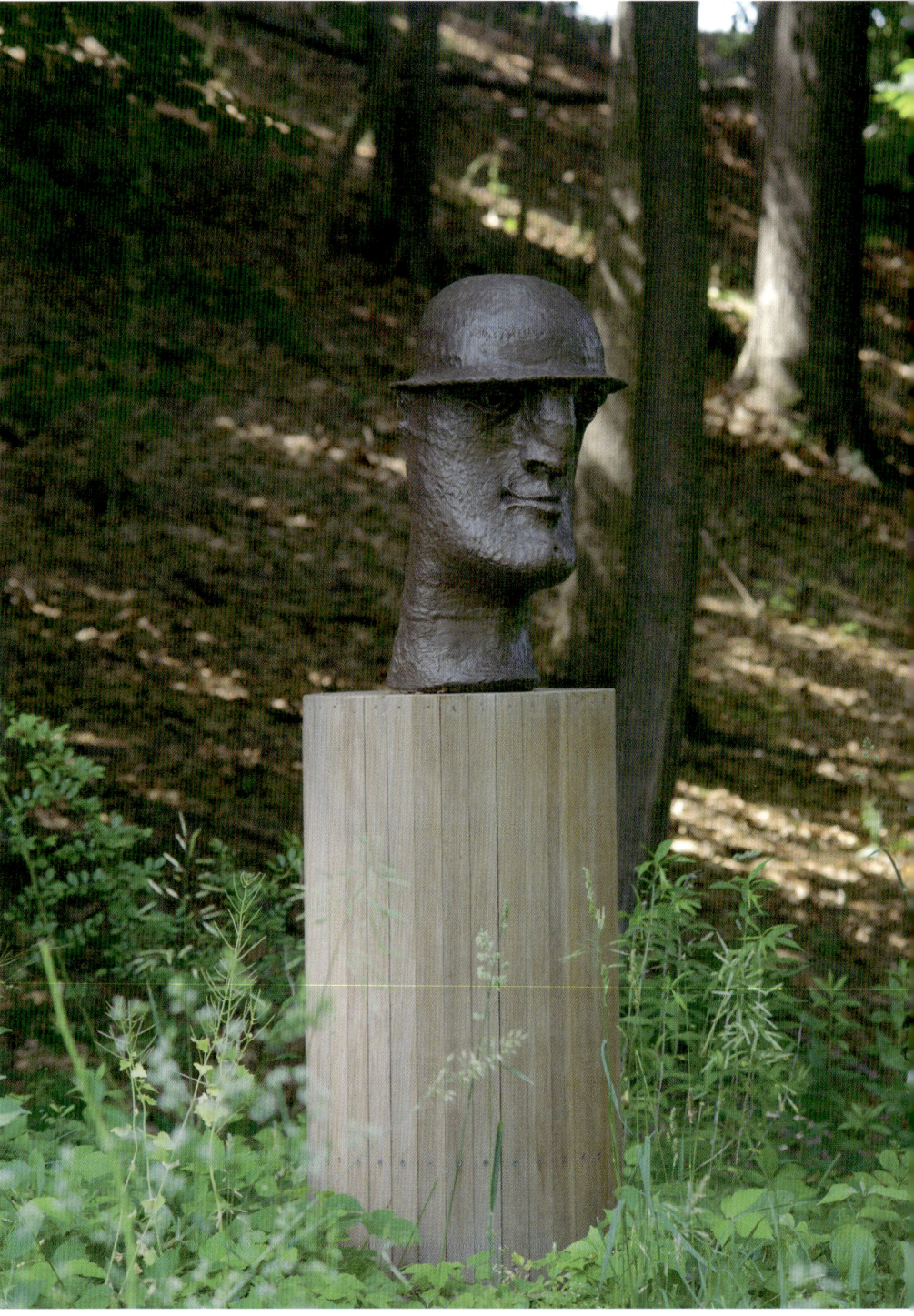

KOSTA ALEX

AMERICAN, 1925–2005

MAN WITH A HAT, #7, 1958
BRONZE
26 ½ x 14 ½ x 13 ½"
GIFT OF THE RALPH E. OGDEN FOUNDATION

In the early part of his career Kosta Alex made symbolic sculptures
reminiscent of Surrealist stage sets. Beginning in the 1950s he turned
to abstract portraiture, a focus that culminated in his "Man with a Hat"
series. Alex claims to have conceived the idea in 1939, but the first known
bust in the series dates from 1951 and depicts a man wearing a Napoleonic-
style hat. By 1969 Alex had made ninety-four variations on the theme;
he stopped making these works after that year. The busts are characterized by abstracted, even schematic facial features and roughly modeled
surfaces. Many are humorous or whimsical in attitude, while others
exhibit a distinctly melancholic mood. According to the artist, this elemental image of a man wearing a hat was originally inspired by his
memory of a man with a Yiddish accent singing the American national
anthem in 1939—on the eve of World War II. This larger than life-size
bronze bust of a man wearing a Derby hat low on his forehead is an
example of the series that has defined Alex's career.

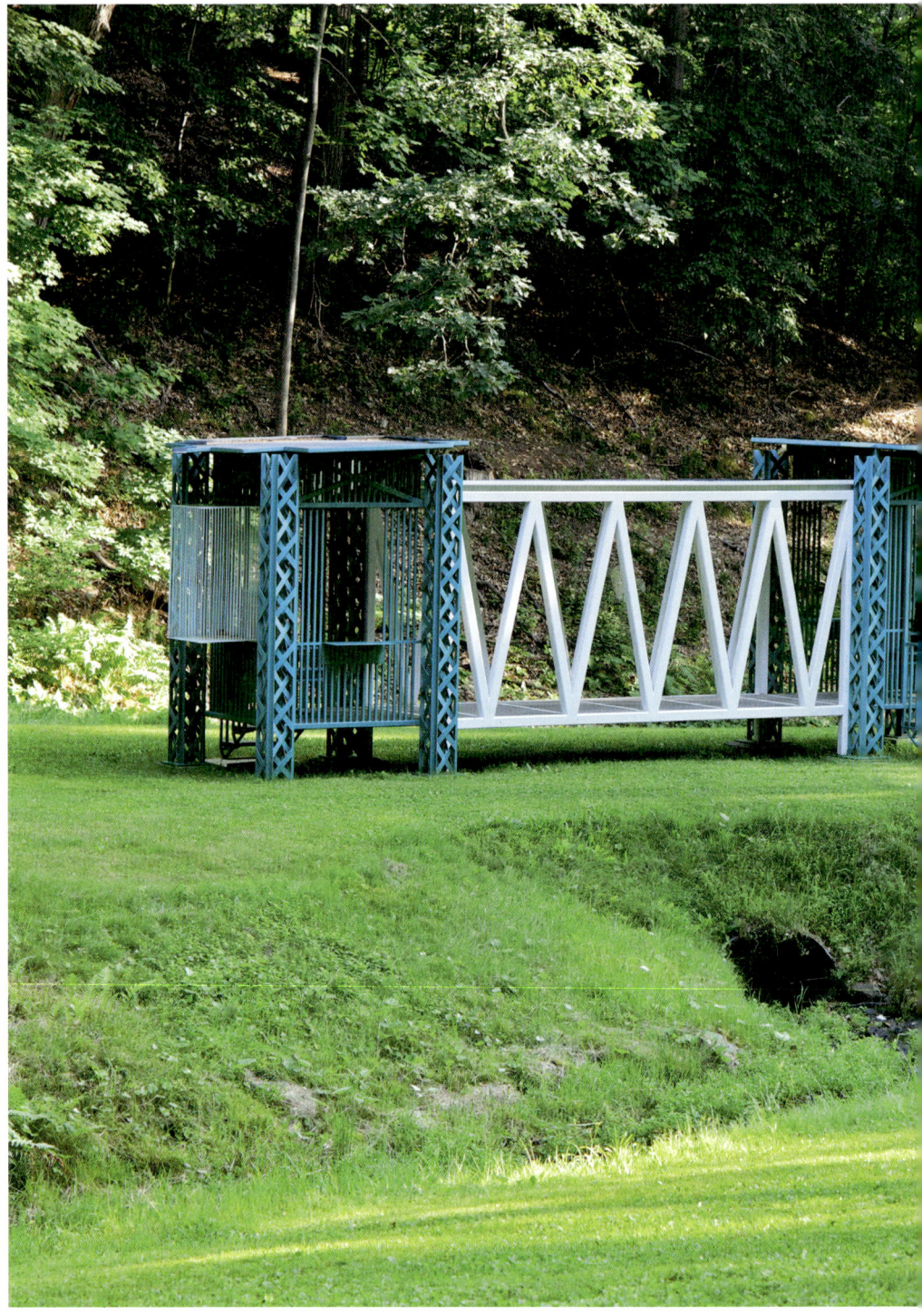

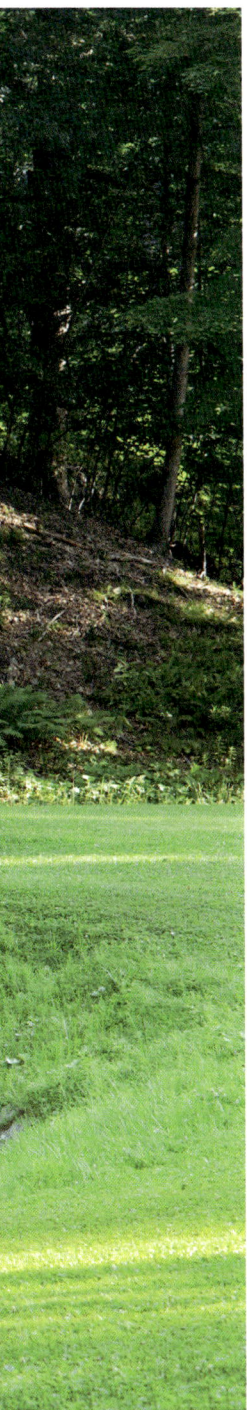

SIAH ARMAJANI

AMERICAN, BORN IRAN, 1939

GAZEBO FOR TWO ANARCHISTS: GABRIELLA ANTOLINI AND ALBERTO ANTOLINI, 1992
PAINTED STEEL AND WOOD
10' 6" x 32' 6" x 8' 5"
GIFT OF THE BROWN FOUNDATION, INC., THE RALPH E. OGDEN FOUNDATION, CYNTHIA HAZEN POLSKY, AN ANONYMOUS FOUNDATION, GIFTS IN MEMORY OF ELIZABETH COLLENS, AND THE JOSEPH H. HAZEN FOUNDATION PURCHASE FUND

Gazebo for Two Anarchists is one of several works Siah Armajani has dedicated to twentieth-century anarchists—in this case, brother and sister Alberto and Gabriella Antolini, the latter of whom was imprisoned for transportation of explosives in the Youngstown Affair in 1918. The open lattice, or truss-work, of *Gazebo for Two Anarchists* suggests incarceration, while the elegance of the design almost belies this interpretation. The two gazebos at each end of the structure appear to symbolize the brother and sister, who are separated but nonetheless connected by the bridge. Each gazebo encloses a large chair with armrests that recall thrones or electric chairs. They are facing one another, suggesting an act of communication. The artist has transformed the gazebo, traditionally a picturesque garden folly, into a vehicle for political expression. It is no longer merely a site to contemplate the natural environment, but to meditate on the nature of democracy.

An Iranian-born American artist, Armajani is known for his politically resonant, large-scale, interactive environmental sculptures that merge sculpture with architecture. His sculptures, walking bridges, and reading rooms are created as functional places for people to use and enjoy. Armajani has created sculpture for plazas, parks, and other urban landscapes, as well as rural locations. The design of *Gazebo for Two Anarchists*, and most of Armajani's structures, is inspired by vernacular American architecture, but here the steel truss-work suggests civic engineering.

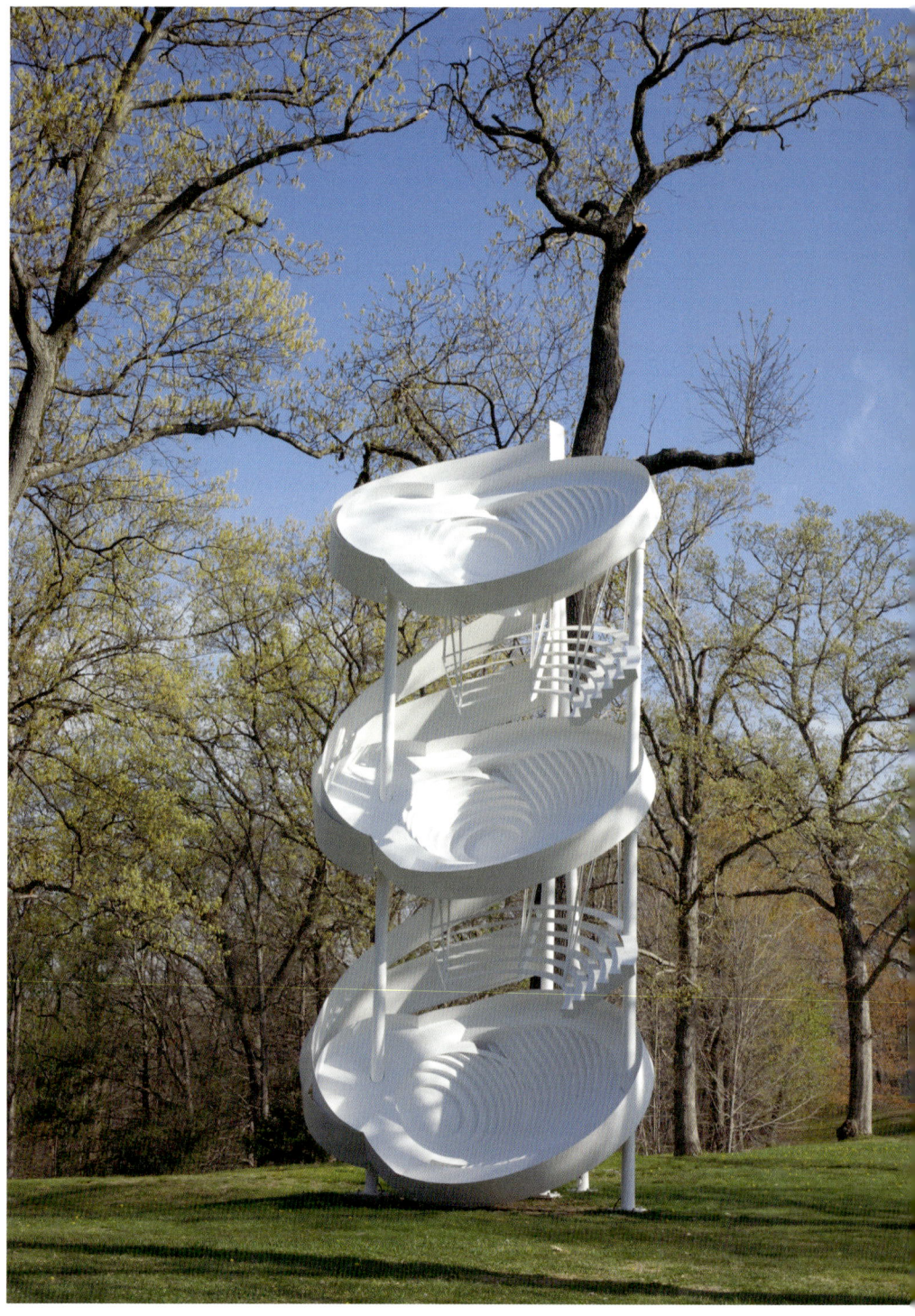

ALICE AYCOCK

AMERICAN, BORN 1946

THREE-FOLD MANIFESTATION II, 1987 (REFABRICATED 2006)
PAINTED ALUMINUM AND STAINLESS STEEL
29'3" x 14' x 12'
GIFT OF THE ARTIST

LOW BUILDING WITH DIRT ROOF (FOR MARY), 1973/2010
WOOD, STONE, AND EARTH
2'6" x 20' x 12'
GIFT OF THE ARTIST

Although the two works by Alice Aycock on view at Storm King—*Low Building with Dirt Roof (For Mary)* and *Three-Fold Manifestation II*—are quite different in aesthetic and significance, both are based in part in Aycock's interest in architectural structures and the archaeology of the ancient Mediterranean. *Low Building with Dirt Roof (For Mary)* was first created in 1973—a time when many artists were working with the earth as an artistic medium—at Gibney Farm, Pennsylvania, land owned by Aycock's family. There, its roof was intended to be planted with whatever crop was growing in the fields surrounding it. Aycock has associated *Low Building* with both a farmhouse and a small cemetery on her family's property. Mary, of the work's title and dedication, was a child in Aycock's family who died prematurely. Aycock also has said that she was inspired by "frontier homes, the tunnels and tombs of Mycenae, the myth of Clytemnestra and Agamemnon, dreams, the memory of my grandparents' attic," and finally adds, "I also have a shelter concept—a sort of physiological need for a 'first house'." The work was re-created at Storm King in 2010.

Aycock's fantastical and complex *Three-Fold Manifestation II* arrived at Storm King in 1987, in advance of a retrospective exhibition of her work. Its form is reminiscent of Roman amphitheaters, one atop the other, and alludes to wide-ranging sources including archeology, science, and astrology. Aycock has noted that her initial inspiration originated with Walter Gropius's unexecuted designs for three theaters. As Aycock has stated of the work, "I was working a lot with these stepped bowl-like forms; I would take astronomical diagrams and imagine the space that would be generated by these diagrams. These bowls or whirling, skewed spaces are tipped, so it's as though you're looking into disoriented worlds…. During the Medieval period and the Renaissance they illustrated people walking off to paradise through a whirling hole in the world, a tumbling structure."

LEFT: *Three-Fold Manifestation II*, 1987 (refabricated 2006)

FOLLOWING SPREAD: *Low Building with Dirt Roof (For Mary)*, 1973/2010

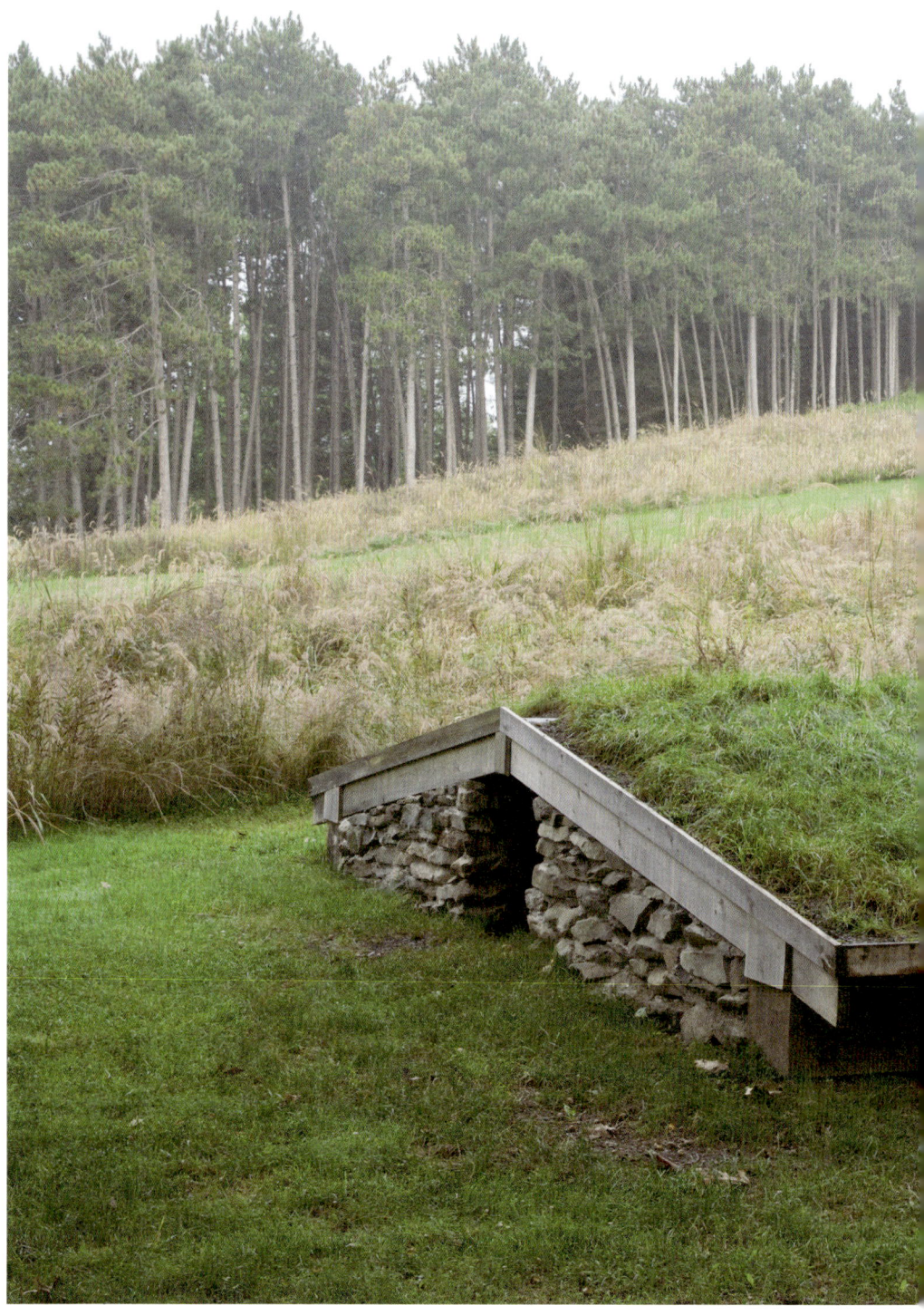

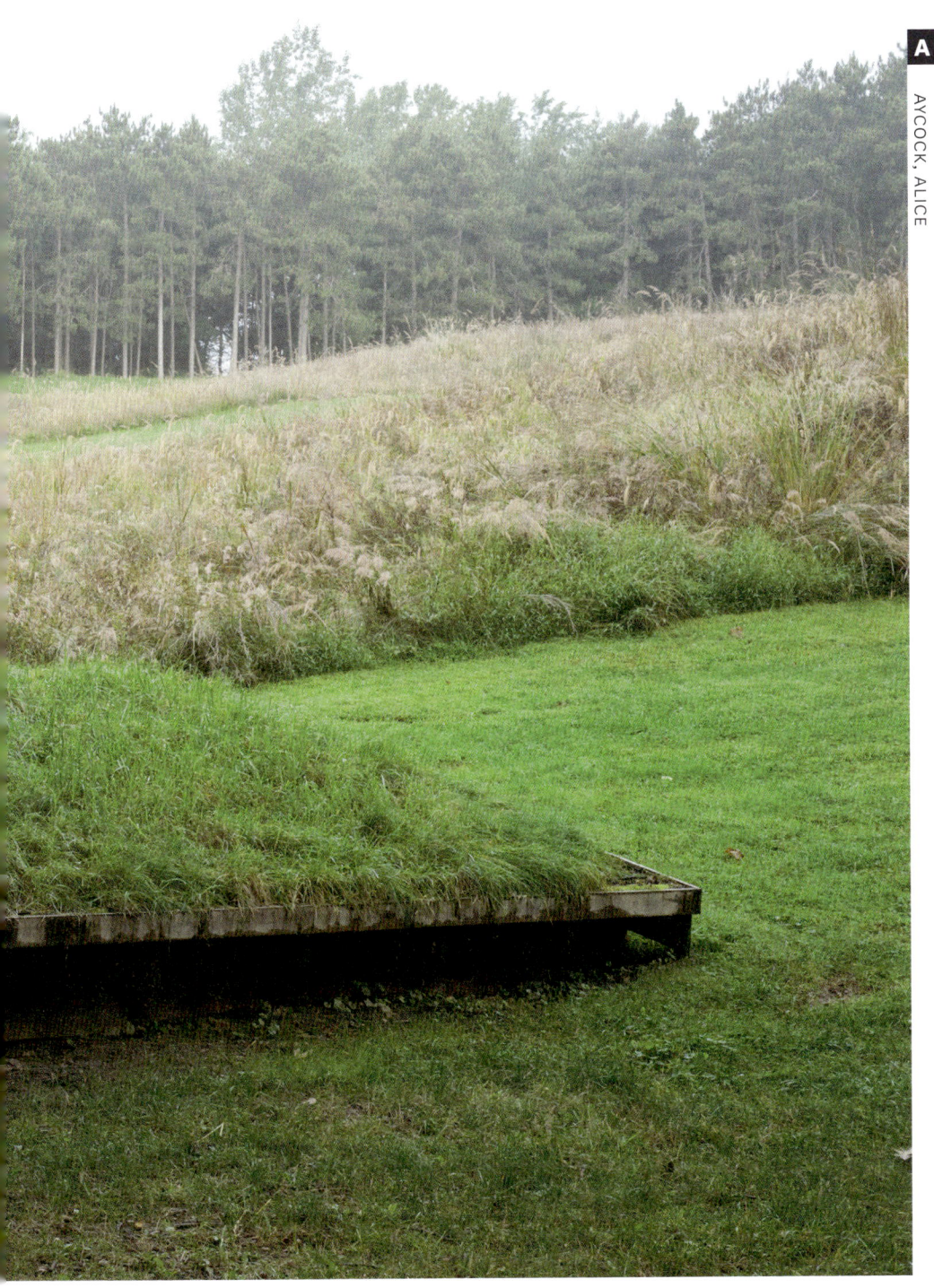

A

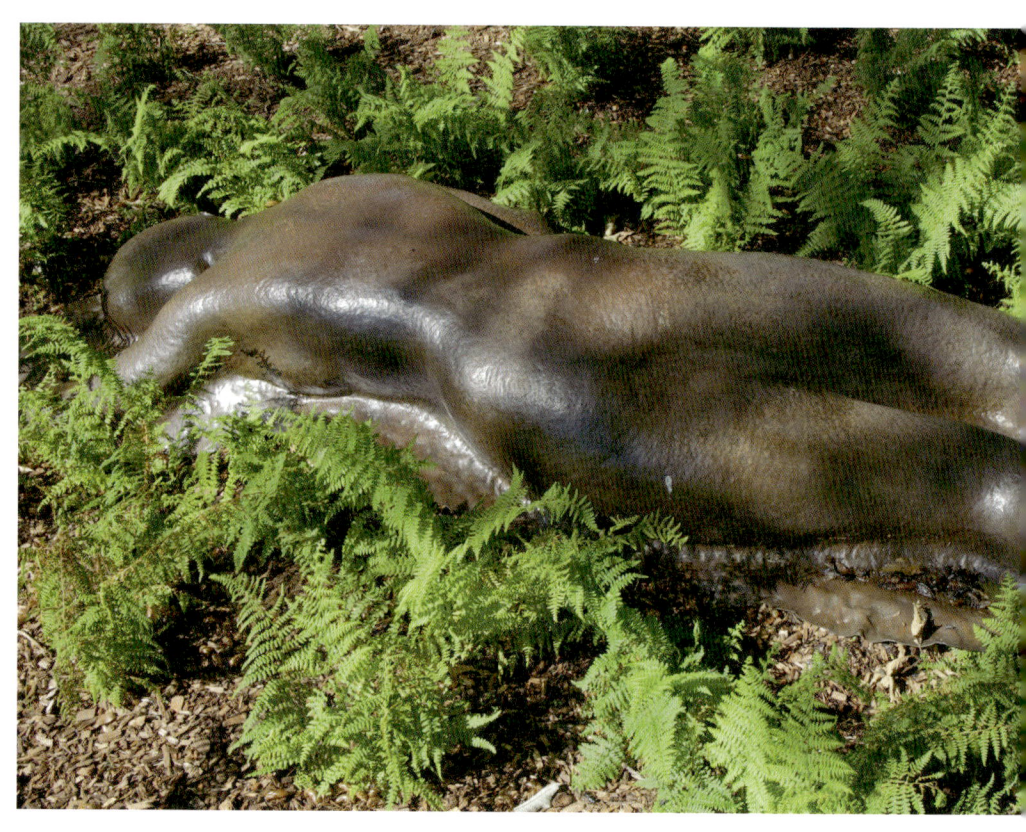

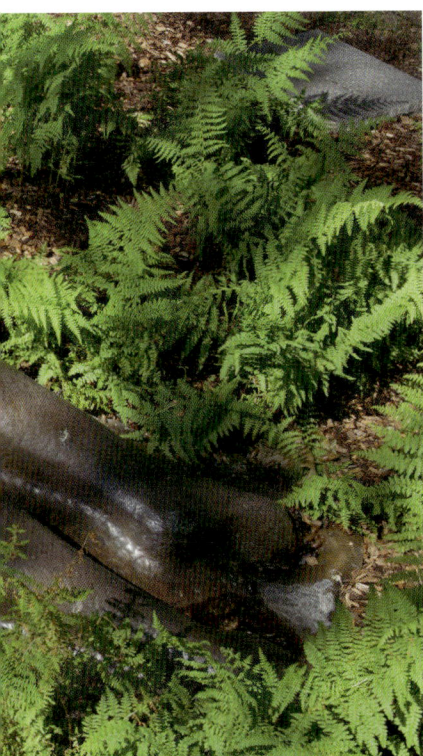

SAUL BAIZERMAN

AMERICAN, BORN RUSSIA, 1889–1957

APHRODITE, CA. 1940–48
HAMMERED COPPER
14" x 8' x 30"
GIFT OF THE RALPH E. OGDEN FOUNDATION

Russian-born American artist Saul Baizerman revitalized the classical tradition of the nude figure with his evocative hammered copper reliefs. In the early 1930s he discovered the expressive power of this direct metal technique while working on small bronzes. His father had been a harness maker in Russia, and had similarly employed hammers in his trade. For the preliminary shaping of the sheet metal, he used a rubber and wooden mallet; the more detailed work was done with a double-headed hammer. He worked both sides of the copper sheet simultaneously in a process central to his artistic expression.

Throughout his long, prolific career, Baizerman remained dedicated to the representation of the human form. He often conceived his figural reliefs on a heroic scale and gave them classicizing titles to impart a universal and timeless vision. Moreover, Baizerman employed the human figure as a metaphor for emotion or nature. He once said, "We sense in these pieces, although of human shape, movements of nature in rivers, in sloping mountains, in the flatness of fields…or the turbulence of the sea." *Aphrodite* is a late work, completed when Baizerman was nearly sixty; it expresses his abiding concern for fluid movement and illustrates his use of the human figure to evoke a force of nature.

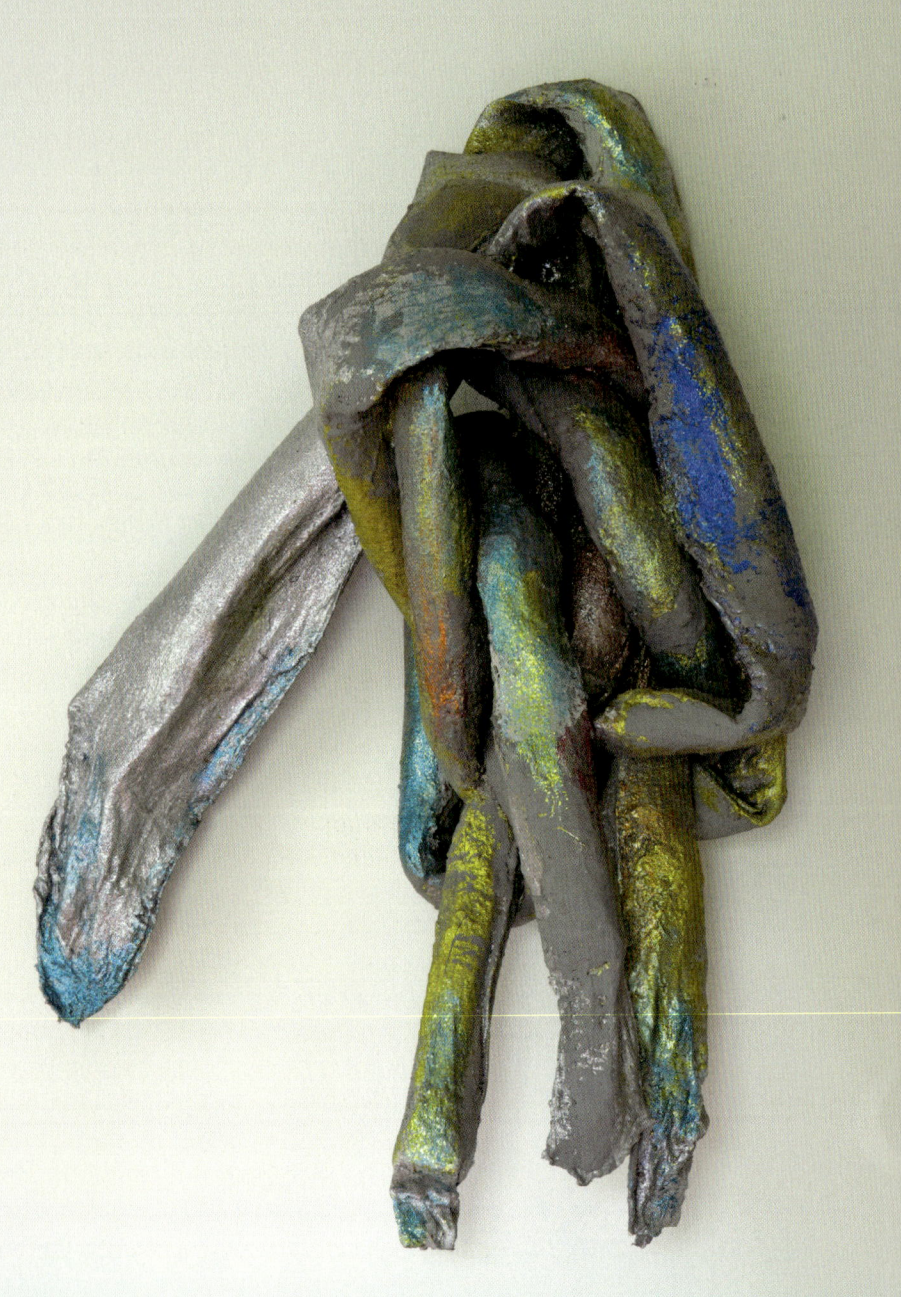

LYNDA BENGLIS

AMERICAN, BORN 1941

NU, 1974
ALUMINUM SCREEN, CHEESECLOTH, PLASTER, METAL, PAINT, AND SPARKLE
43½ x 29 x 15"
GIFT OF THE RALPH E. OGDEN FOUNDATION

Lynda Benglis produced a series of intricate knots made from tubes of wire screening throughout the 1970s. *Nu* is titled after the Greek letter— a reference to Benglis's Greek background. This relatively small, abstract, indoor work was acquired for Storm King's permanent collection in 1974, shortly after it was seen in the artist's one-person exhibition at Paula Cooper Gallery in New York. Although the form is clearly visible in *Nu*, it also captures something inaccessible and unknowable. Its materials are far from obvious, with its rigid metal surface and contradictory organic curves. The sculpture is constructed from several layers, beginning with an aluminum screen, overlaid with cheesecloth, and then covered with plaster, which was still wet when she tied the resulting cylinder into *Nu*'s double knot. Benglis worked with airplane technicians in Los Angeles to metalize her knot pieces, first spraying on a layer of zinc and then a layer of tin. Finishing touches to *Nu* include a few coats of spray paint and flecks of metallic sparkle.

Benglis gained notice in the late 1960s with her gestural works of poured latex and foam. Her practice did not fit neatly within the sharp aesthetics of Minimalism or the overt politics of feminist art of the time. Exploiting the physicality of form, Benglis continues to employ a wide range of materials—from plastics and cast glass to paper and gold leaf— to render dynamic impressions of mass and surface that blur the distinction between hard and soft, flaccid and firm. Her latest sculptures reveal a striking sense of immediacy and physicality even as they seem to defy gravity, and continue to use the body and landscape as primary references.

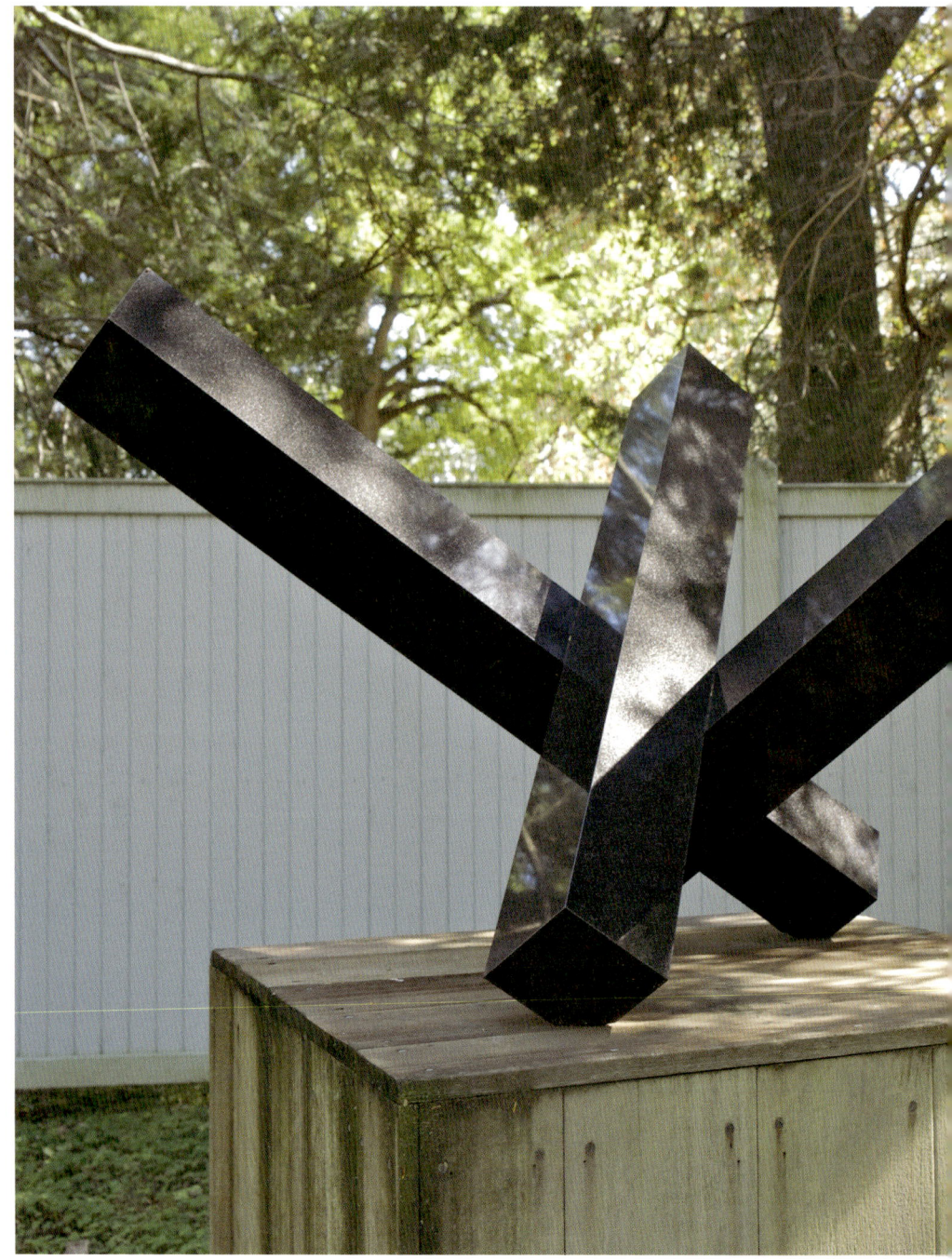

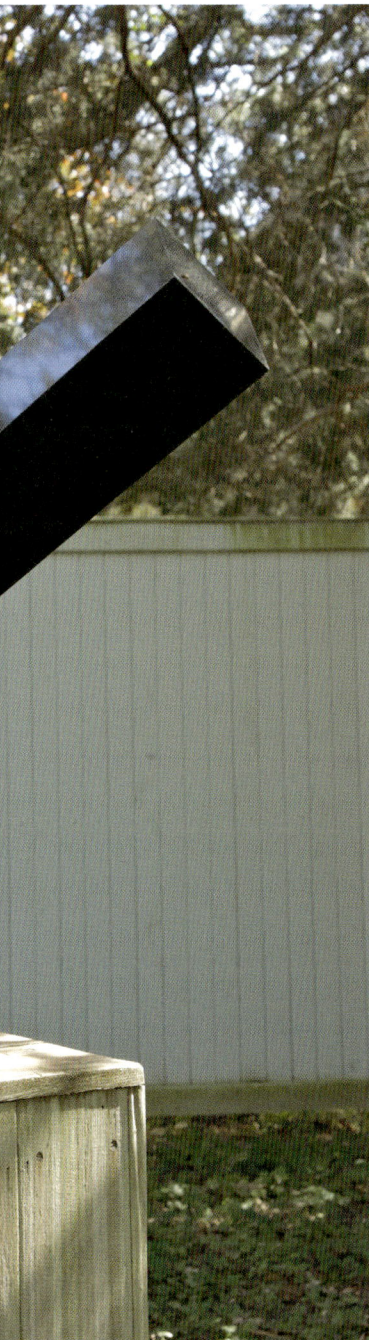

MAX BILL

SWISS, 1908–1994

UNIT OF THREE EQUAL VOLUMES, 1965
BLACK GRANITE
30 x 44 x 44"
GIFT OF THE RALPH E. OGDEN FOUNDATION

Unit of Three Equal Volumes consists of three rectangular bars placed at right angles to each other to create pyramidal voids. The composition exemplifies Max Bill's predilection for precise mathematical organization, while its highly polished surface—a feature the artist admired in the work of Constantin Brancusi—reflects both light and the surrounding space. The compositional formula of three equal volumes presented as a unit occupied Bill for at least a decade.

Bill, a graphic and industrial designer as well as an artist, studied at the Bauhaus in Dessau, Germany, in the late 1920s and was deeply influenced by its mission and practices. The Bauhaus motto, "Unity of Art and Technology," proposes bridging the divide between art and modern life. In 1936 Bill introduced his concept of "Concrete Art" (the term "Art Concrèt" had been coined by Dutch artist Theo van Doesburg in 1930), which came to define his work and Switzerland's artistic landscape. Distinguishing Concrete Art from abstract art, Bill stated that the latter is an arbitrary reduction of natural phenomena while the former is independent of nature. "Concrete Art," he explained, "uses purely aesthetic means to make abstract thoughts become visible and thus create new objects."

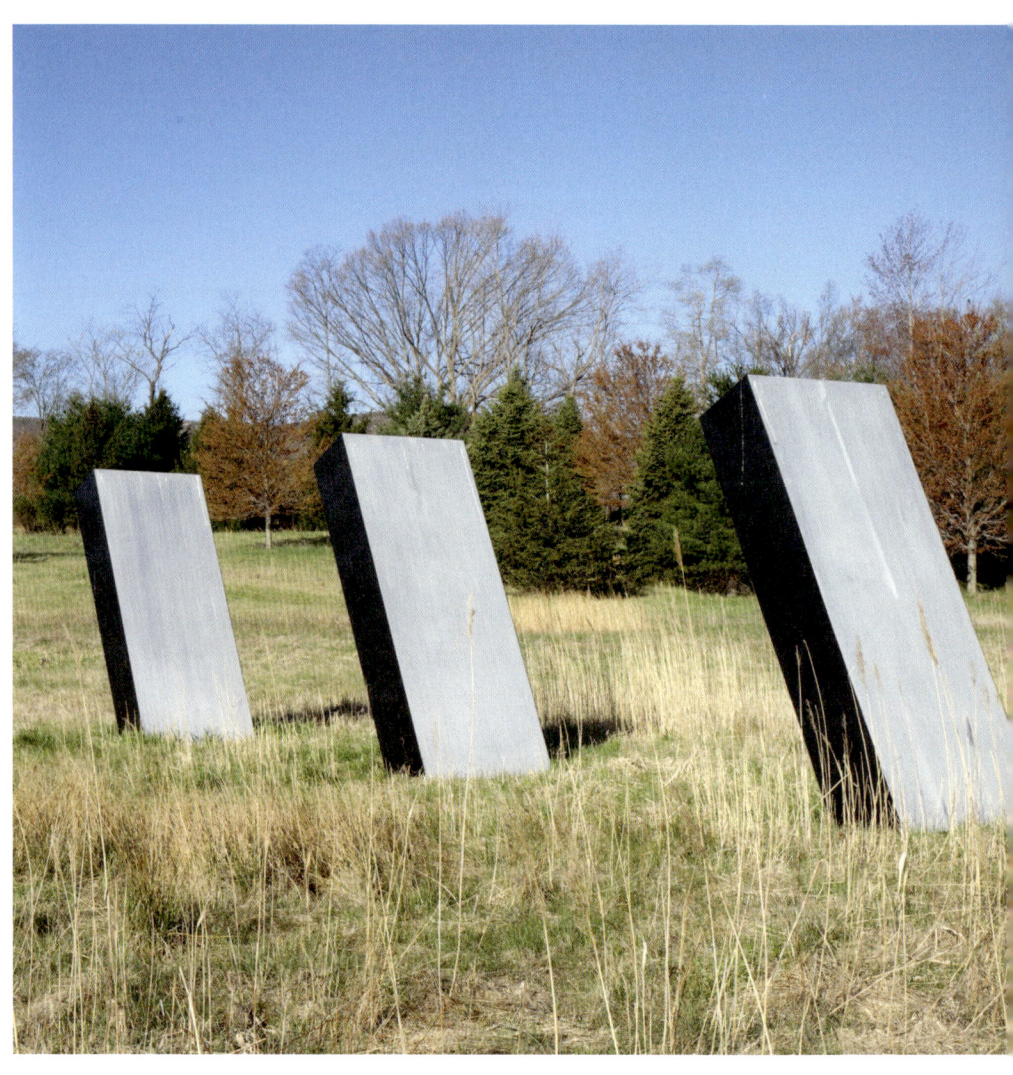

RONALD BLADEN

AMERICAN, BORN CANADA, 1918–1988

UNTITLED (THREE ELEMENTS), 1965 (FABRICATED 1966–67)
BURNISHED AND PAINTED ALUMINUM
EACH ELEMENT 9' x 48" x 21"
EDITION 1 OF 3
GIFT OF MAURICE COHEN AND MARGO COHEN

Ronald Bladen's three-part geometric sculpture exploits the ambiguity and tension between the natural and the non-objective worlds through the lens of geometry, coupling a sense of extreme physicality with precariousness. Composed of identical, acutely angled, tilted elements, its dynamic effect is compounded by the negative spaces between them. Originally made of wood, *Untitled (Three Elements)* was subsequently fabricated in steel, so that it could be installed outdoors. At the time steel was appreciated for its perceived durability in many different climates and for its ability to accurately reproduce geometric forms.

Bladen began his artistic career as a painter in San Francisco, where he had moved in 1939 from his native Canada, and participated in the active community of poets and other artists there. He moved to New York in 1956. In the early 1960s he experimented with collage and relief sculptures. By 1965 Bladen's work expanded dimensionally when he began making room-size sculptures of simplified geometric shapes. These wood constructions had smooth, painted exteriors that masked complexly engineered scaffolding hidden within the forms. Bladen's earliest sculptures of this type were multicolored; *Untitled (Three Elements)* inaugurated a series of starker, mature works. It was included in *Primary Structures*, a landmark exhibition of minimalist art at The Jewish Museum in New York, where it was first shown publicly in 1966.

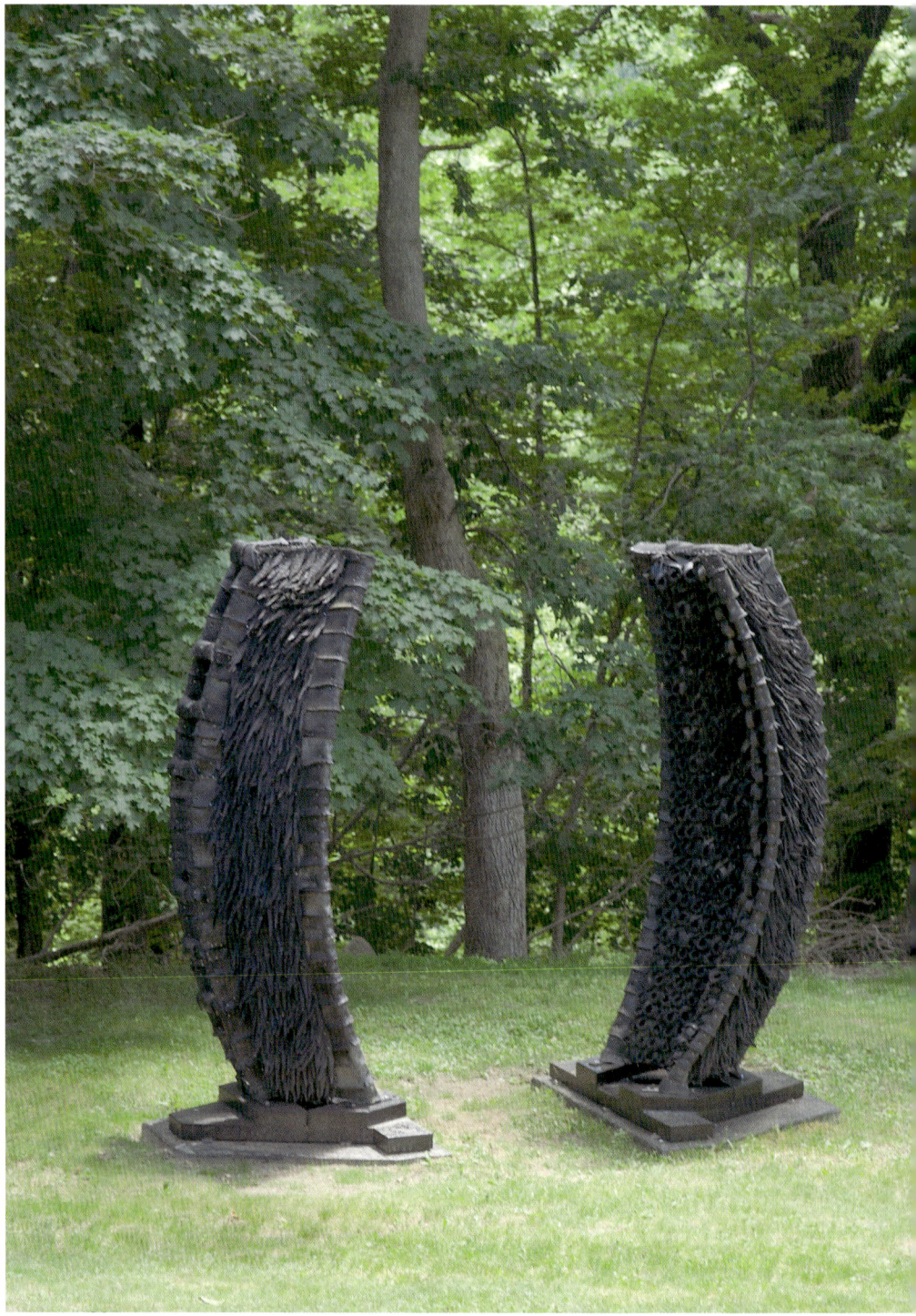

CHAKAIA BOOKER

AMERICAN, BORN 1953

A MOMENT IN TIME, 2004
RUBBER TIRES, STAINLESS STEEL, AND STEEL
10' x 9' 1" x 10' 2" OVERALL
GIFT OF THE HORACE W. GOLDSMITH FOUNDATION

Chakaia Booker works almost exclusively with recycled tires—slicing, twisting, stripping, weaving, and riveting rubber and radials to create and exaggerate the textures, prickled edges, and torqued forms of her radical refashioning. Whether she is creating small-scale wall reliefs resembling ballistic blowouts, suggestively hairy and ovoid pedestal sculptures, or colossal landscape-like tableaux, Booker transforms tires— iconic symbols of urban waste and blight—into extraordinary compositions of renewal.

A *Moment in Time* conveys multiple meanings that crisscross historical, social, political, and cultural contexts. The different tonalities of the rubber, for instance, from brown- and blue-, to green- and red-black, are linked to issues of African-American identity as well as to the history of black as a color in modern art. As commercial objects, tires symbolize the rise and fall of industrial revolutions, the movement of populations across the landscape, the growth of the suburbs, and the decay of urban centers. Discarded and now re-used, the tires are also metaphors for the modern cycle of industrial manufacture and waste in an era of global expansion. A *Moment in Time* alludes not only to environmental degradation and decay but also to the possibility of transformation and redemption through the artist's own brand of environmental spiritualism.

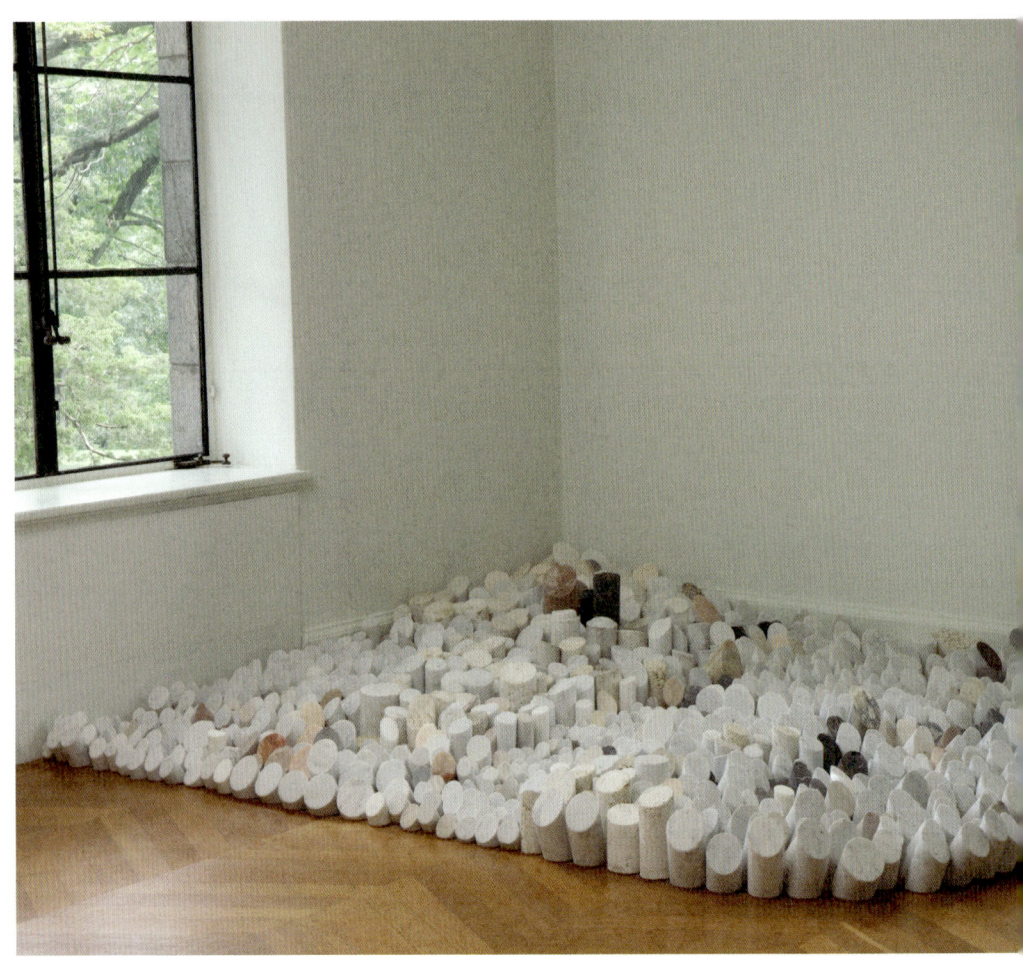

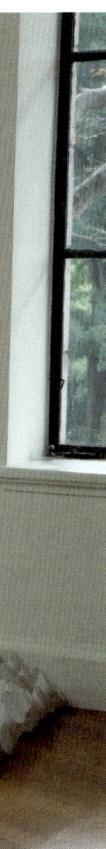

LOUISE BOURGEOIS

AMERICAN, BORN FRANCE, 1911–2010

NUMBER SEVENTY-TWO (THE NO MARCH), 1972
MARBLE
13 ½" x 8' 6" x 7' 1"
PURCHASED WITH THE AID OF FUNDS FROM THE NATIONAL ENDOWMENT
FOR THE ARTS AND GIFT OF THE RALPH E. OGDEN FOUNDATION

Number Seventy-Two (The No March) is one of Louise Bourgeois's most complex and politically charged works. This intricate sculpture—a floor work made from 1,200 individual cylindrical pieces of marble and travertine—was created in homage to a non-violent protest against the Vietnam War. Bourgeois also imbued the work with a more universal meaning, noting: "*The No March* also means accepting you're almost nobody. You have to merge with thousands like you." The work is installed in a tightly packed rectangle in the corner of an indoor gallery in the Museum Building. Varying in size, color, and textures and cut at various angles, no piece is taller than fourteen inches. *Number Seventy-Two (The No March)* inspired a 2007 exhibition at Storm King comprised of a group of twenty works that demonstrate Bourgeois's use of the clustered form.

Though often rooted in personal experiences—particularly her painful childhood and dysfunctional family—Bourgeois's work deals poignantly and sometimes disturbingly with broad themes of anxiety, loneliness, betrayal, sex, and death. Her emphasis on organic forms, the subconscious, and states of metamorphosis can be traced to her interest in the French Surrealists; she had met and been influenced by Marcel Duchamp, Max Ernst, and André Breton while attending the École des Beaux-Arts in the 1930s. While much of her work may legitimately be viewed in the context of Surrealism, Abstract Expressionism, and other movements, Bourgeois was a singular artist whose work eludes categorization.

In 1938 Bourgeois moved to New York. There she created drawings, paintings, and prints with haunting, dreamlike scenes. Her first sculptures—tall, spindly wooden totems—date from the late 1940s. All but ignored when she exhibited with the Abstract Expressionists in the 1940s and '50s, Bourgeois was rediscovered by feminists in the 1970s, and finally, at the age of seventy-one, received international recognition with a retrospective exhibition at the Museum of Modern Art, New York, in 1982.

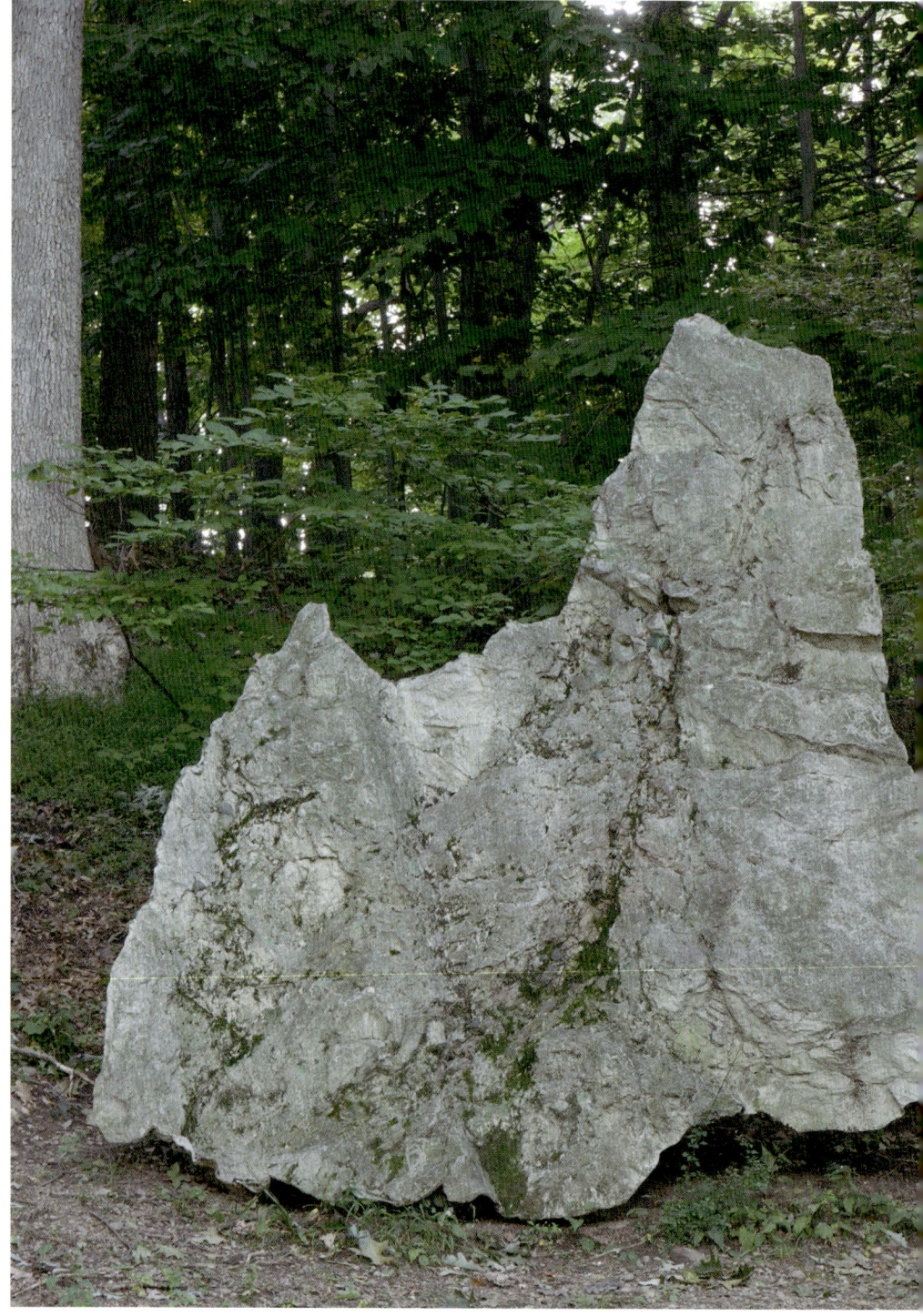

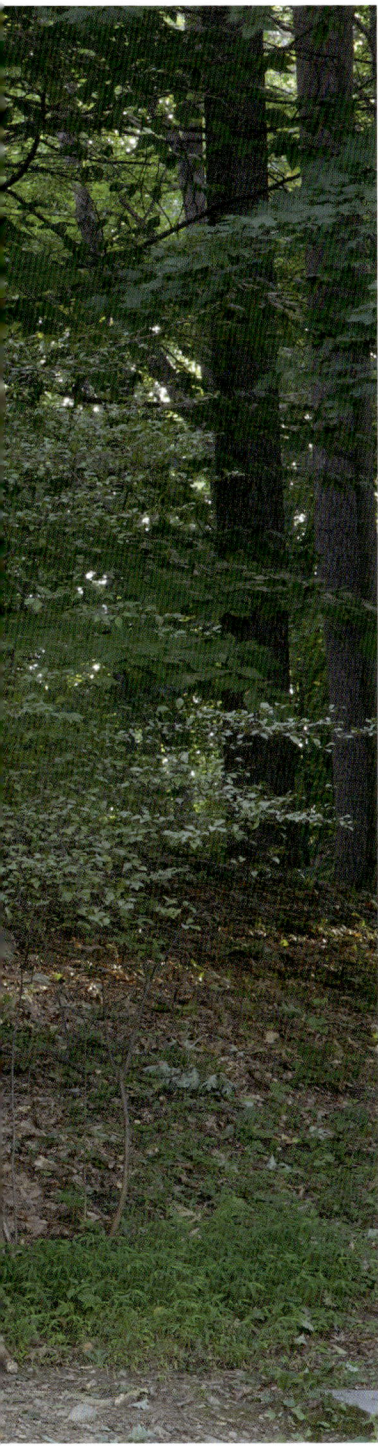

MANUEL BROMBERG

AMERICAN, BORN 1917

CATSKILL, 1968
POLYESTER, FIBERGLASS, AND ROCK AGGREGATE
15' 8" x 12' x 24"
GIFT OF THE RALPH E. OGDEN FOUNDATION

Manuel Bromberg attracted early attention when in 1940 he won a commission for a Works Progress Administration post office mural, and his design appeared with others in *LIFE* magazine. Three years later the War Department sent him abroad to document the fighting in sketches and paintings, for which he was awarded a Citation for the Legion of Merit. After the war he abandoned figurative painting and adopted a hard-edge abstract style. During the 1950s Bromberg was closely associated with Buckminster Fuller and his early explorations of geodesic domes. In the early 1960s he experimented with painting and cutting plaster for mural work. One nine-hundred-foot mural in Teaneck, New Jersey, produced in 1963, was surfaced in ten thousand pounds of cement, which was applied by union plasterers.

Bromberg became a professor at the State University College at New Paltz, New York, in 1961, and in 1968 received a grant from the university to cast a twenty-two-foot-high polyester and fiberglass cliff in the Catskill Mountains. Bromberg presented one fifteen-foot section of the cliff to the college in memory of Martin Luther King, Jr. Storm King acquired the second section. Now the artist's best-known work, *Catskill* demonstrates an early concern for environmental issues, while also reflecting the Romantic painting heritage of the Hudson River.

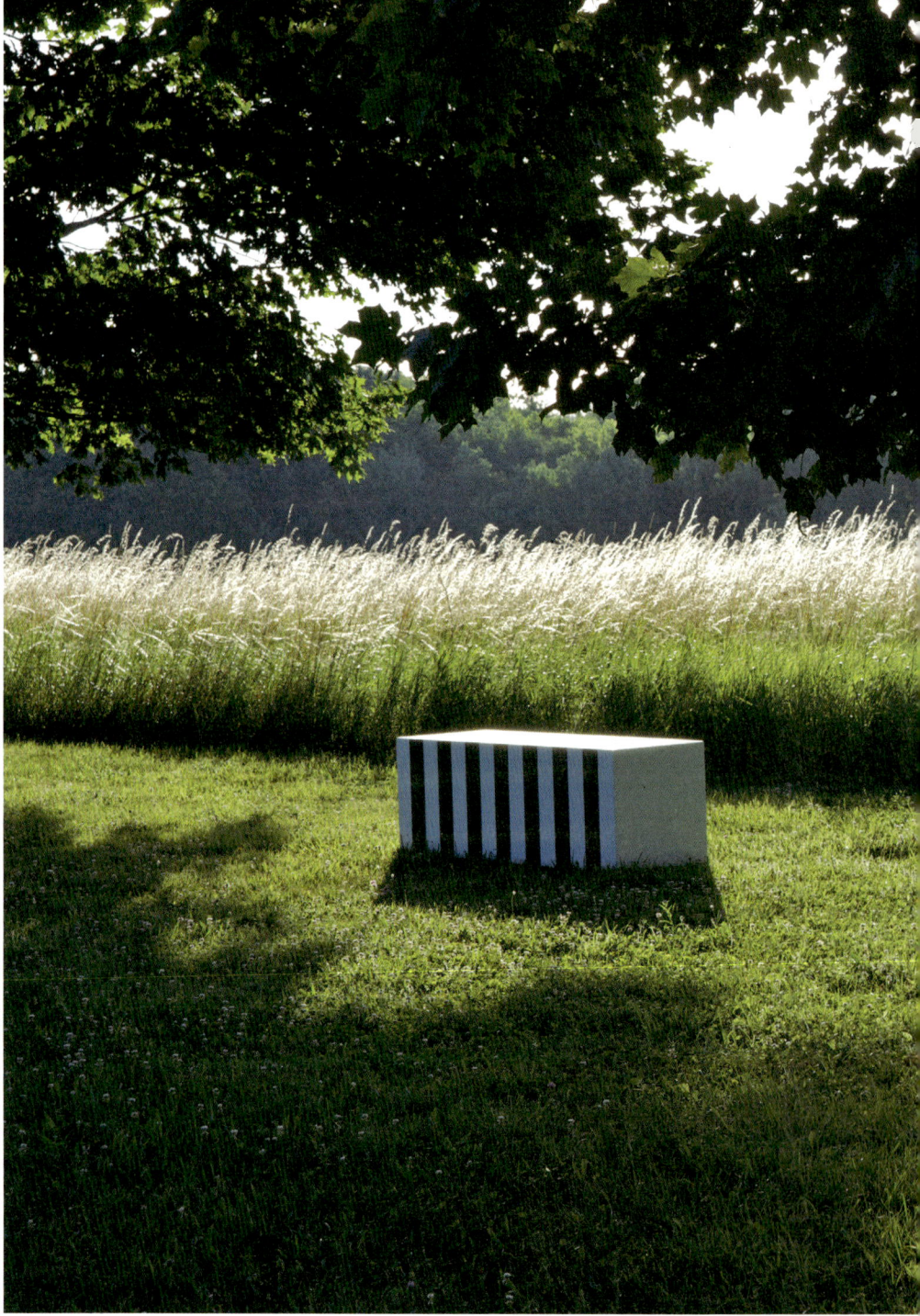

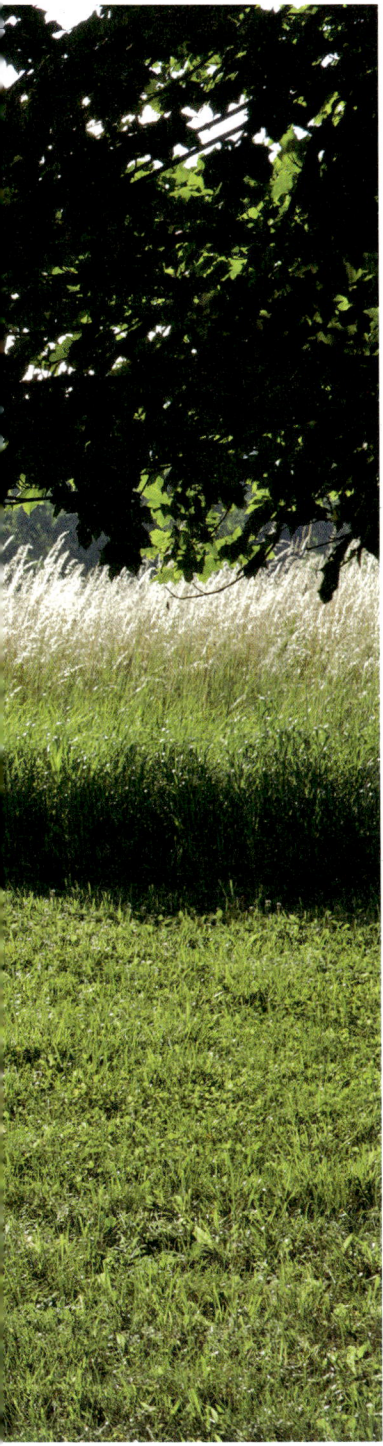

DANIEL BUREN

FRENCH, BORN 1938

SIT DOWN, 1998 (REFABRICATED 2010)
PAINTED ALUMINUM
17 ¾ x 17 ¾ x 53 ⅛" EACH
GIFT OF THE RALPH E. OGDEN FOUNDATION

Daniel Buren's group of ten green-and-white striped benches, titled *Sit Down*, functions doubly as seating and as art objects. Inspired by the natural surroundings, the work was conceived in response to a series of visits Buren made to Storm King for this commission. Originally made of marine plywood before being refabricated in aluminum and painted with Buren's patented alternating dark green and white stripes, the simple cubic design permits seating in any orientation. The siting of the benches changes according to the needs of Storm King. Envisioned as "signals" in the landscape, the benches are always meant to be displayed in groups, however, so that they are visually linked to one another as they punctuate their terrain, and a visitor sitting on one can readily see another.

Buren began his career as a painter in the 1960s, at a particularly active time of cultural ferment and artistic change in France. In 1965, while he was in a Paris flea market looking for canvas to paint on, he was captivated by a vertically striped, commercially available fabric that he subsequently adopted. He has gone on to use this infinitely expandable, non-hierarchic, non-art module to create site-specific installations since 1970.

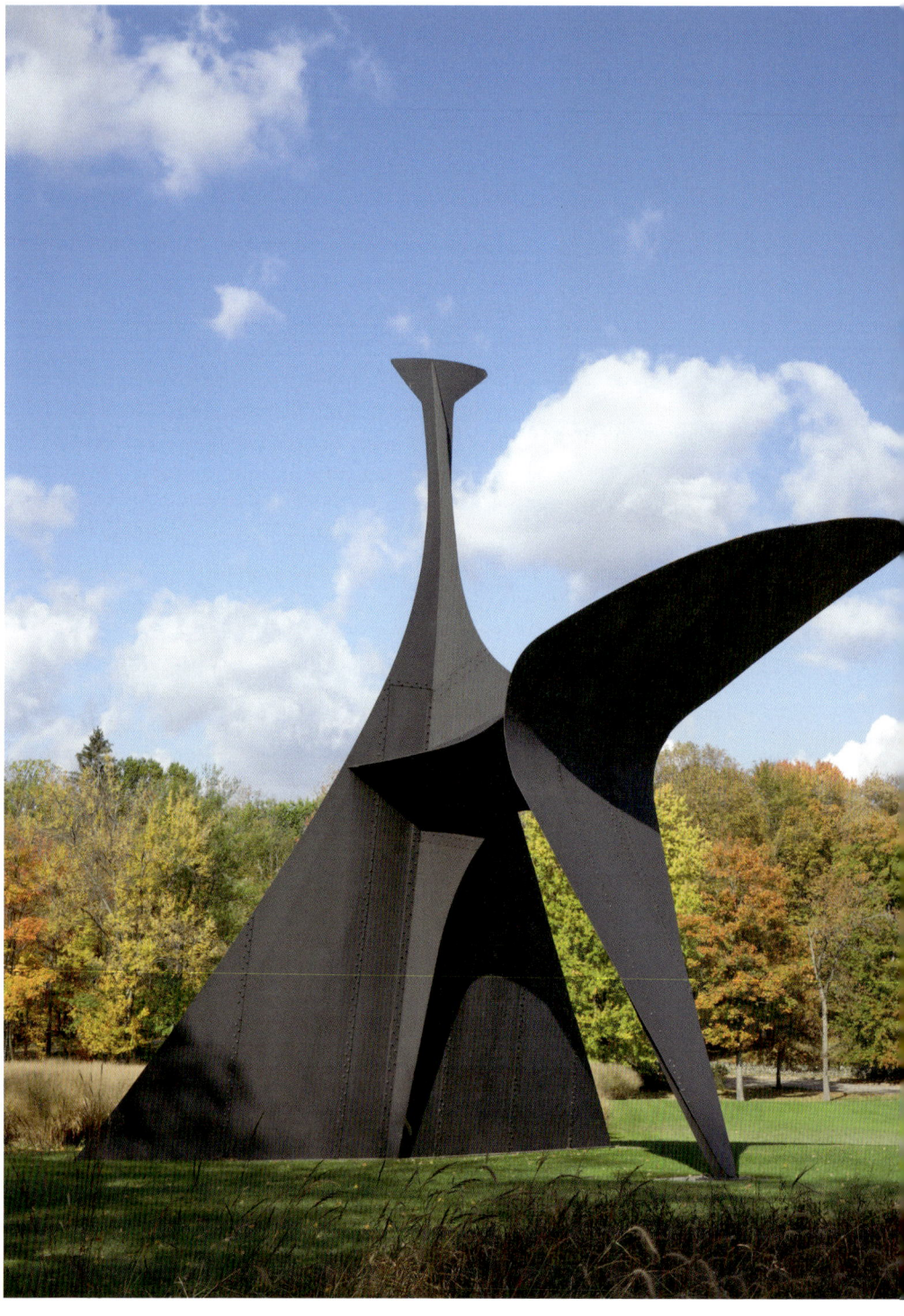

ALEXANDER CALDER

AMERICAN, 1898–1976

SELECTED WORKS:
THE ARCH, 1975
PAINTED STEEL
50' x 41' 6" x 34' 10"
PURCHASE FUND AND GIFT OF THE RALPH E. OGDEN FOUNDATION

BLACK FLAG, 1974
SHEET METAL, BOLTS, AND PAINT
23' 5" x 19' 9" x 17' 2"
CALDER FOUNDATION, NEW YORK

FIVE SWORDS, 1976
SHEET METAL, BOLTS, AND PAINT
17' 9" x 22' x 29'
CALDER FOUNDATION, NEW YORK

The Arch is among the last of the monumental works Alexander Calder created before his death in 1976. Based on a nineteen-inch-high model that the artist conceived around 1940, *The Arch* was enlarged from a twelve-foot-high black-painted steel maquette in 1975. Its dramatic composition melds the biomorphic and architectonic aspects that characterize Calder's work and creates an impressive, multi-layered image. The full-scale, painted steel sculpture is set in a field of tall native grasses. The open parabolic arch, an element from the vocabulary of building, is meant to entice visitors to pass through its portal and discover its buoyant forms from unexpected vantage points. Passage through Calder's arch draws attention to the work itself as well as to the rural surroundings.

The sculpture is composed of three elements: a bent "boomerang" on one side, joined by a central arch to a tall, concave fan shape, with an elongated upper portion capped by a small triangular "tail." The work offers many different views, depending on the angle of approach. At certain vantage points, the black surface looks flat, punctuated by the many lines of bolts securing the steel. From another angle, the structurally supportive ribs give the inert steel structure a sense of grace and movement. The tall, triangular element seems to grow straight up from the ground, monumental but not overbearing.

Calder is renowned as a pioneer of abstract sculpture. He studied mechanical engineering before he attended the Art Students League in New York. His artistic sensibility flourished in the heady climate of

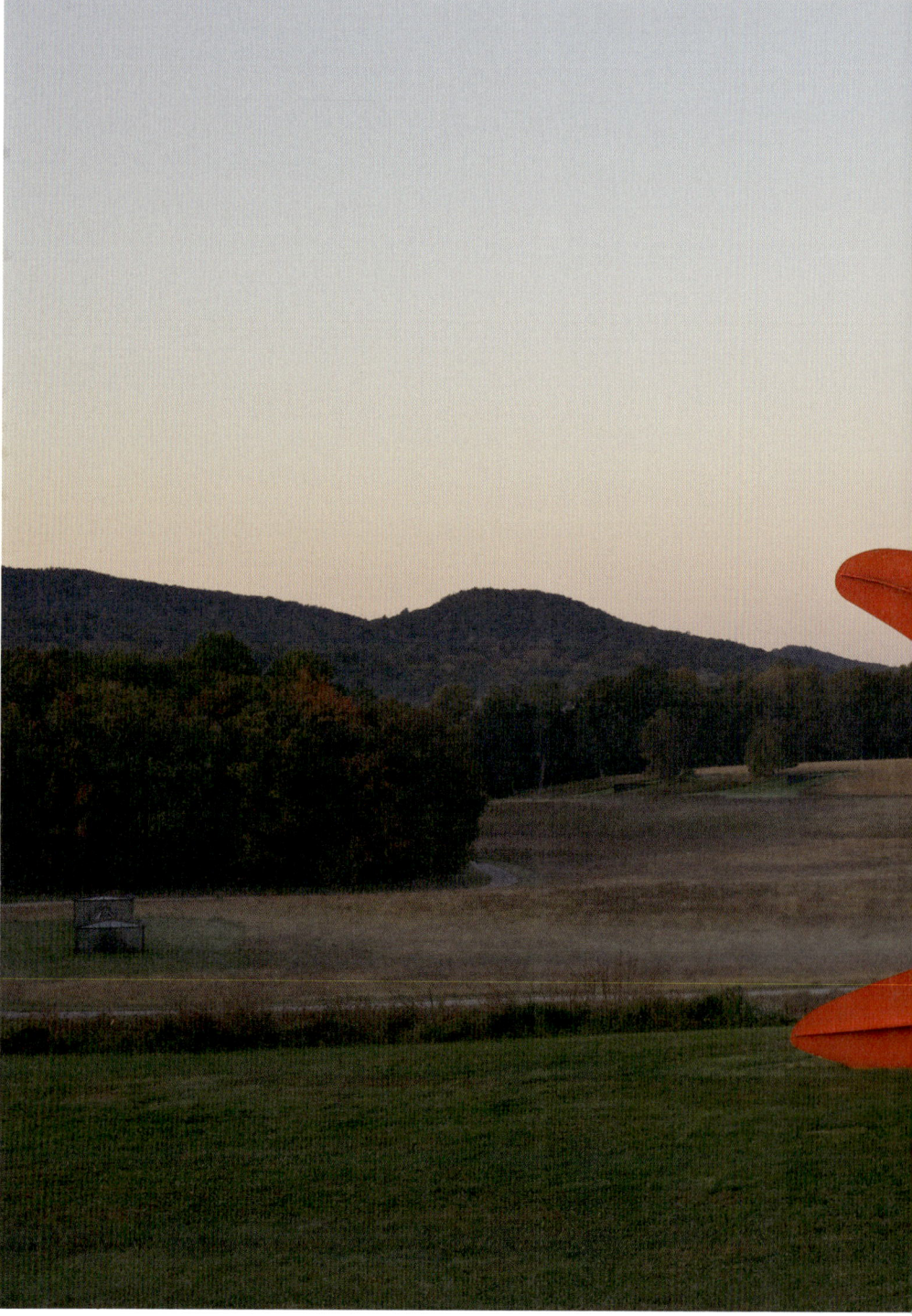

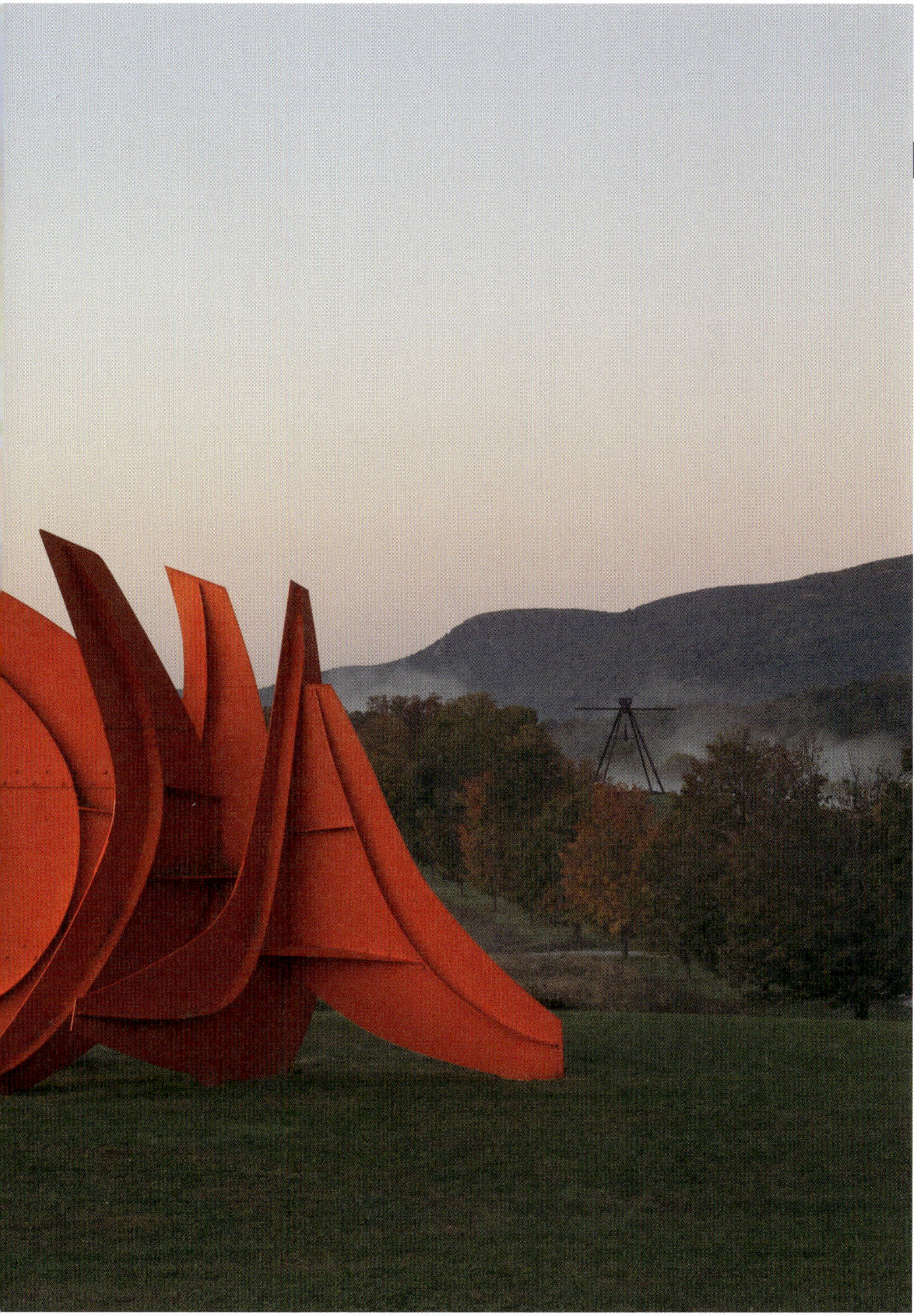

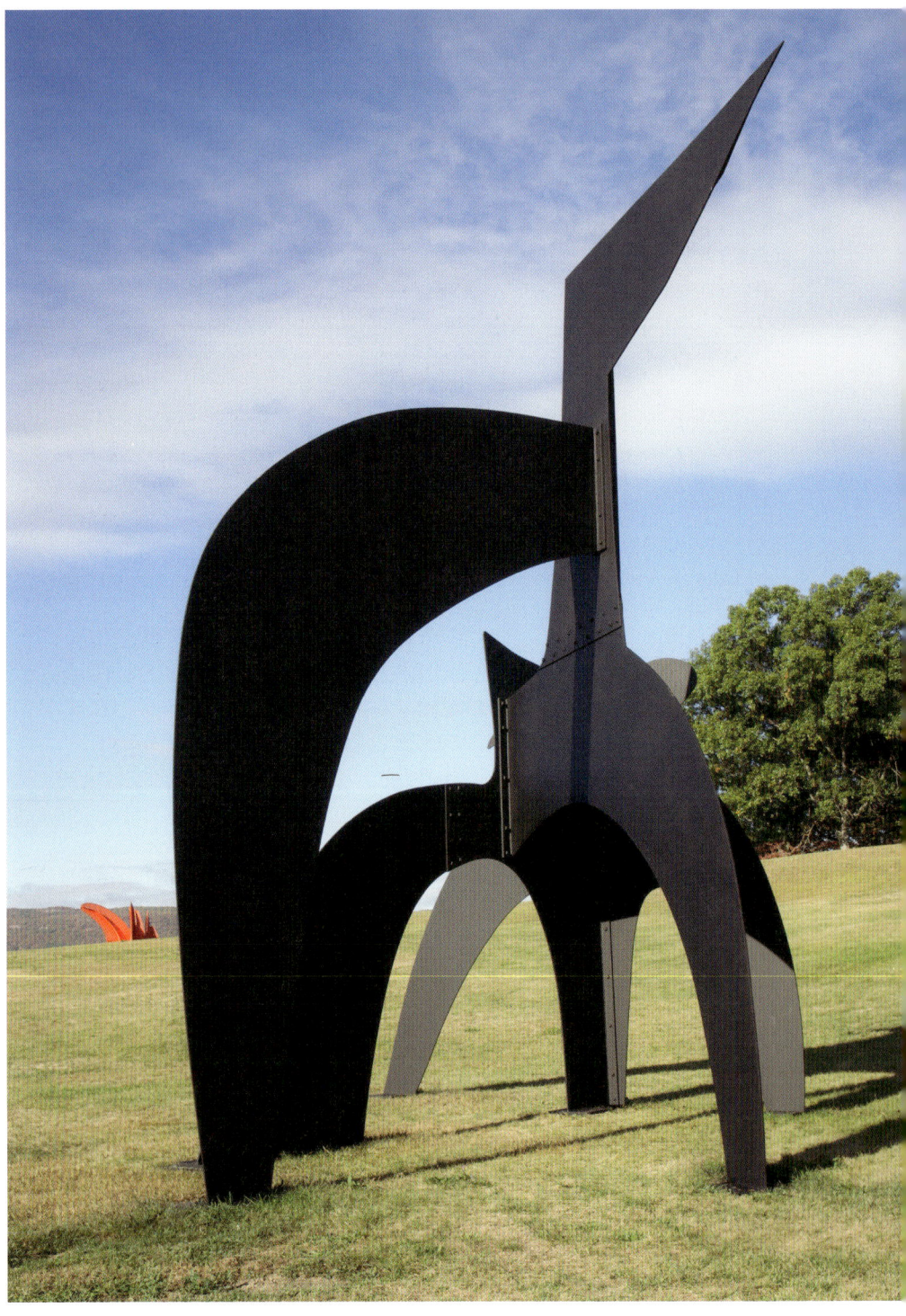

1920s Paris, where he befriended Joan Miró and Paul Klee. Calder's mature works reflect these early influences in his combination of direct methods with Surrealist, often biomorphic, imagery. He began making abstract constructions after a visit to Piet Mondrian's studio in 1930. A year later he conceived his first *mobiles*, a term invented by Marcel Duchamp to describe Calder's new kinetic sculptures. Jean Arp, in response to Duchamp, dubbed Calder's motionless painted metal constructions *stabiles*. During the 1960s and 1970s the stabiles gained colossal proportions, appropriate to the public sites for which they were often commissioned.

The Arch was fabricated at Segre Ironworks in Waterbury, Connecticut, in 1975, the year before Calder's death. In spring 1978 *The Arch* arrived at Storm King as a loan from the Estate of Alexander Calder and Knoedler Gallery; it was acquired in 1982 and painted at Storm King. The work was placed on a slightly raised mound shaped by a few feet of gravel, a site created by the late William A. Rutherford, Sr., Storm King's landscape architect. It sits in the same location today—on the left side of the road leading to the Museum Building.

In the 1980s Rutherford designed a hillside near the Museum Building to expand exhibition space and create broad, gently sloping walking paths to sculptures located in the South Fields. *Black Flag* was installed on the site in 1999. Storm King has presented three exhibitions featuring works by Calder here, including a landmark installation of monumental sculpture outdoors, from 2001 through 2003. Occasionally the works on view on this hillside change. *Five Swords*, however, has been in the same location for more than twenty-five years.

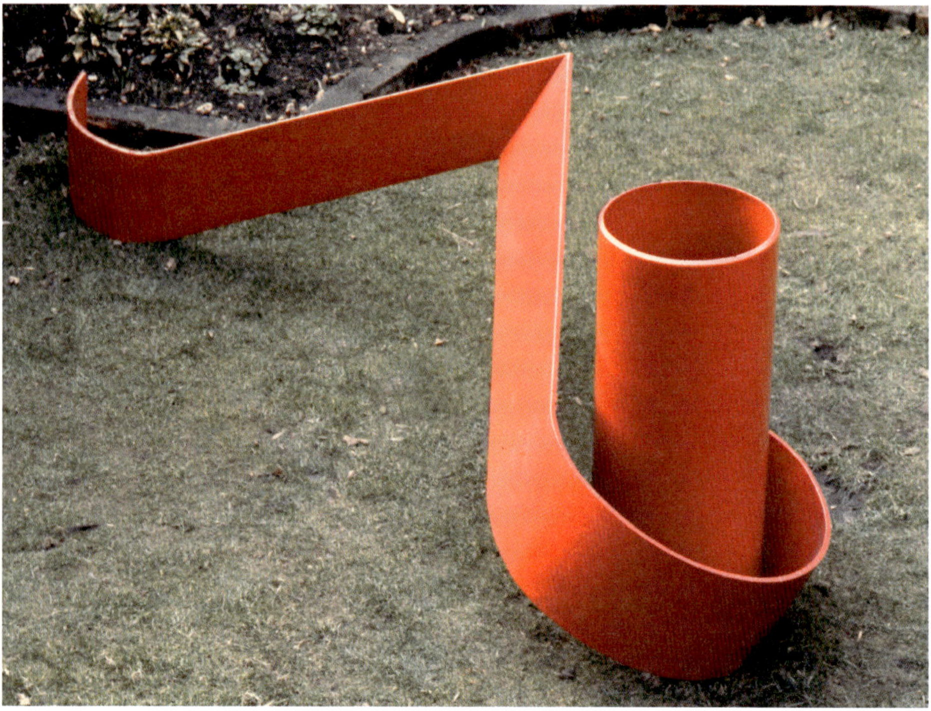

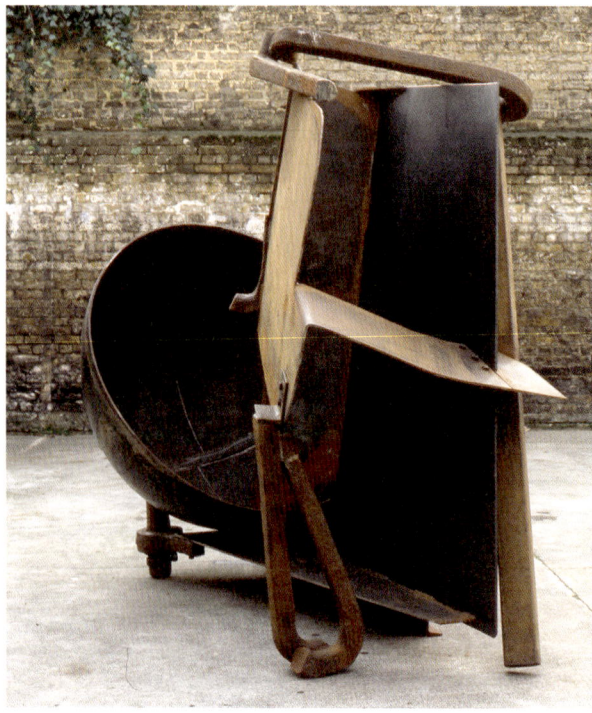

ANTHONY CARO

BRITISH, 1924–2013

REEL, 1964
PAINTED STEEL
34 ⅜" x 9'3" x 40"
GIFT OF THE RALPH E. OGDEN FOUNDATION

BITTER SKY, 1983
STEEL AND PAINTED STEEL
7'10" x 7'9" x 60"
GIFT OF JAMES H. OTTAWAY JR., THE HORACE W. GOLDSMITH FOUNDATION,
AND THE RALPH E. OGDEN FOUNDATION

Sir Anthony Caro profoundly influenced a younger generation of sculptors, several of whom are represented at Storm King, when he taught at Saint Martin's School of Art, London, in the 1950s and 1960s. In 1960 he began working with welded metal immediately following a six-week, grant-funded trip to the United States and Mexico, where he encountered works by David Smith and Kenneth Noland, and was influenced by Clement Greenberg's art criticism. Upon returning to London Caro promptly bought his own welding equipment and began to create abstract, welded steel sculptures made from industrial materials.

Reel and *Bitter Sky* represent two distinct stylistic periods in Caro's sculpture. Works dating from the 1960s, such as the low-slung, curvilinear *Reel*, are horizontally oriented, painted a uniform color, and placed directly on the ground, tending to appear to float or hover. *Bitter Sky*, made almost two decades later, is characteristically darker, vertical, planar, and more architectonic. Bolts and seams joining the assemblage parts remain clearly visible; integrated seamlessly into the whole structure, they are not "hidden" as in the earlier work. *Bitter Sky* reflects Caro's renewed interest in the heritage of Cubism, with its overlapping planes and volumes and explorations of volume and mass in space—precisely those issues that he rejected two decades earlier in works such as *Reel*.

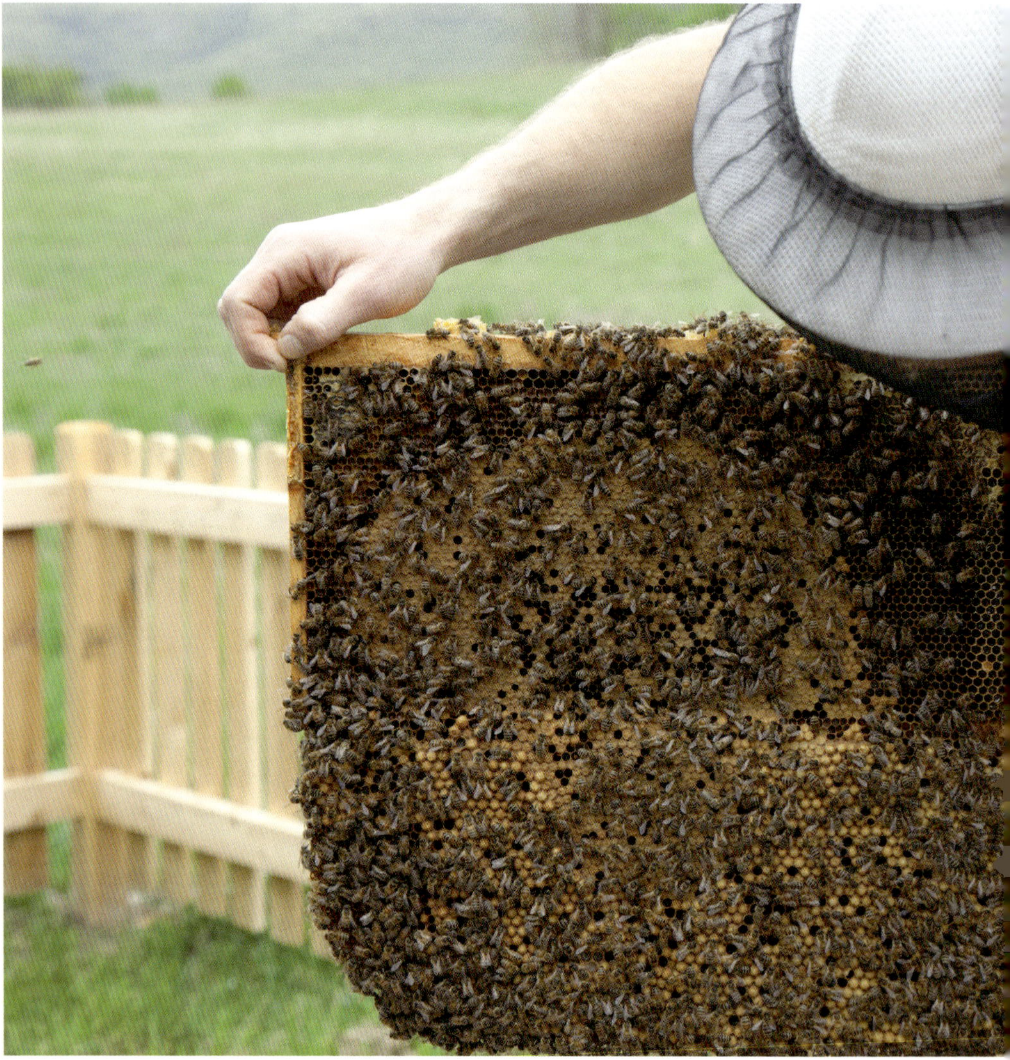

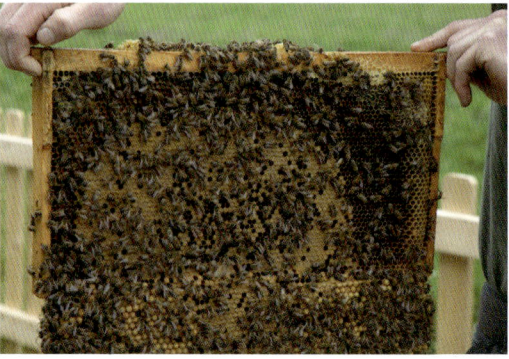
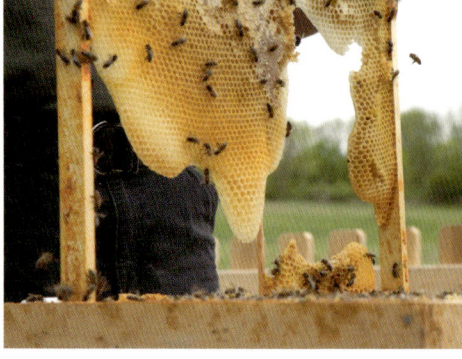

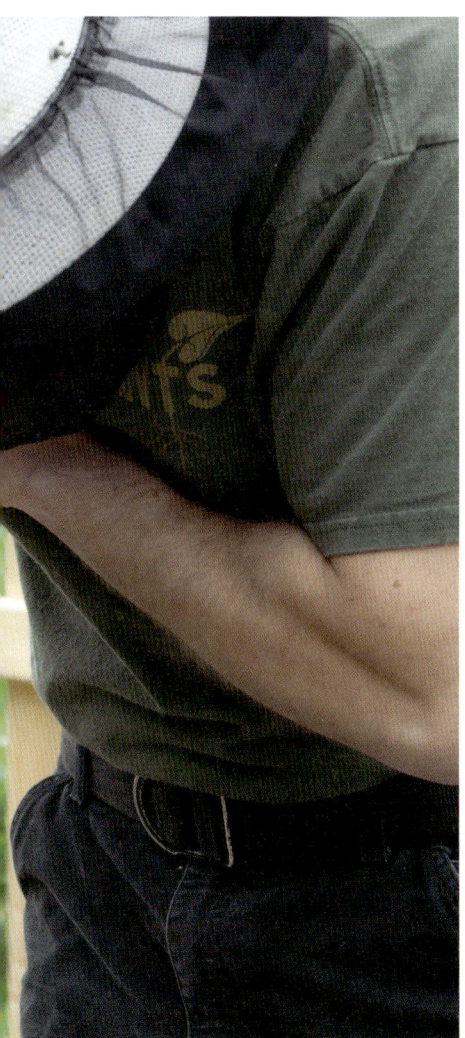

PETER COFFIN

AMERICAN, BORN 1972

UNTITLED (BEES MAKING HONEY), 2012
BEEHIVES AND HONEY BEES
DIMENSIONS VARIABLE
COURTESY THE ARTIST

Peter Coffin's practice involves working with familiar things—here, the sun, bees, honey—to see them anew. This project comprises an apiary at the far edge of Storm King's property, where a beekeeper leads tours, educating participants about honeybees and their dependence on the sun for communication and survival. Tour participants receive a gift of local honey: a proposed answer to the artist's whimsical question, "What does light taste like?"

Please consult the Storm King Calendar of Events for a current listing of tour dates and times.

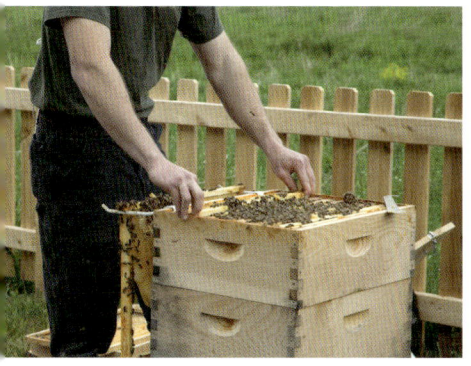

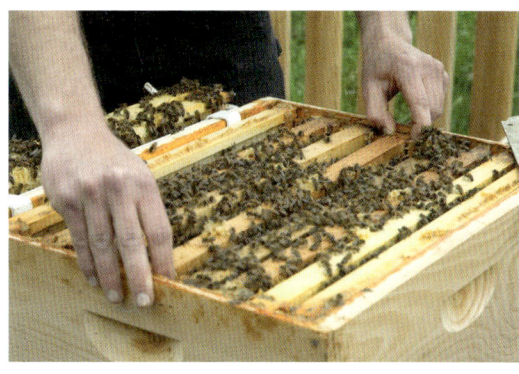

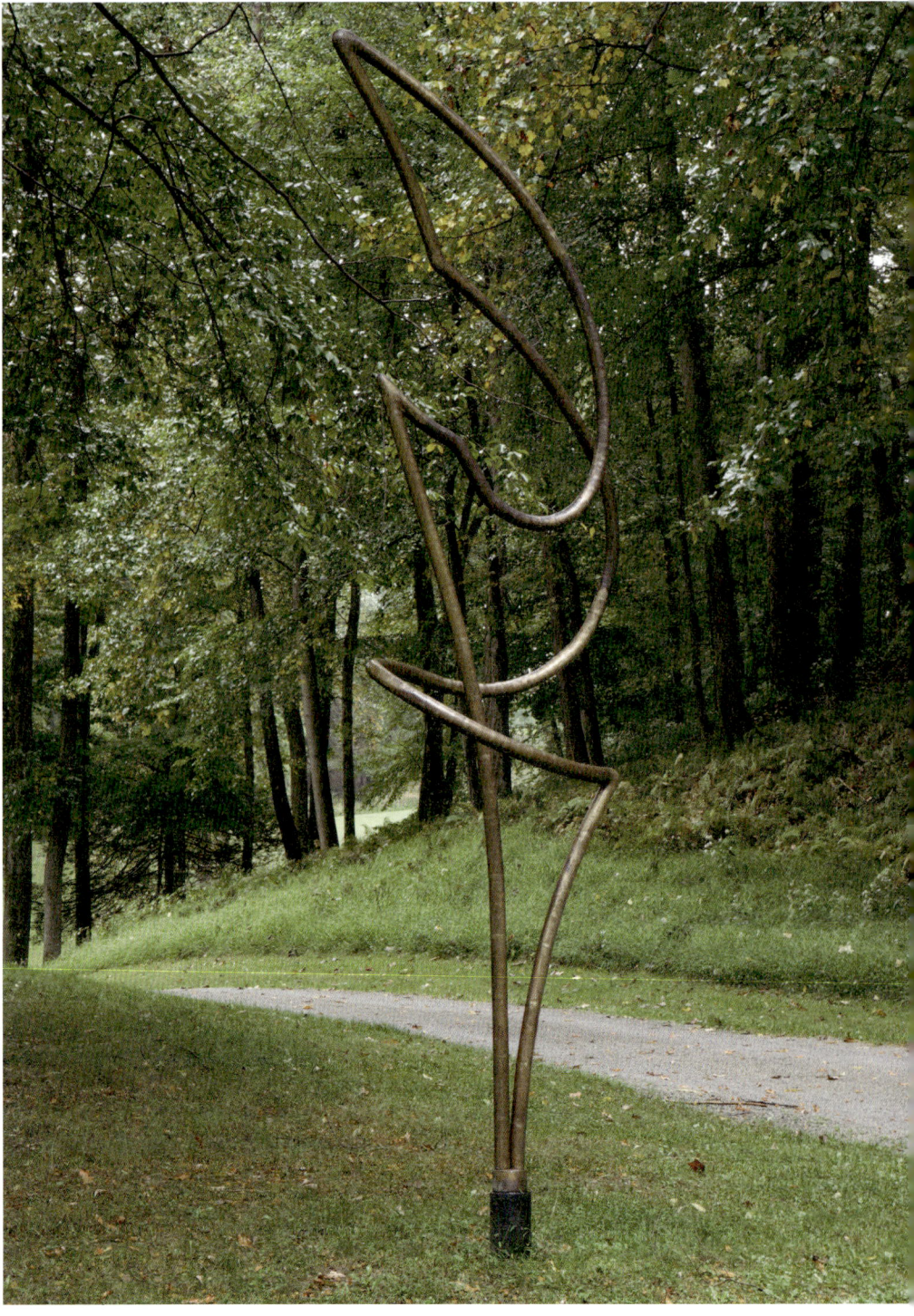

VICTOR CONTRERAS

MEXICAN, BORN 1941

INFINITE FLIGHT, 1995
BRONZE
20½" x 13'6" x 43"
GIFT OF THE V. M. CONTRERAS FOUNDATION

Victor Contreras melds abstract form with a symbolic subject in this spare sculpture. A vertically oriented abstract bronze with remarkably little mass, its tubular forms look like a drawing in space that proceeds upward from the base, crossing the central axis, up, around, and back down again toward and into the base. The artist has interpreted the work in two ways. In 2000 he revealed visual and narrative references, noting, "This sculpture was inspired by two white 'mariposas' [butterflies] in flight, which ancient Indian Mexican legends say are souls coming back to comfort their beloved." Indeed, Contreras has often re-created Mexican legends in the visual language of abstraction, integrating his culture into the flow of contemporary art. In 2005 he spoke more broadly of *Infinite Flight* as "a symbolic work of art, symbolizing the infinity of time." In reference to his work as a whole, he has said, "The Hands of God, Human Unity, and Good and Evil are all themes of my public works. I create these sculptures for the benefit of the public, so that people can be moved and inspired to realize the greater themes of life."

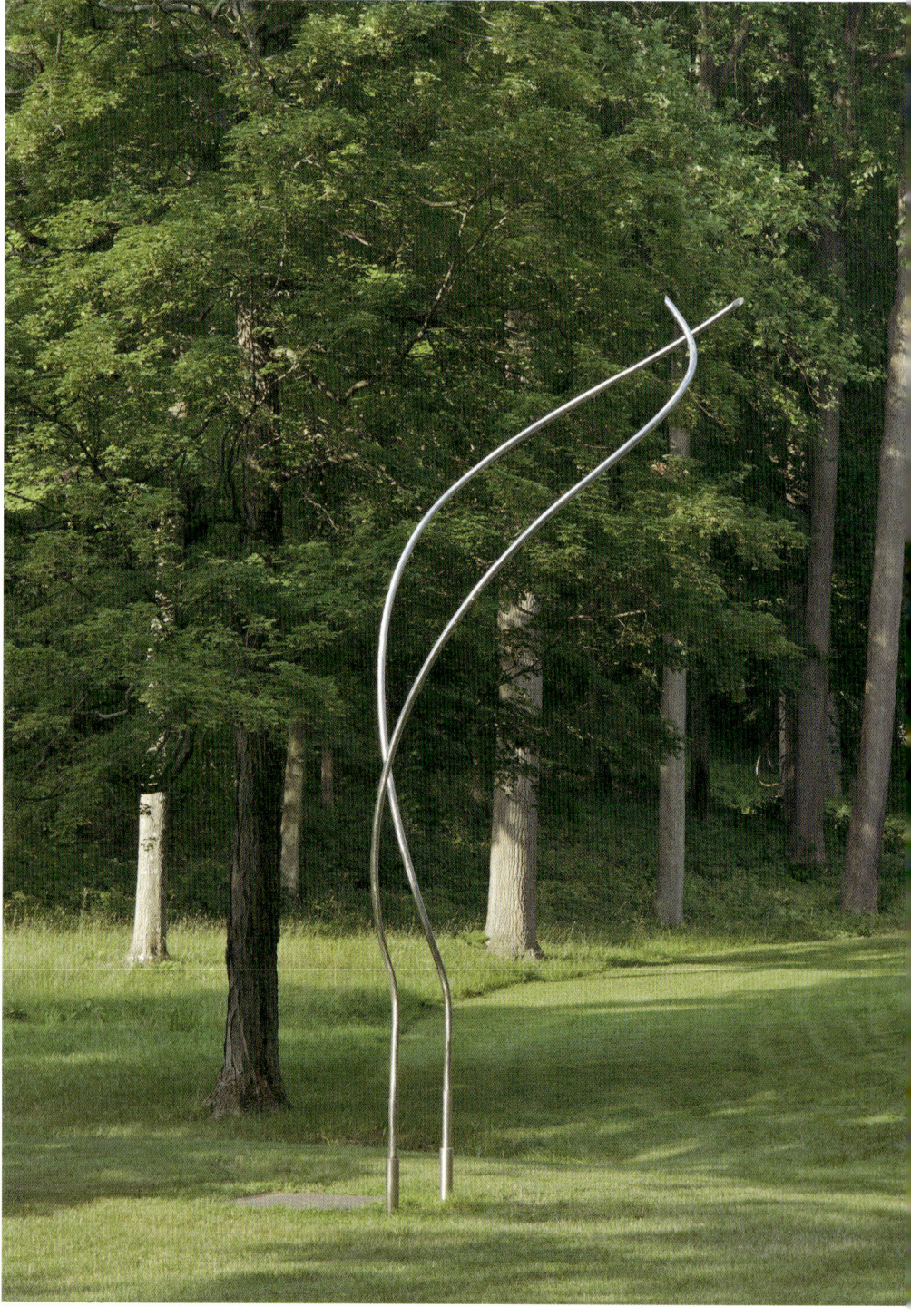

GEORGE CUTTS

BRITISH, BORN 1938

SEA CHANGE, 1996
STAINLESS STEEL
20' 5" x 11' x 13' 9"
GIFT OF THE RALPH E. OGDEN FOUNDATION, THE HORACE W. GOLDSMITH
FOUNDATION, AND THE MARGARET T. MORRIS FOUNDATION

George Cutts's *Sea Change* is composed of two identical, slender, curving, stainless steel poles that turn slowly in opposite directions. The poles are anchored to motorized disks that are sunk below ground and encased in a concrete box. Electricity comes from an underground line, powering the only motorized sculpture at Storm King. The slow, synchronized rotations of the poles produce fluid, undulating movement as the poles seem to sway and flex, blending the mechanical with the natural. Moving ambiguously, the poles at times appear to rotate in opposite directions and at others in the same direction. As the sculpture moves and as one's vantage point changes, the relationship between the two poles also seems to change, as they visually weave together then separate, shifting the space between them. An experienced deep sea diver, Cutts has noted that he intends this lyrical, kinetic sculpture to evoke the motion of seaweed as it moves with the flow of ocean waves and currents.

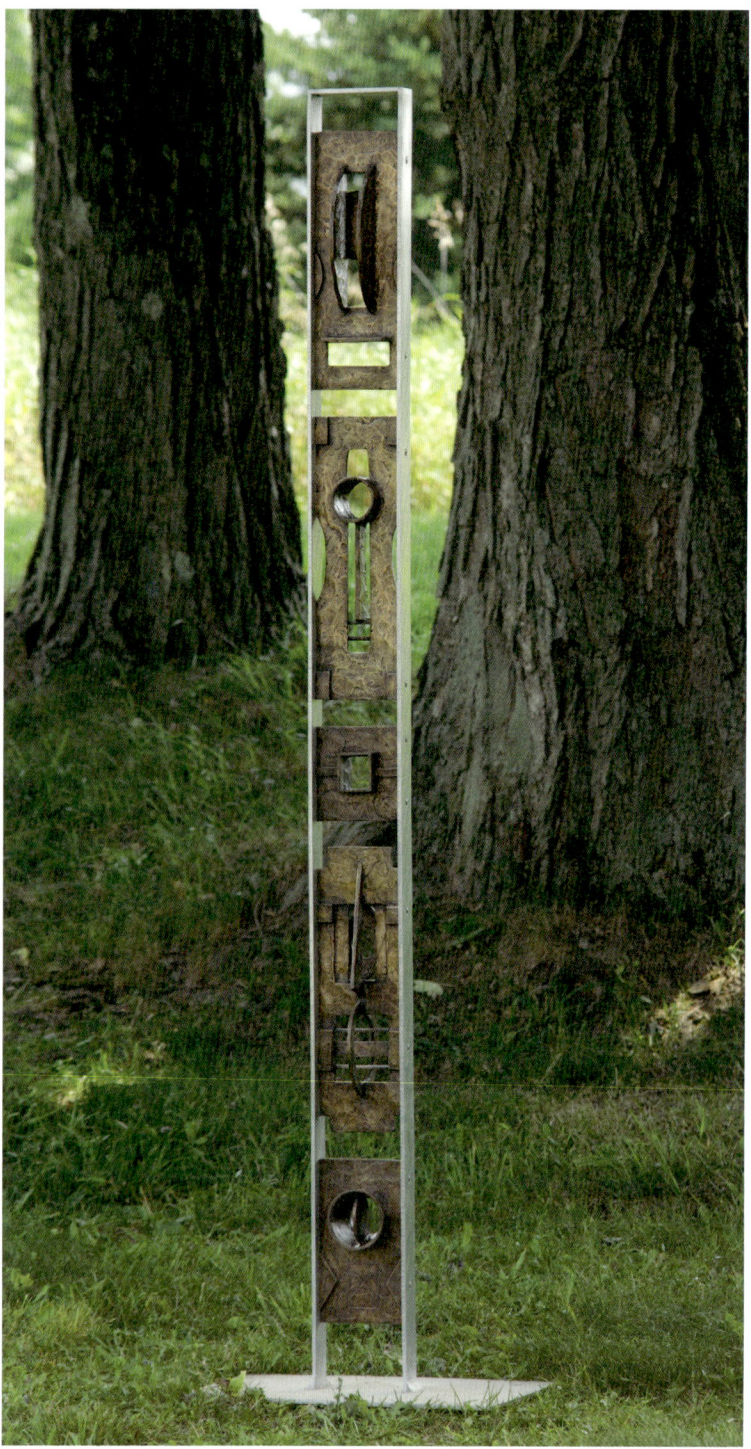

DOROTHY DEHNER

AMERICAN, 1901–1994

CENOTAPH #4, 1972
BRONZE AND ALUMINUM
6' 4" x 20" x 14"
ANONYMOUS GIFT

A painter and printmaker, Dorothy Dehner did not become a sculptor until she was in her fifties—four years after her divorce from sculptor David Smith, whose work is also represented in Storm King's collection. Dehner created her earliest sculptures in wax, which emphasizes contour and rich textural effects, but in 1955, she started to cast her sculpture in bronze. In the 1960s Dehner began to explore a rectilinear formal language, and the scale of her works increased. Her horizontal works often suggest landscapes, while her vertical sculptures, notably *Cenotaph #4*, exhibit a distinctly totemic or iconic presence. Dehner created several cenotaphs— "empty tombs" or markers honoring someone whose remains are located elsewhere—placing rows of bronze, geometric shapes incised with symbols and designs inside a thin, rectangular frame. The open negative space of *Cenotaph #4* exposes the surrounding environment, while the positive spaces speak to Dehner's enduring concern for intricately worked surfaces. Throughout her long career, Dehner remained committed to abstraction, creating sculpture until her death at the age of ninety-two.

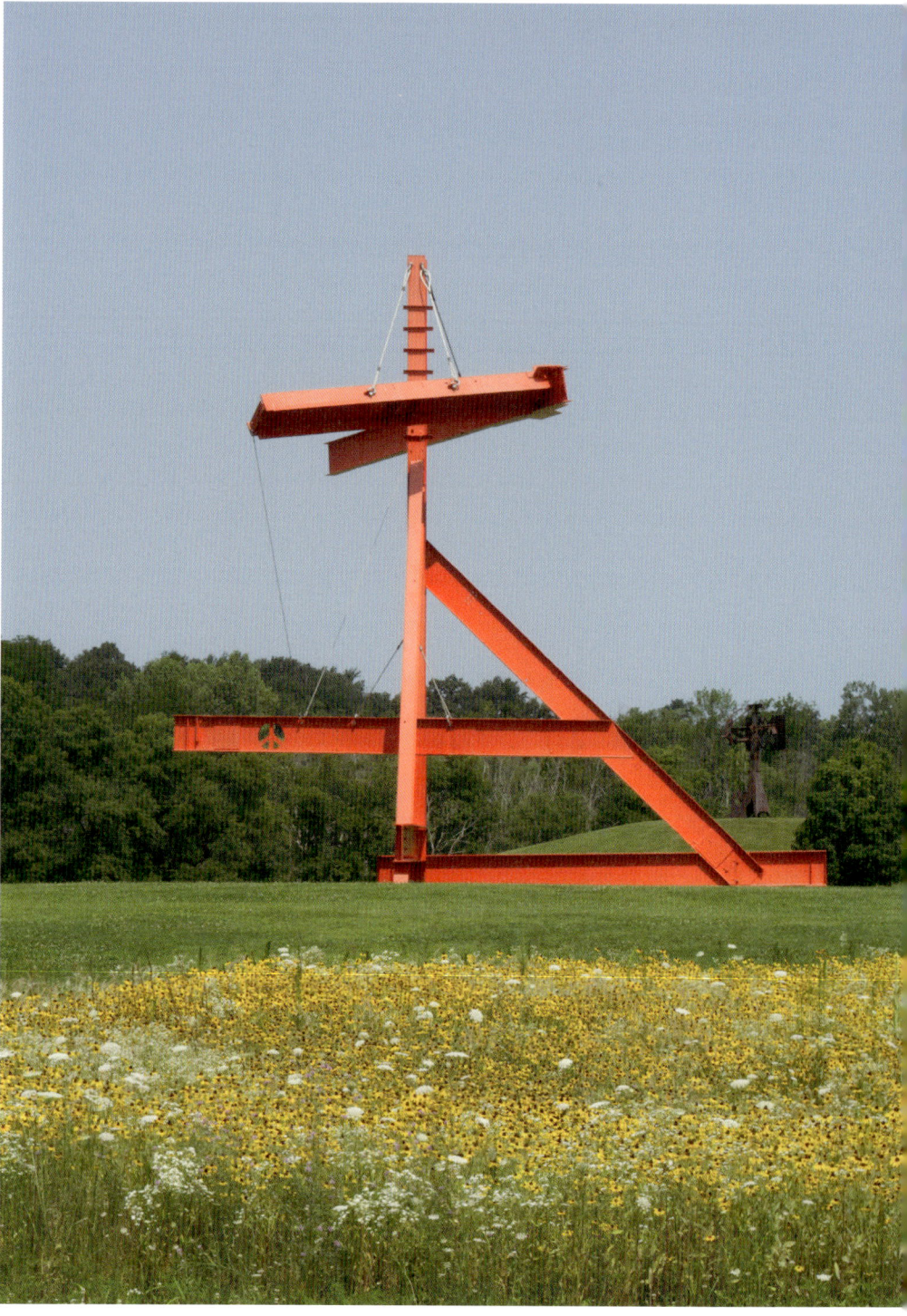

MARK DI SUVERO

AMERICAN, BORN CHINA, 1933

SELECTED WORKS:
MOTHER PEACE, 1969–70
PAINTED STEEL
41' 8" x 49' 5" x 44' 3"
GIFT OF THE RALPH E. OGDEN FOUNDATION

MON PÈRE, MON PÈRE, 1973–75
STEEL
35' x 40' x 40' 4"
GIFT OF THE RALPH E. OGDEN FOUNDATION

PYRAMIDIAN, 1987/1998
STEEL
56 x 46 x 46'
GIFT OF THE RALPH E. OGDEN FOUNDATION

Mark di Suvero often works on an architectural, monumental scale, creating spatially dynamic sculptures largely from industrial steel I-beams, each weighing many tons. His primary tools are the crane, the cherry picker, and cutting and welding torches. Di Suvero's bold, open, steel sculptures and the broad expanses of Storm King seem made for each other—together they create a unique environment in which the dynamism of art and nature reinforce one another. Storm King has presented four landmark exhibitions of di Suvero's work: the first, a twenty-five year retrospective of sculptures and drawings in 1985; the second, a ten-year retrospective in 1995 and 1996 that included a group of di Suvero's paintings shown in the United States for the first time; a unique exhibition highlighting di Suvero's relationship with his longtime gallerist and friend Richard Bellamy in 2005 and 2006; and most recently, a major exhibition of twelve monumental outdoor works sited on Governors Island in New York in 2011 and 2012.

Di Suvero came to public prominence in 1975 with a display of his work in the Jardin des Tuileries in Paris—the first for any living artist—and a major retrospective that same year at the Whitney Museum of American Art in New York, which featured his large-scale sculpture in public sites through all five boroughs of the city. It was after the Whitney retrospective that a group of di Suvero's outdoor works were first brought to Storm King, at the invitation of its co-founder and president, H. Peter Stern. Since then, Storm King has presented more than ninety sculptures by di Suvero, and currently owns an unrivaled group of five of his large-scale sculptures—*Mother Peace, Mon Père Mon Père, Pyramidian, Mozart's Birthday,* and *Mahatma.*

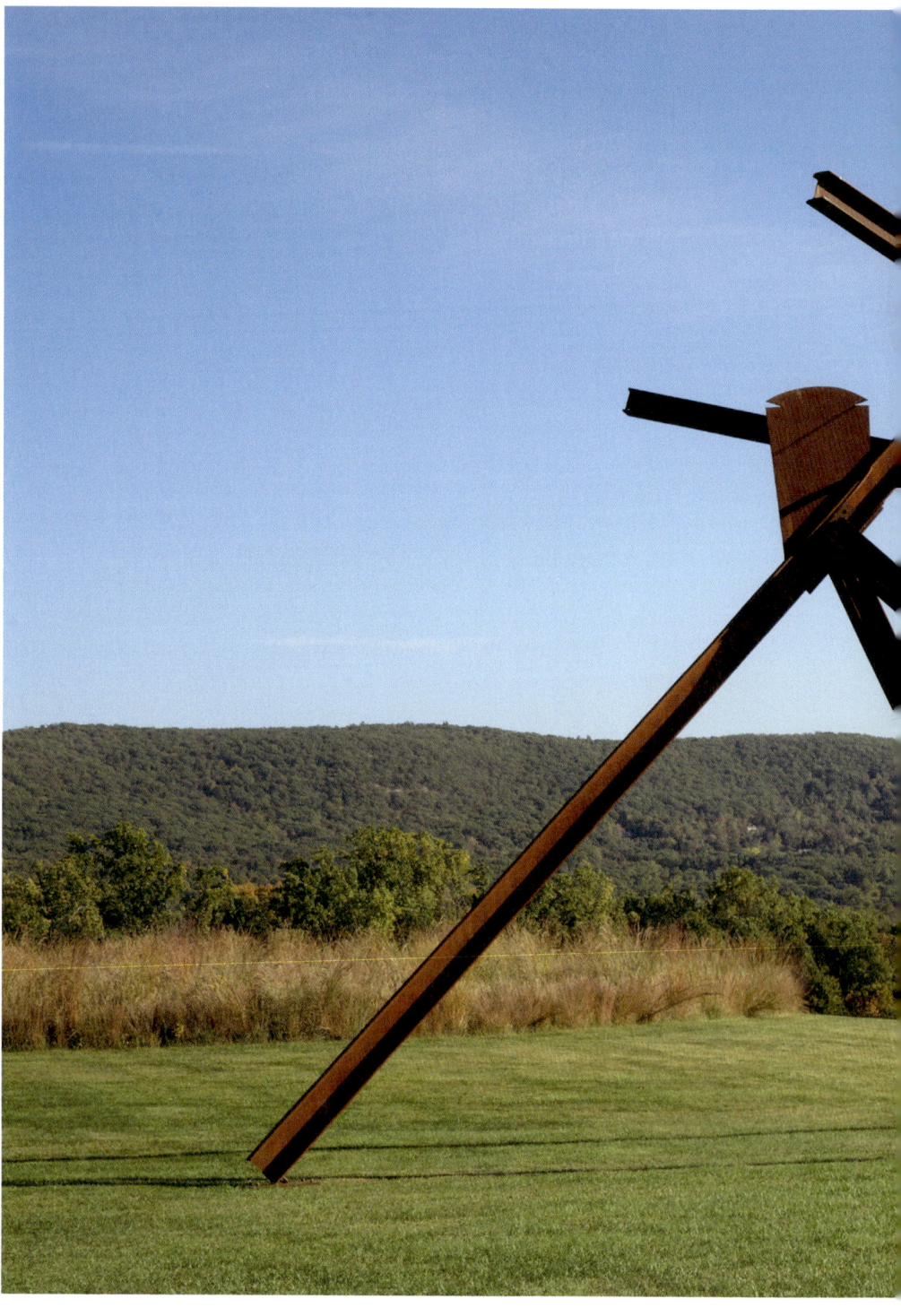

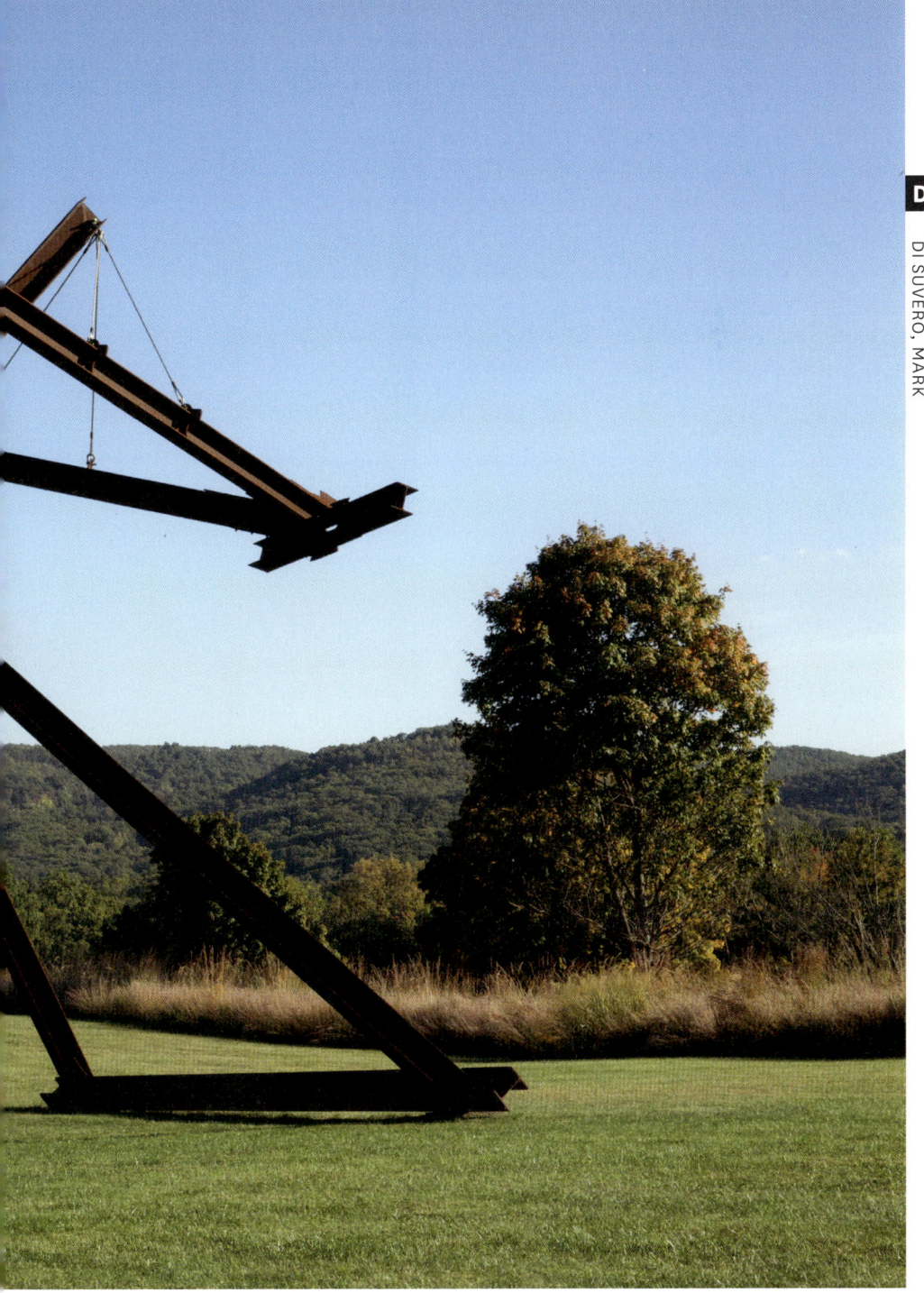

These were the first works to be sited in the South Fields at Storm King, when the first group of his sculpture arrived in 1976.

Di Suvero is a politically committed artist. In 1966 he designed the fifty-five-foot-high *Peace Tower* (now destroyed) in Los Angeles as a protest against the war in Vietnam. Soon after, he left the United States for several years, in voluntary exile as an antiwar protest. Leaving North America in 1971, he traveled first to Eindhoven, Holland, working in a factory there. In 1972 he moved to Venice, his father's ancestral home. There, he established a small painting and drawing studio, taught at the Università Internazionale dell'Arte, and collaborated with engineers to design a system of locks to prevent canal flooding. Shortly thereafter di Suvero relocated to the industrial French town of Chalon-sur-Saône, living until 1974 on a houseboat anchored next to a waterfront shipyard, where he used cranes and cherry pickers to create a series of large-scale sculptures, including *Mon Père, Mon Père*.

In 1985 di Suvero turned an abandoned warehouse into a studio on the waterfront in Long Island City, across the East River from Manhattan. Since that time he has created many works that are more visually complex, comprising a varied repertoire of flat circular shapes and acute angles. Recently the artist has experimented with incorporating different materials into his compositions, including burnished stainless steel and titanium. Di Suvero's smaller works explore balance, movement, and intricate design on an intimate scale. A series of puzzle sculptures made in the early 1980s, for example, invites viewers to rearrange calligraphic cut steel shapes into new compositions. Foregoing preparatory drawings and improvising as he constructs, di Suvero continues to invent new shapes, new forms, and material combinations that enliven space, enrich experience, and convey poignant human emotion.

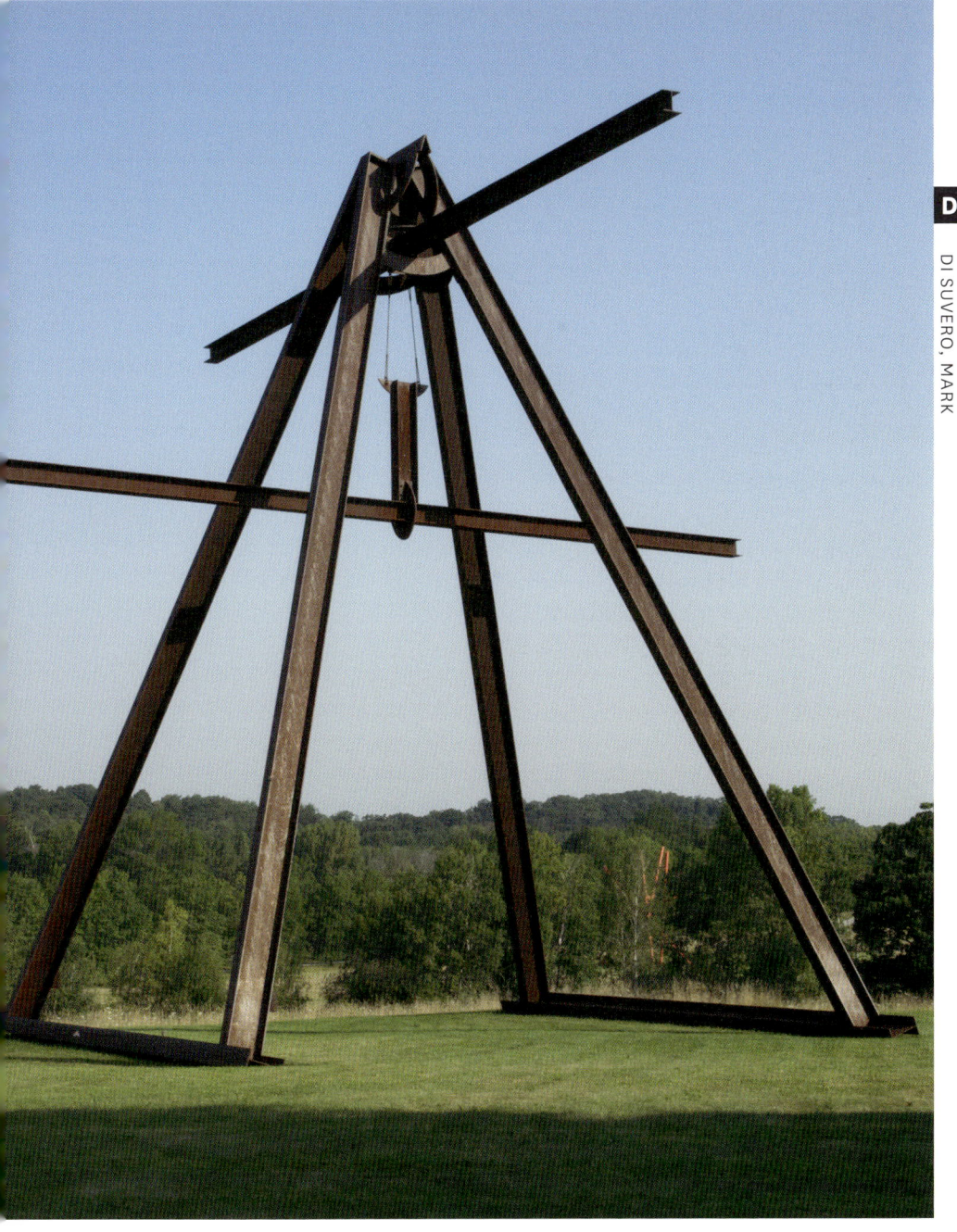

59   PREVIOUS SPREAD: *Mon Père, Mon Père*, 1973–75; ABOVE: *Pyramidian*, 1987/1998

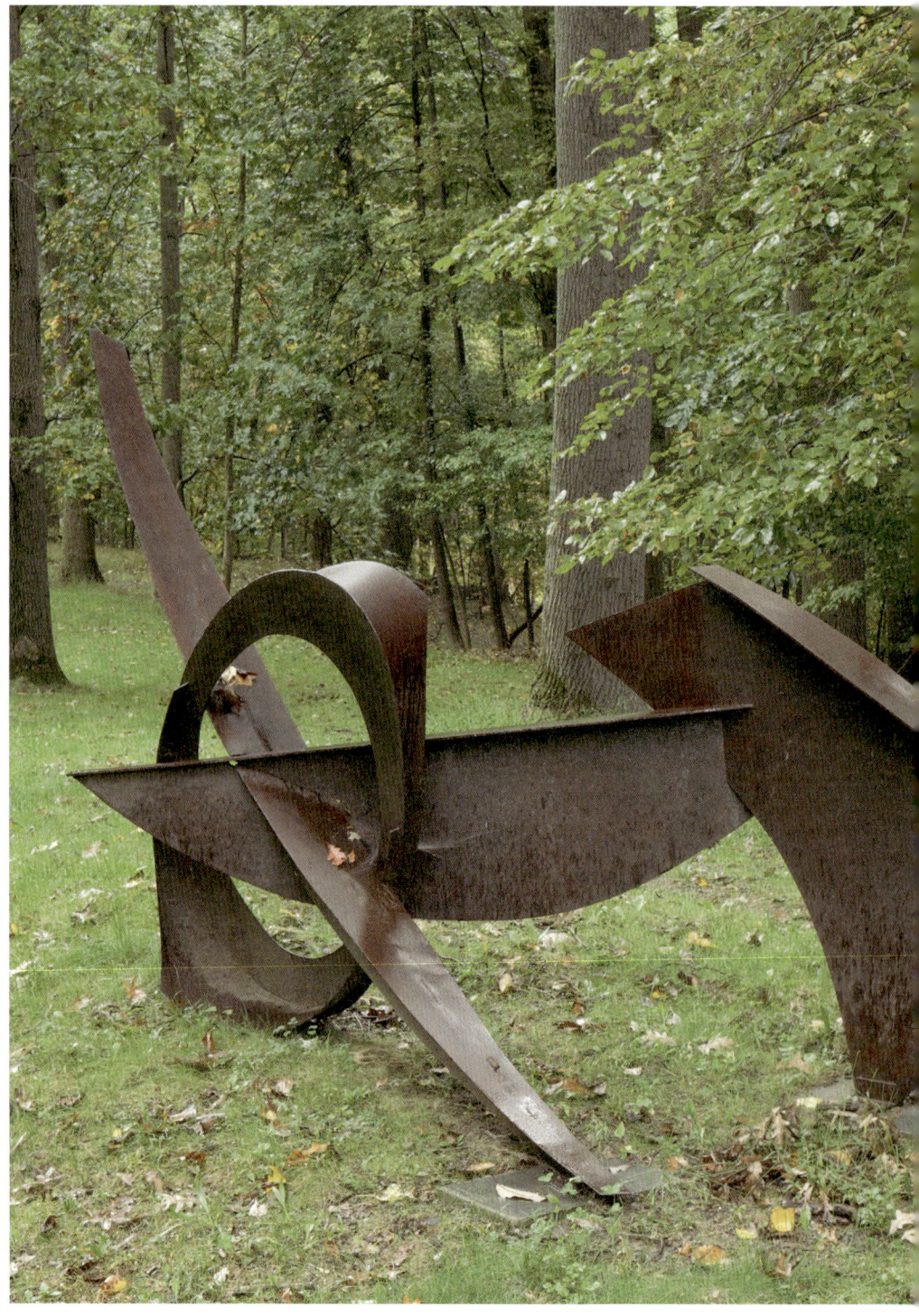

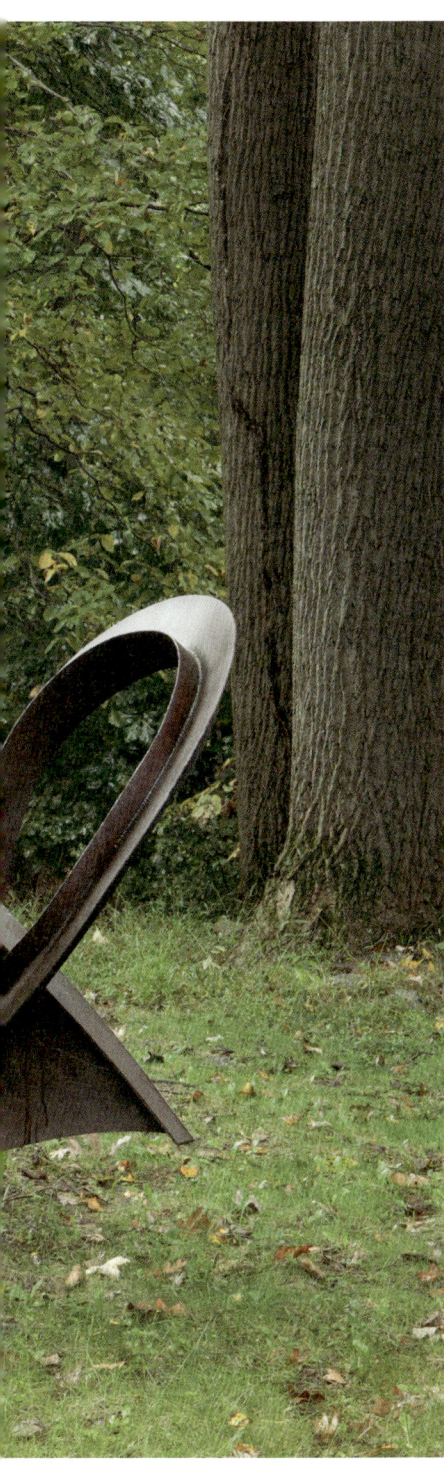

HERBERT FERBER

AMERICAN, 1906–1991

SELECTED WORK:
KONKAPOT II, 1972
WEATHERING STEEL
69" x 10' x 48"
PURCHASED WITH THE AID OF FUNDS FROM
THE NATIONAL ENDOWMENT FOR THE ARTS AND
GIFT OF THE RALPH E. OGDEN FOUNDATION

Herbert Ferber's dynamic, open-form, welded works pierce space and seem to defy gravity. As he once observed, "Where sculpture had been solid, closed, it is now an art of open, airy, discontinuous forms, suspended in space." *Konkapot II* is one in a group of works Ferber created in the early 1970s in which he sought to convey a sense of calligraphy and a relief-like quality. He referred to these lyrical works, distinguished by a lateral rhythm of arcs and circles, as "horizon sculptures." *Konkapot II* conjures the fluidity of nature in steel. Spreading curves and arcs balance segmented planes so the sculpture seems to rest and to move at the same time. The piece is named after a river near the artist's home in the Berkshires in Massachusetts.

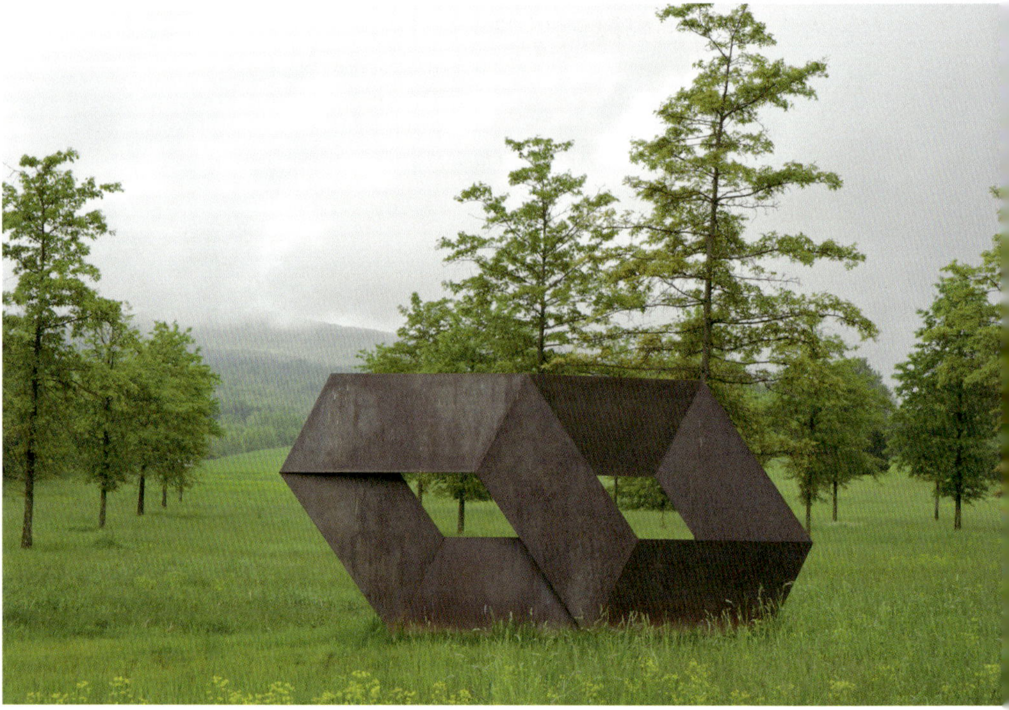

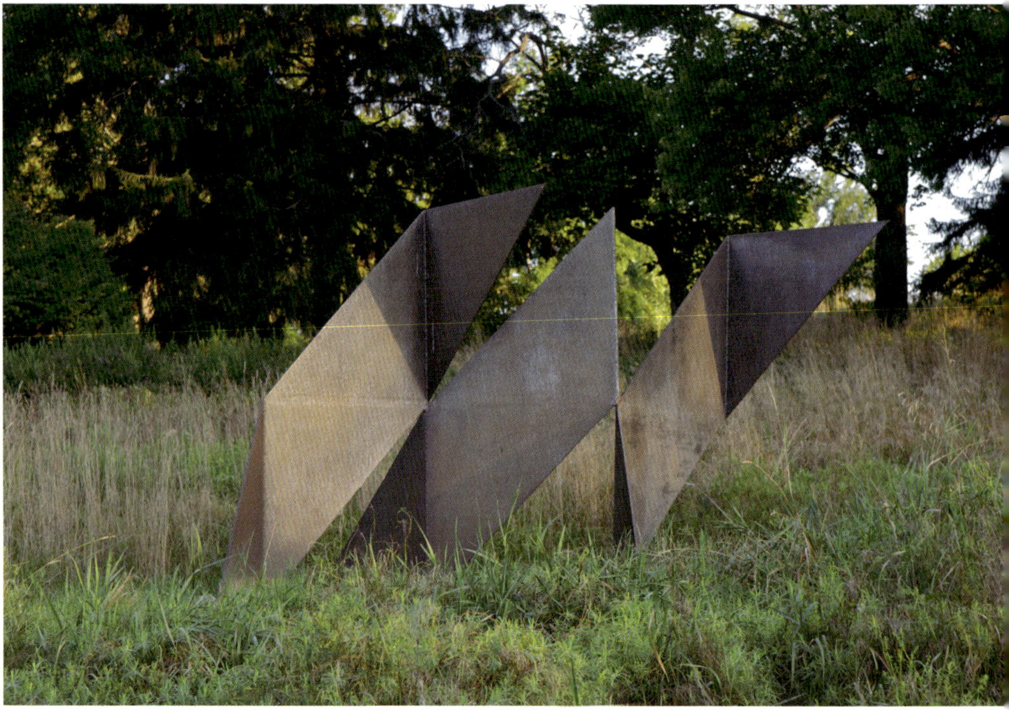

CHARLES GINNEVER

AMERICAN, BORN 1931

SELECTED WORKS:
FAYETTE: FOR CHARLES AND MEDGAR EVERS, 1971
WEATHERING STEEL
7' 10 ½" x 16' 10" x 18"
GIFT OF THE RALPH E. OGDEN FOUNDATION

PROSPECT MOUNTAIN PROJECT (FOR DAVID SMITH), 1979
WEATHERING STEEL
8' x 14' x 12' 4"
PURCHASED WITH THE AID OF FUNDS FROM THE NATIONAL ENDOWMENT
FOR THE ARTS AND GIFT OF THE RALPH E. OGDEN FOUNDATION

Throughout his career Charles Ginnever has been interested in creating works whose visual complexities belie the relatively simple forms they first suggest. Many of his sculptures are bold, geometric sets of interconnected steel planes that seem to vacillate between flatness and cubic volumes as the viewer moves around them. In a sense, Ginnever invites the viewer to meditate on the nature of perception.

Fayette: For Charles and Medgar Evers is named for two brothers who were prominent leaders in the civil rights movement. Medgar was killed by a sniper in 1963. Charles continued their work and was elected mayor of Fayette, Mississippi, in 1971. Ginnever made this sculpture that same year, taking part in public art's long tradition of honoring important people and commemorating heroic achievements and allying him with the aims of the civil rights movement.

Prospect Mountain Project honors David Smith, a pivotal figure in the history of modern sculpture and a central presence in the Storm King collection. The work was first exhibited as part of *Prospect Mountain Sculpture Show: An Homage to David Smith*, a 1979 exhibition near Smith's home in Bolton Landing, New York, which featured works by artists including Mark di Suvero and Isaac Witkin. The piece consists of three steel structures, each resembling folded paper objects, arranged to give an impression of delicate balance. Ginnever's work, like much of Smith's, draws inspiration from Cubism and explores the ambiguity between perception and reality.

FROM TOP: *Fayette: For Charles and Medgar Evers*, 1971;
63   *Prospect Mountain Project (For David Smith)*, 1979

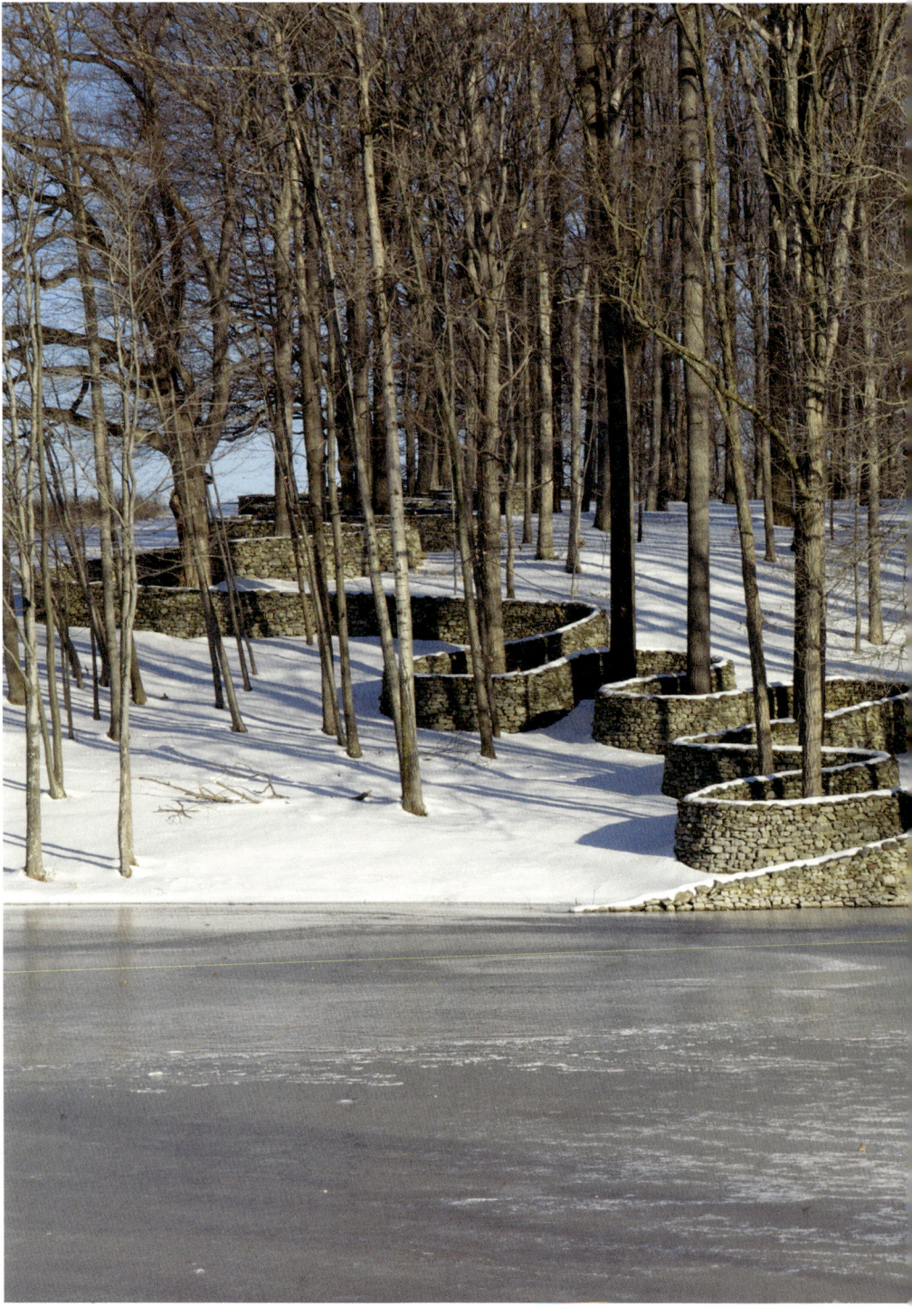

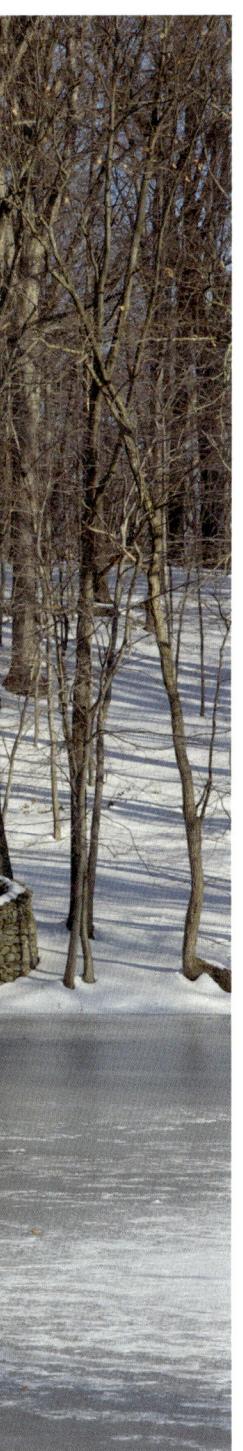

ANDY GOLDSWORTHY

BRITISH, BORN 1956

STORM KING WALL, 1997–98
FIELDSTONE
APPROX. 60" x 2,278' 6" x 32" OVERALL
GIFT OF THE RALPH E. OGDEN FOUNDATION, MR. AND MRS.
JOEL MALLIN, MRS. W. L. LYONS BROWN, JR., MR. AND MRS.
JAMES H. OTTAWAY, JR., THE MARGARET T. MORRIS FOUNDATION,
THE HORACE W. GOLDSMITH FOUNDATION, THE HAZEN FUND,
THE JOSEPH H. HAZEN FOUNDATION, INC., MR. AND MRS.
RONALD N. ROMARY, DR. WENDY SCHAFFER AND MR. IVAN GJAJA,
AND AN ANONYMOUS FOUNDATION

FIVE MEN, SEVENTEEN DAYS, FIFTEEN BOULDERS, ONE WALL, 2010
FIELDSTONE
APPROX. 60" x 309' x 32" OVERALL
COURTESY THE ARTIST AND GALERIE LELONG, NEW YORK

Storm King Wall—Andy Goldsworthy's first museum commission for a permanent work in the United States and his
largest single installation to date—exemplifies his nature-
based methodology, which includes building this and other
dry stone walls that draw on British agricultural tradition.
Storm King Wall was originally imagined as a 750-foot-long
dry stone wall snaking through the woods, but when it
reached its planned endpoint, at the foot of a large oak tree,
it seemed only natural to the artist for the wall to continue
downhill to a nearby pond. Soon after the wall's trajectory
was extended again; it now emerges from the other side
of the pond and continues uphill to Storm King's western
boundary at the New York State Thruway—totaling 2,278
feet overall.

The work was built, in some parts, stone-by-stone upon
the remnants of an old farm wall that Goldsworthy found
in the woods overlooking Moodna Creek, at Storm King's
eastern boundary. Rising to a maximum height of about five
feet, it follows a path the artist chose—winding through a
row of trees that grew from seeds to saplings to maturity in
a line alongside the original, dilapidated wall. Goldsworthy
has speculated that these trees played a role in the slow
collapse of the farm wall, and thus the new wall's path winds
through the trees instead of alongside them.

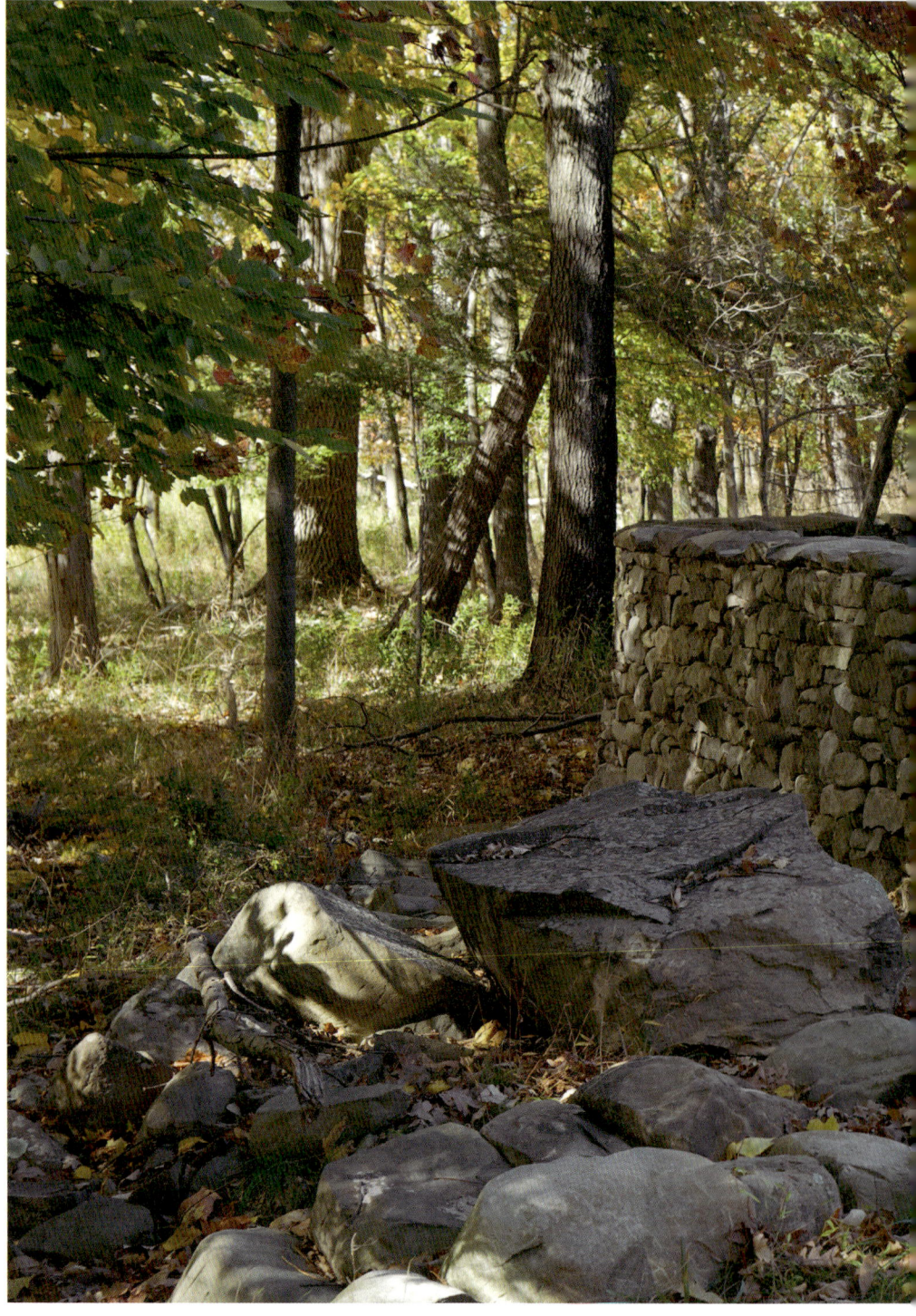

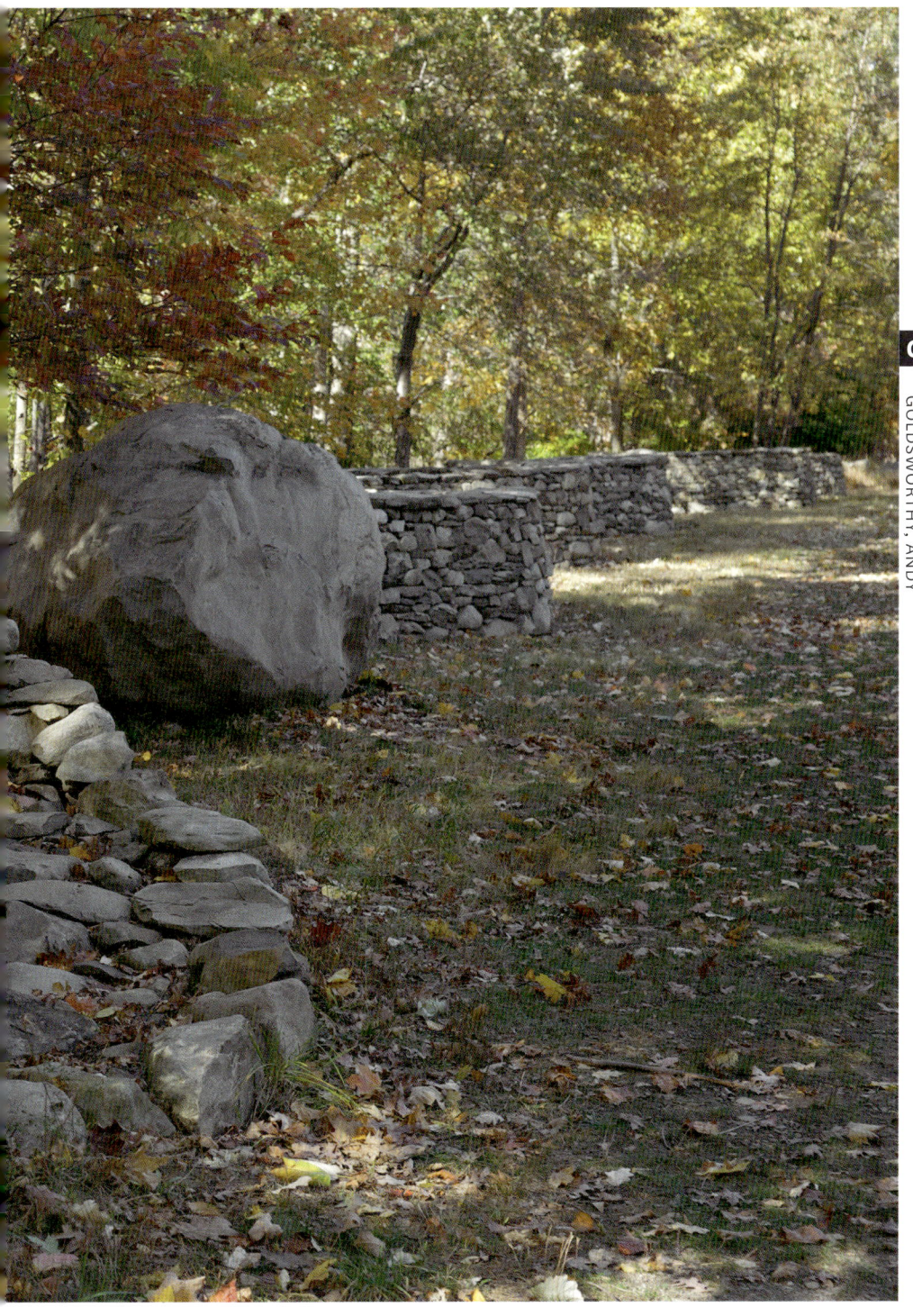

While Goldsworthy conceived *Storm King Wall* and supervised its construction, the roughhewn structure was built by a team of British wallers, who explained to Storm King staff exactly what kinds of stone to harvest and sort in preparation for their work: chunky foundation stones, a smaller, rounder variety for the wall's midsection, large "through stones," and flat cap stones for the top layer. The British team built the wall by placing one stone on top of another while chipping and shaping each one to fit snugly; no concrete was used in stacking the wall's 1,579 tons of fieldstone. The stones can be as captivating as the wall itself.

On the occasion of Storm King's fiftieth anniversary in 2010, Goldsworthy and the same team of British wallers returned to build *Five Men, Seventeen Days, Fifteen Boulders, One Wall* in a field that had interested Goldsworthy upon his first visits to Storm King. Using 250 tons of stones found on the property, Goldsworthy and the wallers altered a 309-foot dilapidated wall in the field over seventeen days. The five men built up a major span of the wall, while allowing the ends to taper off gently, evoking an ancient ruin. The wall winds around fifteen boulders along a grove of trees. Reflecting on his walls at Storm King, Goldsworthy has noted, "Trees, stone, people—these are the ingredients of the place and the work."

From the beginning of his career, Goldsworthy has worked outdoors, rejecting the traditional studio as constraining. From 1976 until 1984, he constructed ephemeral works in natural environments that were not shown as such, but rather as photographs of the works, which would soon disappear or disintegrate. His more recent works are generally permanent installations; their construction involves interaction with landowners and builders, providing a foil to the solitary ephemeral creations. Goldsworthy calls the stone walls of the British countryside "a living part of the landscape." Indeed, stone walls connect to both the present and to the history of any place where they happen to be.

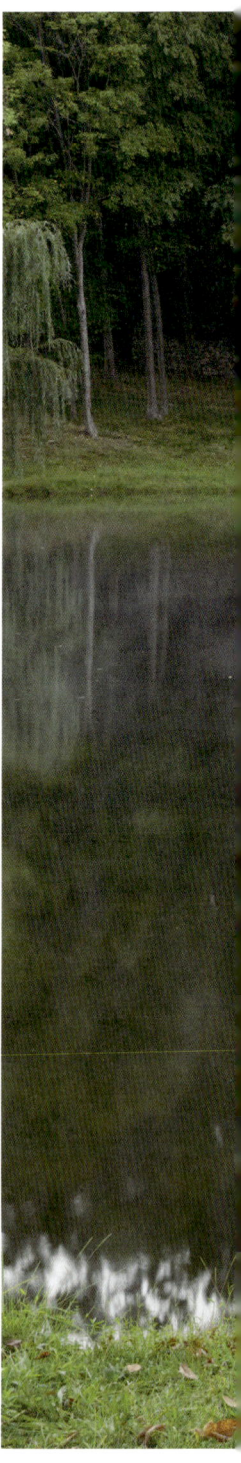

PREVIOUS SPREAD: *Five Men, Seventeen Days, Fifteen Boulders, One Wall*, 2010; RIGHT: *Storm King Wall*, 1997–98

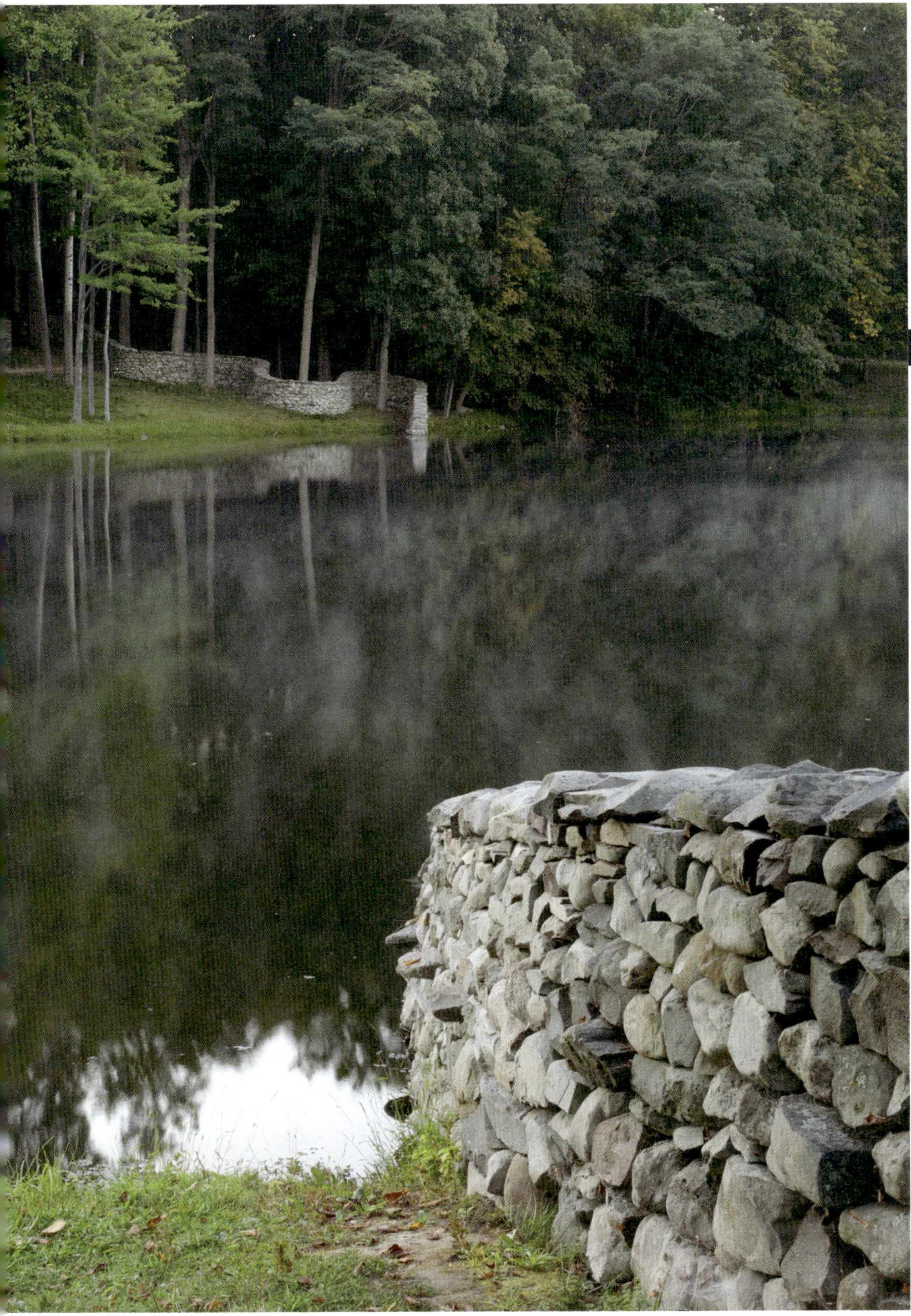

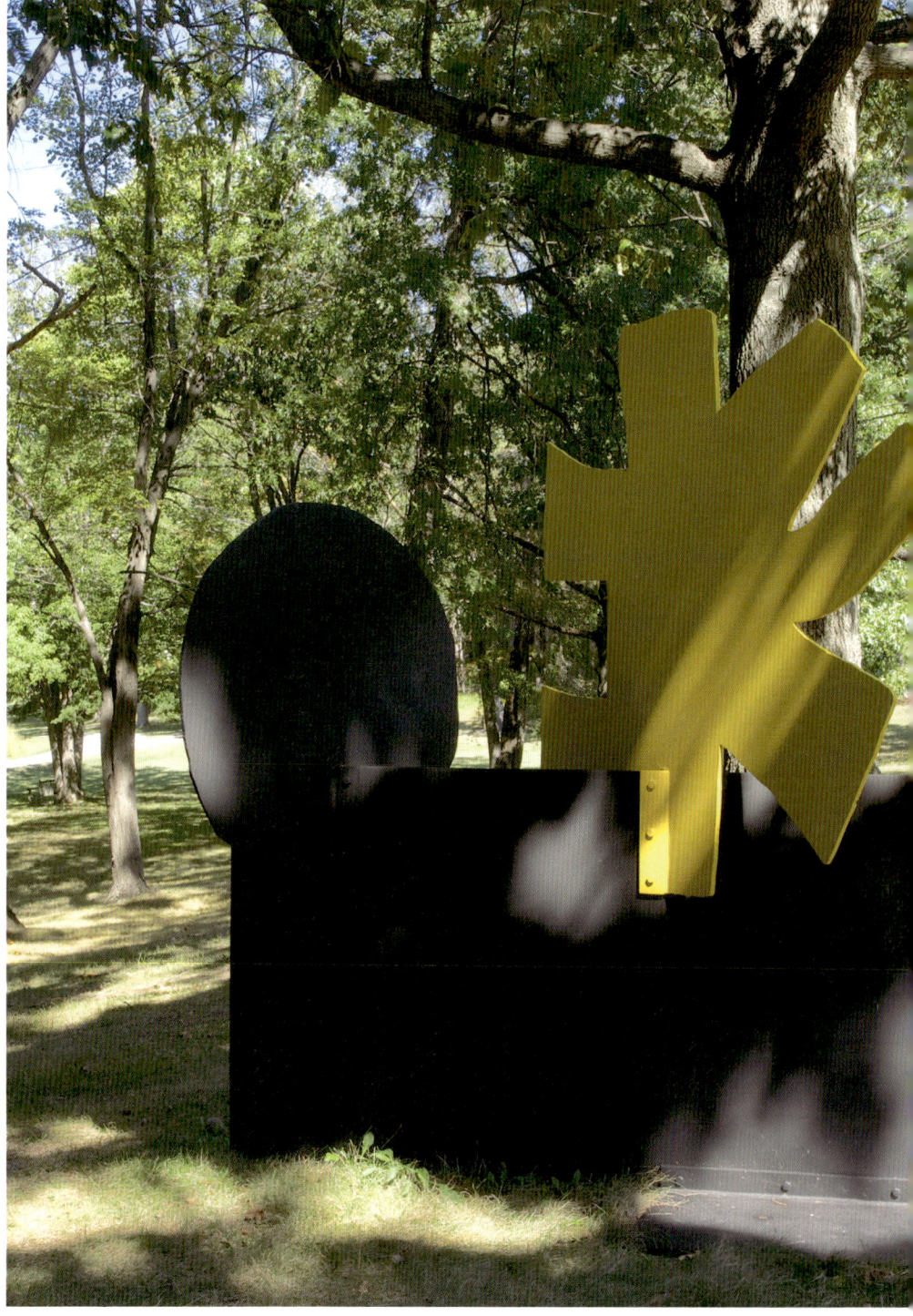

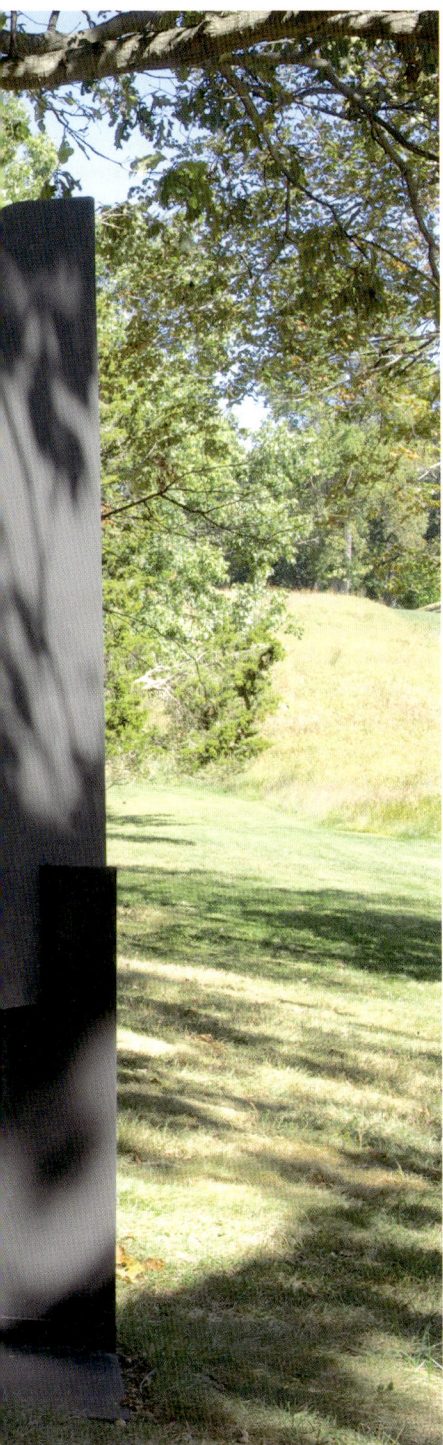

ADOLPH GOTTLIEB

AMERICAN, 1903–1974

PETALOID, 1967–68
PAINTED STEEL
8' 6" x 8' x 37"
GIFT OF THE ADOLPH AND ESTHER
GOTTLIEB FOUNDATION

In the late 1960s Adolph Gottlieb—the prominent painter associated with the Abstract Expressionist movement of the late 1940s and '50s—began experimenting with three-dimensional works. Most were realized only in the form of small maquettes, and *Petaloid* is one of only three large-scale sculptures Gottlieb made. Gottlieb's sculptures can be interpreted as an extension of the experimentation with form and shape in which he engaged in his paintings. In the early 1950s Gottlieb painted a series of imaginary landscapes divided into distinct horizontal celestial and terrestrial zones, a duality that crystallized in his *Burst* pictures of 1956–57, which depict sun-like disks suspended over explosive, irregular black masses. In *Petaloid*, a planar, rectilinear, horizontal element supports a bright yellow petal-like form resting on the top edge, flanked by a black vertical rectangle on one side and a black circle on the other. The imagery of this sculpture roughly approximates that of his paintings: the bright yellow flower dominates the sculpture just as dazzling sunbursts illuminated his canvases.

G

GOTTLIEB, ADOLPH

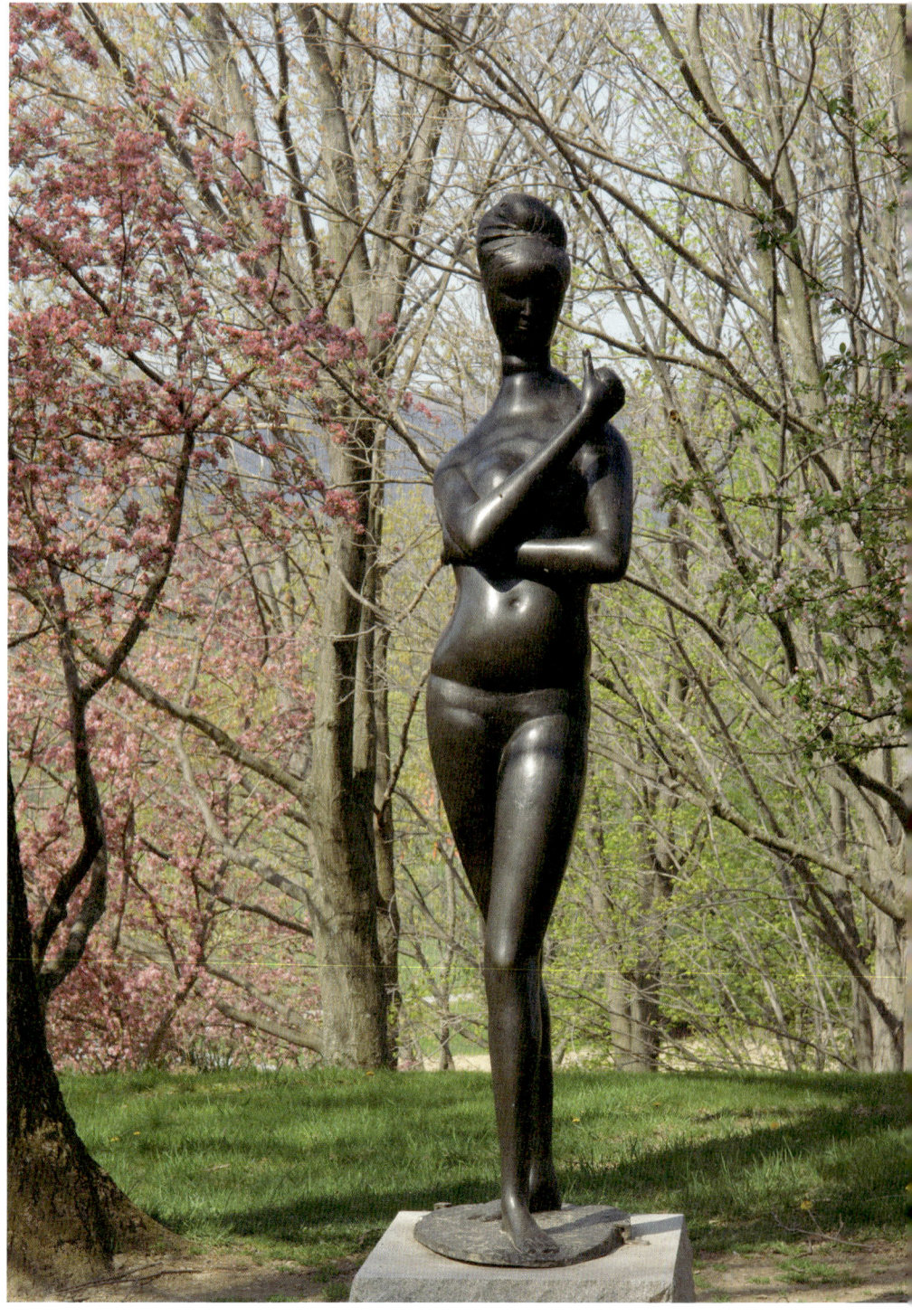

EMILIO GRECO

ITALIAN, 1913–1995

TALL BATHER NO. I, 1956
BRONZE
6'11" x 18" x 28"
GIFT OF THE RALPH E. OGDEN FOUNDATION

Tall Bather No. I is the first in a series of seven variously posed sculptures of female bathers, a central theme in Emilio Greco's sculptural work. Greco noted that he considered his seven *Large Bathers* as dancers, and their movements and poses as a progressive choreography. He planned to create twelve *Bathers* on this scale and place them around a pool or pond but the final five were never realized.

   Tall Bather No. I stands in a relaxed but contained contrapposto pose: her torso is slightly curved and she leans back on a straightened leg while her front leg bends slightly. She wraps her arms around her upper body in a gesture of modesty. Her head is slightly tilted and her eyes look downward, perhaps suggesting pensiveness and inwardness. The soft swelling of her body and the elegance of the sculpture as a whole suggest the stylistic quality of sixteenth-century Italian Mannerist painters. These classical associations are, however, disrupted by some decidedly stylized, modern elements of the figure, such as her hairstyle and the tight-fitting bikini bottom.

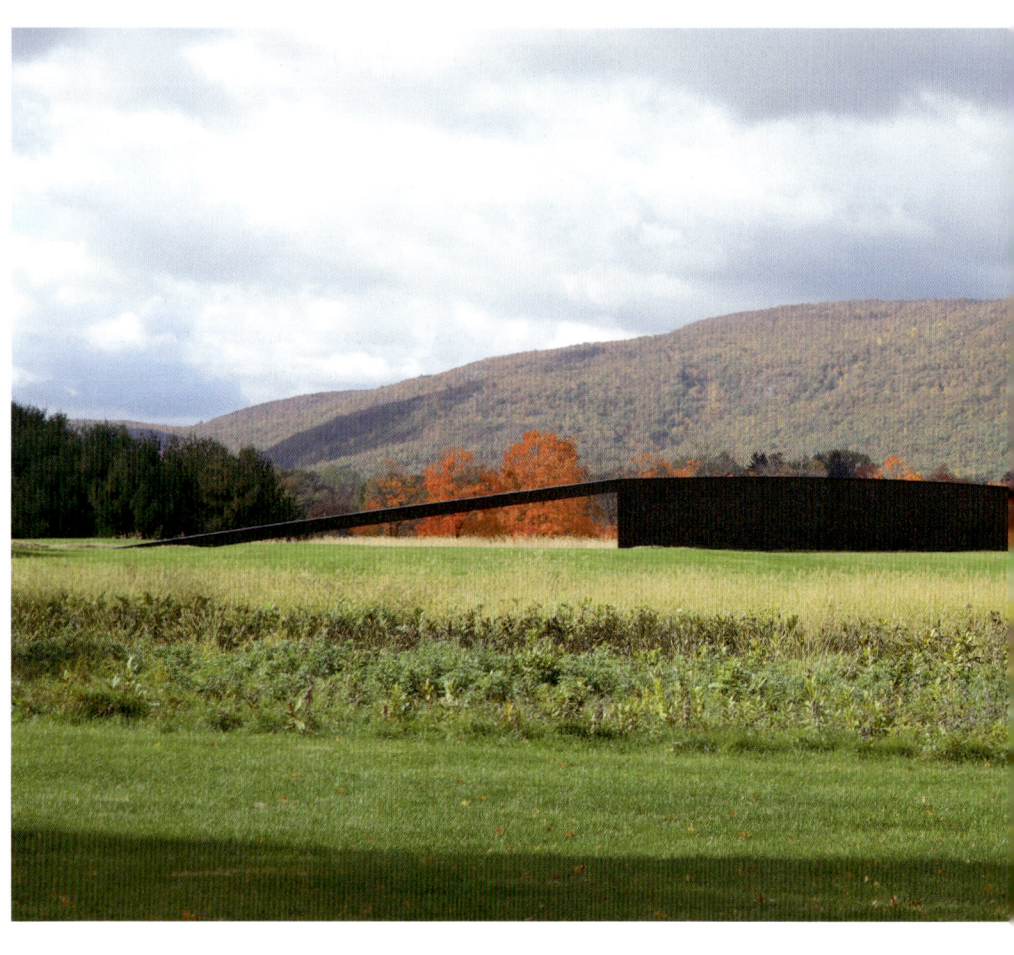

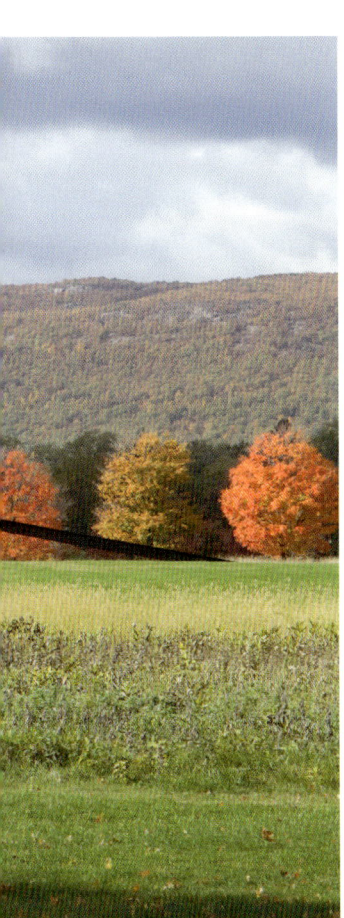

ROBERT GROSVENOR

AMERICAN, BORN 1937

UNTITLED, 1970
PAINTED WEATHERING STEEL
10' x 212' 5½" x 12"
GIFT OF THE RALPH E. OGDEN FOUNDATION

Robert Grosvenor's *Untitled* was the second site-specific commission to be installed at Storm King, in 1974. This expansive horizontal structure measures 212 feet long and only 12 inches wide. It spans a relatively flat field along an approximate east-west axis, drawing the viewer's eye to the panoramic view of the distant Hudson Highlands and Schunnemunk Mountain ridge. The potential for industrial materials (like Grosvenor's) and nature to enhance each other is a key element of Storm King's ethos.

Although its spine appears to be made of a single, long I-beam, *Untitled* is actually composed of several I-beams joined together and painted black to appear as a seamless whole. Seen head-on, the central wall focuses the viewer's attention on the thin frontal plane of the sculpture, blocking the view through the work's central core and heightening the viewer's sensitivity to the natural world visible through the negative spaces that flank the central plane. This broad expanse appears to disappear, becoming two-dimensional and linear, when the work is viewed from either end.

Storm King co-founder Ralph E. Ogden became interested in Grosvenor's work in 1971 after seeing one of his large pieces in a private collection in nearby New City, New York. Ogden contacted Grosvenor, who visited Storm King that summer. Grosvenor did not design a completely new work for Storm King. He felt that the location was perfect for a long, thin piece with a central panel that he had envisioned in 1970. Hence, the work is dated 1970, but was fabricated and installed in 1974.

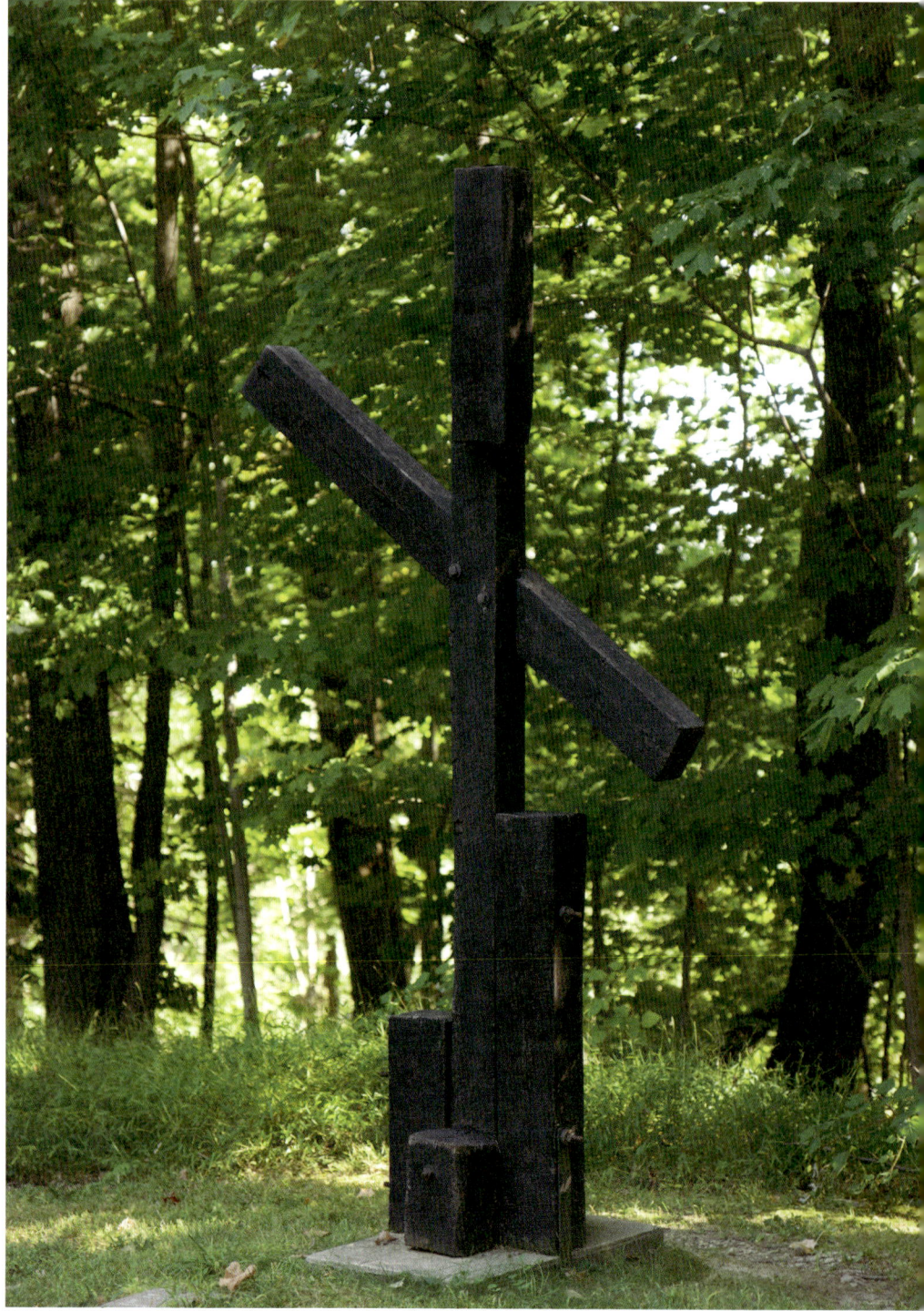

GILBERT HAWKINS

AMERICAN, BORN 1944

SELECTED WORK:
EX, 1971
WOOD AND STEEL
9'1" x 60" x 20"
GIFT OF THE RALPH E. OGDEN FOUNDATION

After Gilbert Hawkins visited Storm King in 1972 and dropped off photographs of his work, Storm King co-founder Ralph E. Ogden sought him out and made arrangements to exhibit his *Blue Moon*, a steel constructivist piece, for a year. Ogden ultimately purchased and commissioned several sculptures by Hawkins, both for Storm King and for his private collection. *Ex*, a totemic wood assemblage, is composed of simple geometric forms. Various rectangular wood blocks are attached to a central vertical piece. A single notch, approximately one-third of the way down from the top, animates the work. A separate timber attached to the back is set at an oblique angle, forming the work's *X* shape, which inspired its title.

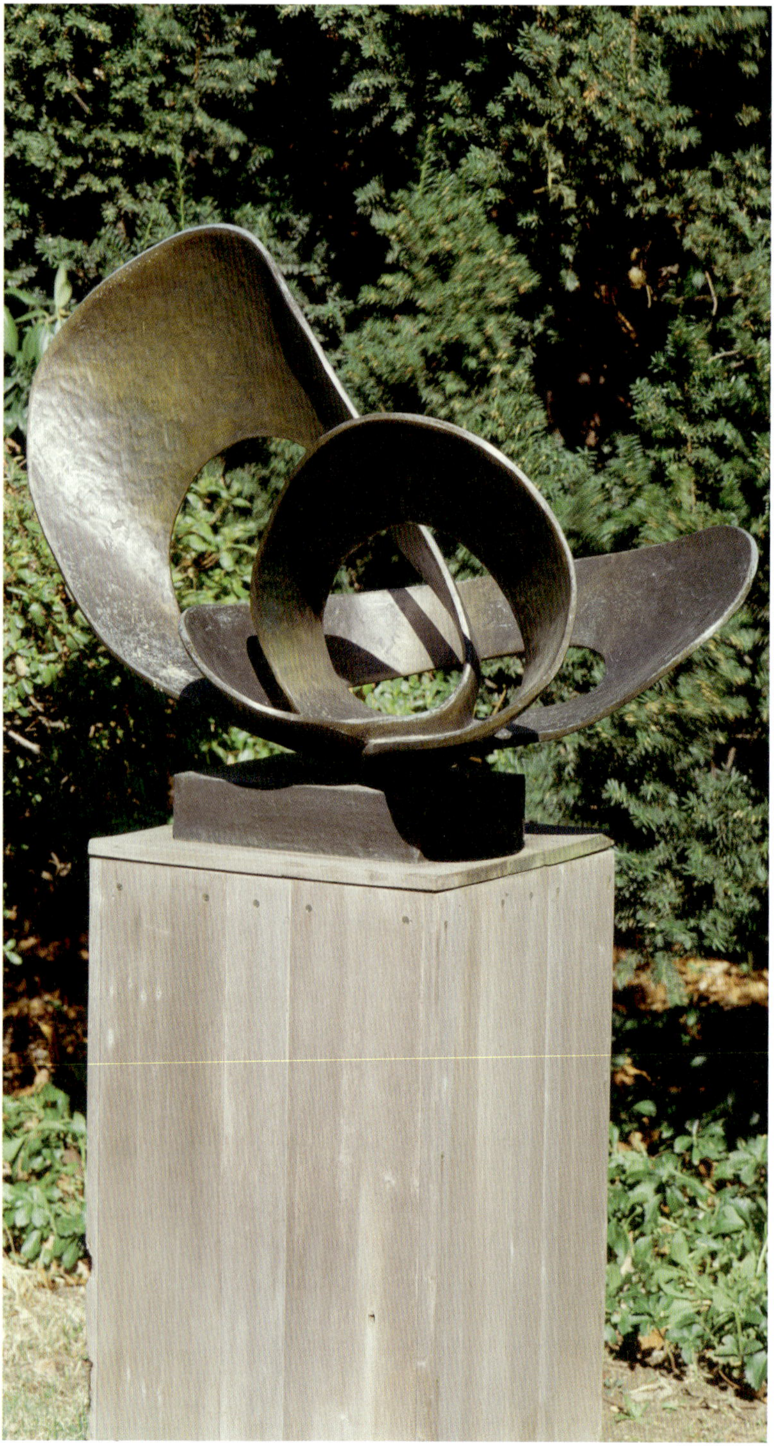

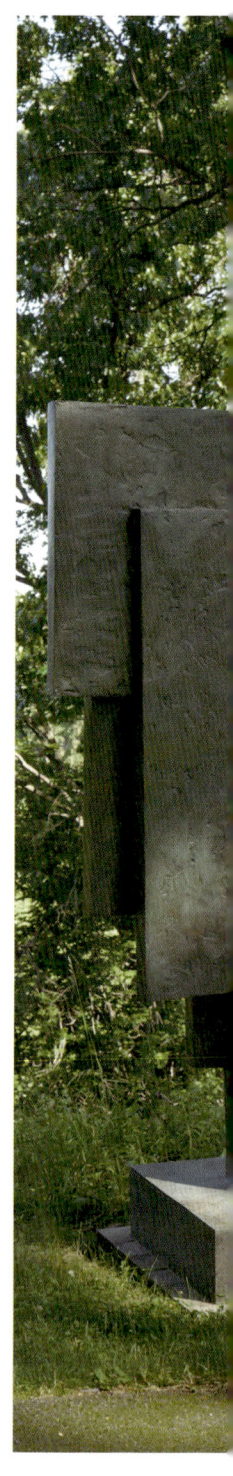

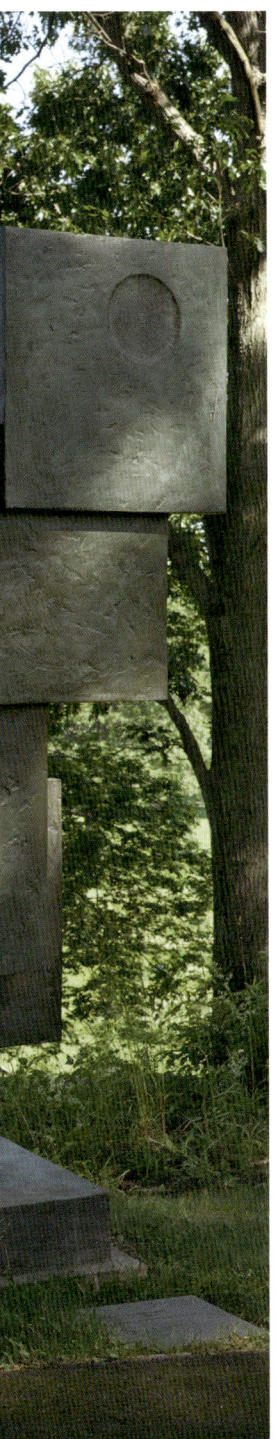

BARBARA HEPWORTH

BRITISH, 1903–1975

FORMS IN MOVEMENT (PAVAN), 1956 (CAST 1967)
BRONZE
29½ x 43 x 22"
GIFT OF THE RALPH E. OGDEN FOUNDATION

SQUARE FORMS WITH CIRCLES, 1963
BRONZE
8'6" x 58" x 27¾"
GIFT OF THE RALPH E. OGDEN FOUNDATION

Barbara Hepworth, who played a key role in the creation of a new sculptural style in England in the twentieth century, became renowned for sculptures that are often pierced by a hole, a device she conceived in 1931. *Forms in Movement (Pavan)* is a graceful, open work with interlaced, looped forms reflecting the artist's interest in dance. The sculpture has a natural feeling to it, enhanced by the off-center placement and irregular shape of the three loops.

Hepworth began to work with cast bronze in 1956. The medium enabled her to experiment with a greater variety of shapes than stone and wood afforded, as well as to work on larger-scale and outdoor works. *Forms in Movement (Pavan)* exemplifies how Hepworth integrated her expertise as a carver in using a material that was new to her. The piece was created in three phases: the first incarnation was made in 1956 of metalized plaster (plaster built up over an aluminum armature), then carved to make the final form; a 1959 version was made in concrete; and in 1967, an edition of seven bronzes was cast from the concrete original.

Hepworth often talked about her interest in the figure in landscape, but she never represented actual objects or people. The abstract works instead become something like figures. In *Square Forms with Circles*, for example, the subtle placement of the square and rectangular forms and their delicately scraped and carved surfaces convey a mysterious personality. Placed in natural settings, her sculptures create a contrast between the geometry of their clear edges and nature's curving shapes and lines.

FROM LEFT: *Forms in Movement (Pavan)*, 1956 (cast 1967); *Square Forms with Circles*, 1963

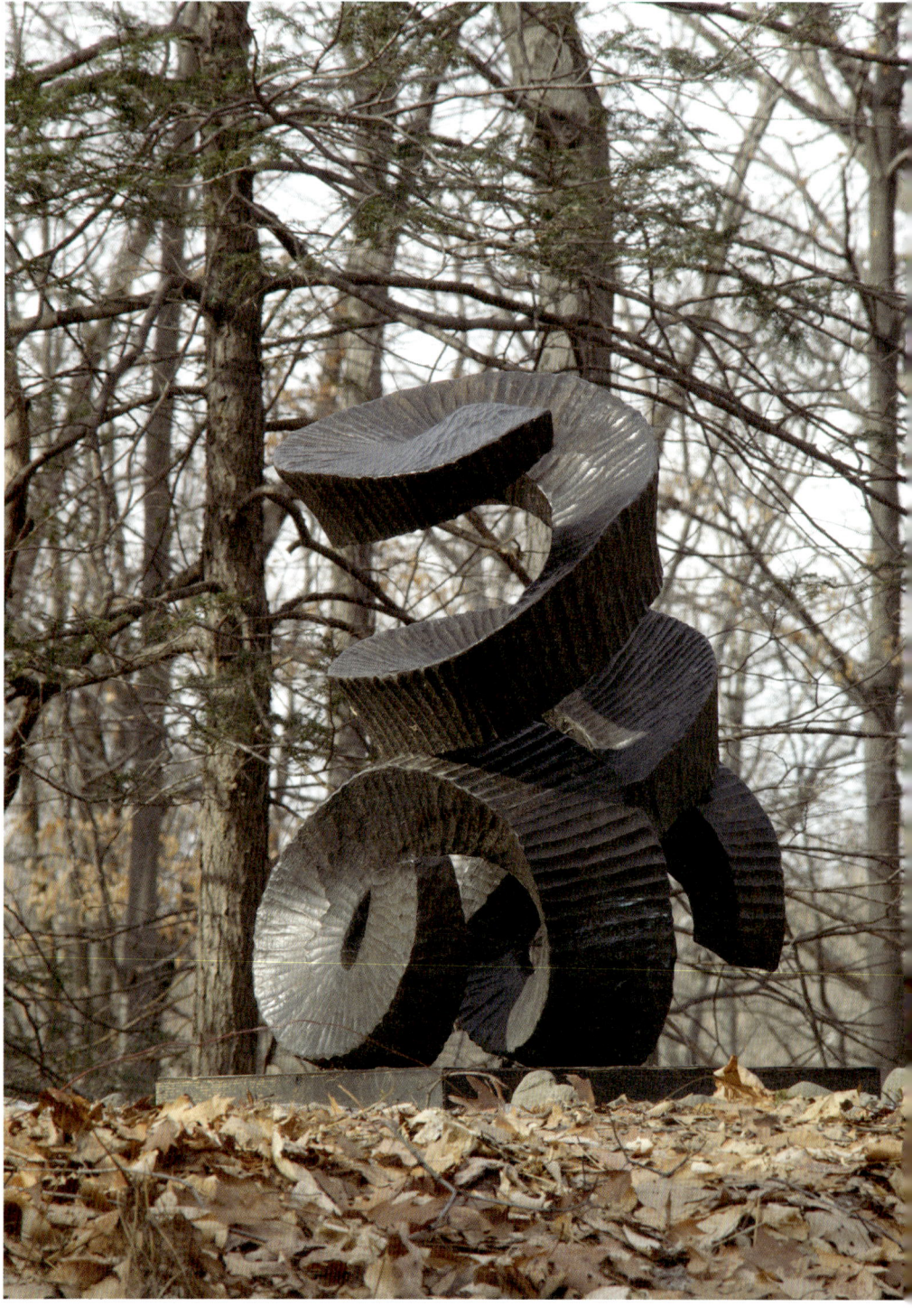

HANS HOKANSON

SWEDISH, 1925–1997

HELIXIKOS NUMBER 3, 1969
BRONZE
36 ½ x 25 x 22"
GIFT OF THE RALPH E. OGDEN FOUNDATION

The original version of *Helixikos Number 3* was conceived and executed in wood; after the original sustained substantial damage, the piece was re-created in bronze. Hans Hokanson's training as a carpenter influenced his early sculptural techniques; he carved from tree trunks and stumps found at Northwest Creek, near his home in East Hampton, on New York's Long Island. The tactile, rippled surface of *Helixikos Number 3*, with its centrifugally curved, ribbon-like forms, is characteristic of Hokanson's early forays into three-dimensional work. The sculpture is abstract, but has a decorative quality that is further enhanced by the grooved surface pattern produced by the carving tool. The work's title contains in it the word "helix," a coiled, twirled, or twisted shape that aptly describes the sculpture's form.

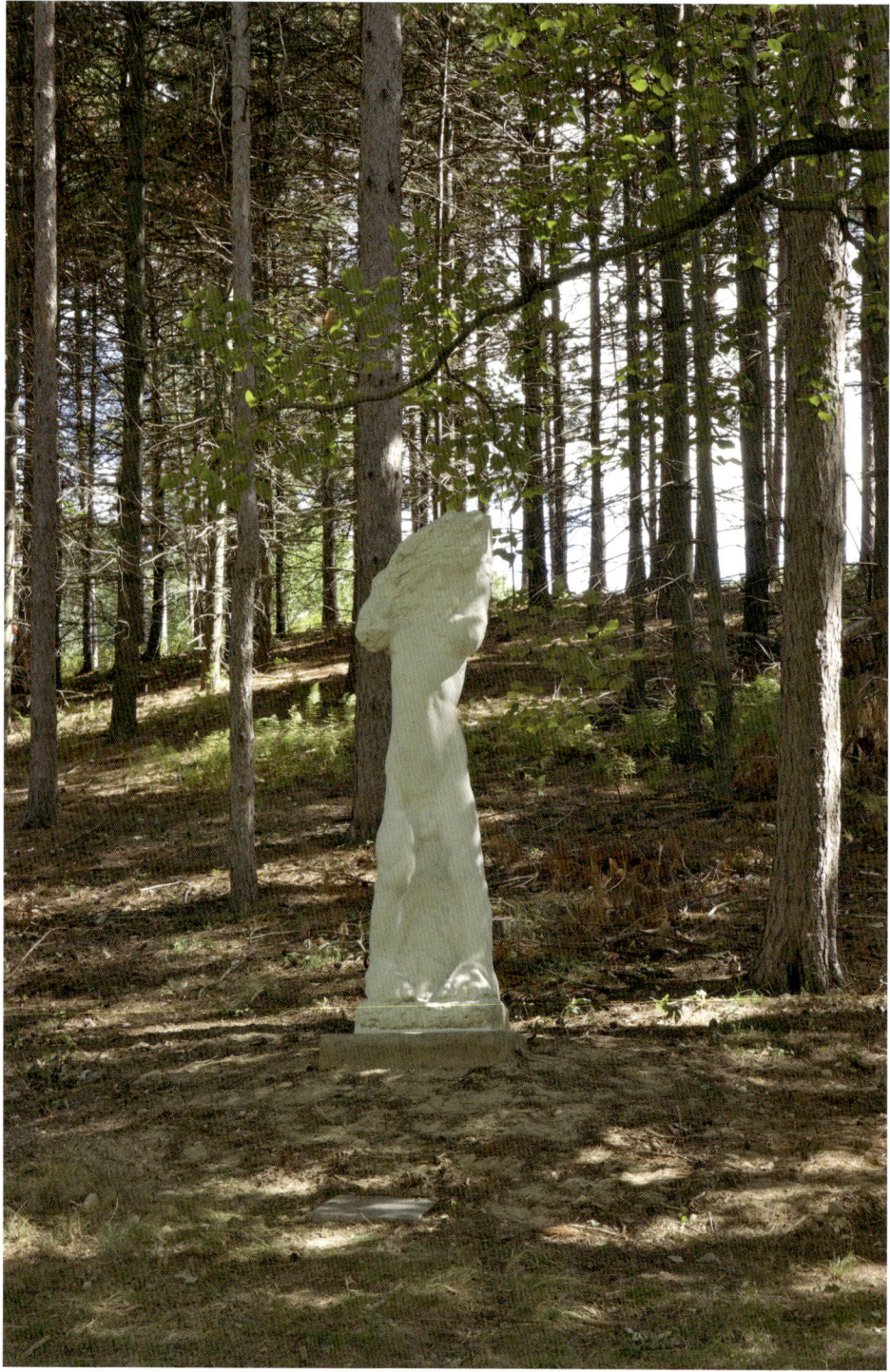

ALFRED HRDLICKA

AUSTRIAN, 1928–2009

GOLGATHA, 1963
WHITE GREEK MARBLE
7' 3 ¾" x 23" x 19 ½"
GIFT OF THE RALPH E. OGDEN FOUNDATION

Alfred Hrdlicka is one of several Austrian artists represented at Storm
King, including Fritz Wotruba, Hrdlicka's teacher at the Academy of
Fine Arts in Vienna from 1953 to 1957. Hrdlicka, in contrast with Wotruba,
insisted on using his artistic tools to expressive rather than formal or
naturalistic ends. Concentrating on the male figure, predominantly the
torso, Hrdlicka had been developing a "body language" based on expressive contortions and sagging flesh—a vocabulary he had studied as a
"professional voyeur" in the meatmarket halls and bars where he earned
his living while studying in the Academy. The figure in *Golgatha* is typical
of Hrdlicka's style of the period, its limp muscles suggesting that the
body is no longer alive. The work takes its name from a hill outside of
Jerusalem, a biblical reference to the site of the Crucifixion.

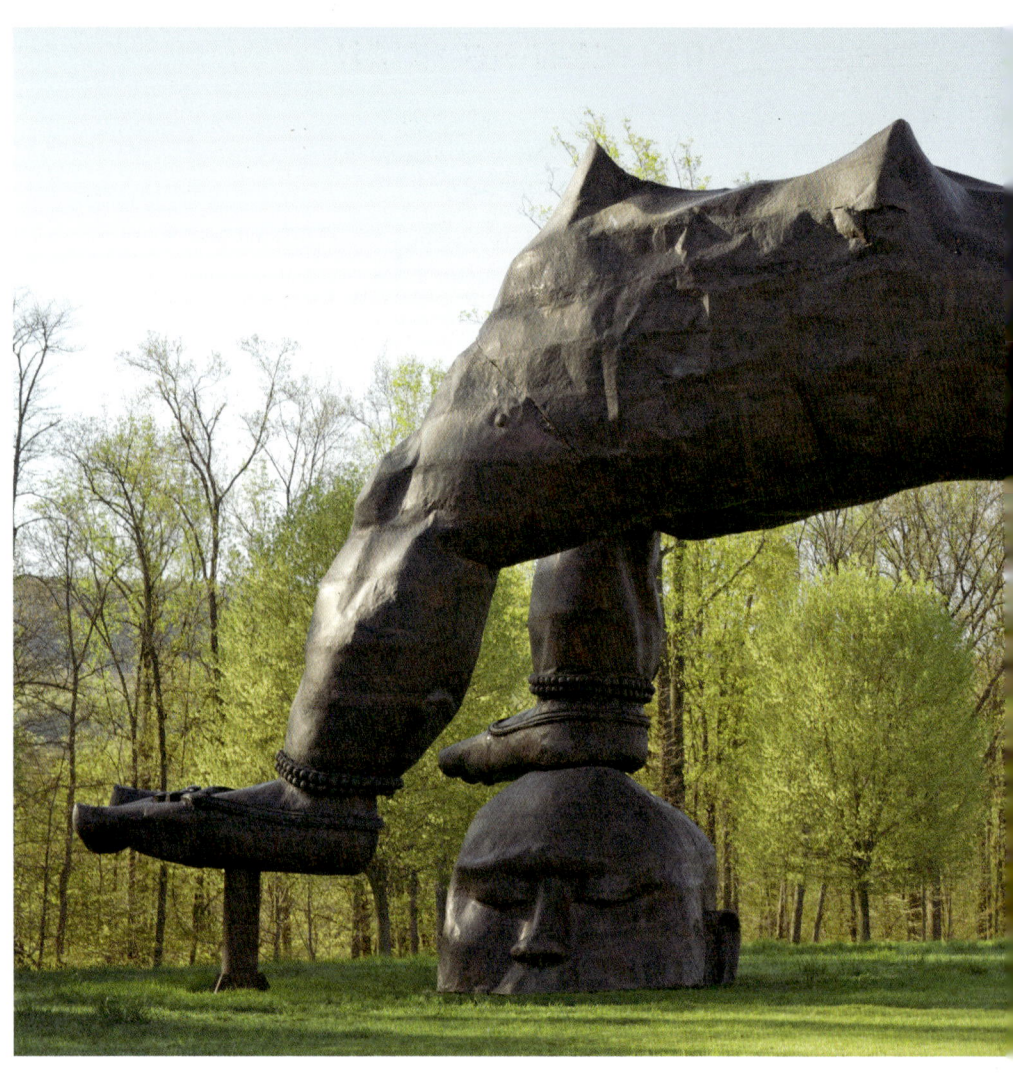

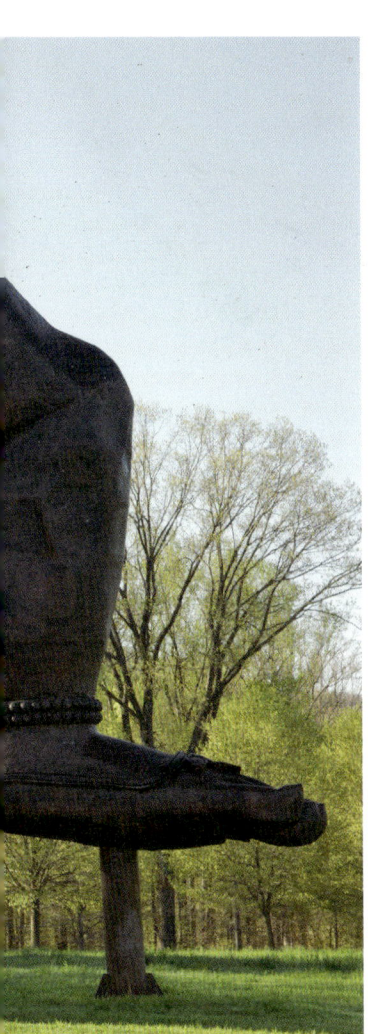

ZHANG HUAN

CHINESE, BORN 1965

THREE LEGGED BUDDHA, 2007
STEEL AND COPPER
28' 2½" x 42' x 22' 7⅝"
GIFT OF ZHANG HUAN AND PACE GALLERY

Zhang Huan's work engages with Buddhist philosophy and rituals and with the artist's notion that the contemporary condition is continually revitalized through an engagement with the past. *Three Legged Buddha*—a copper and steel sculpture standing twenty-eight feet high and weighing more than twelve tons—represents the bottom half of a sprawling, three-legged figure, one of whose feet rests on an eight-foot-high human head that appears to be either emerging from or sinking into the earth. The work is comprised of nine sections of copper "skin," each with an interior steel armature, held together with bolts and welds.

While the legs of *Three Legged Buddha* are modeled closely after fragments of bronze Buddha sculptures that Zhang encountered on a trip to Tibet in 2005, the sculpture's face—visible only from the nostrils upward—is a self-portrait. Zhang folds himself into his creation, much as he took his own body as subject in the 1990s, when he came to prominence for performance-based work. *Three Legged Buddha* further alludes to performance and to the process of making a sculpture in both the perforations and hatches on the copper surface. Zhang designed the hatches to provide access to the sculpture's interior so that incense might be burned inside, with the resultant smoke emanating through holes in the Buddha's toes and through the head's open nostrils and eyes.

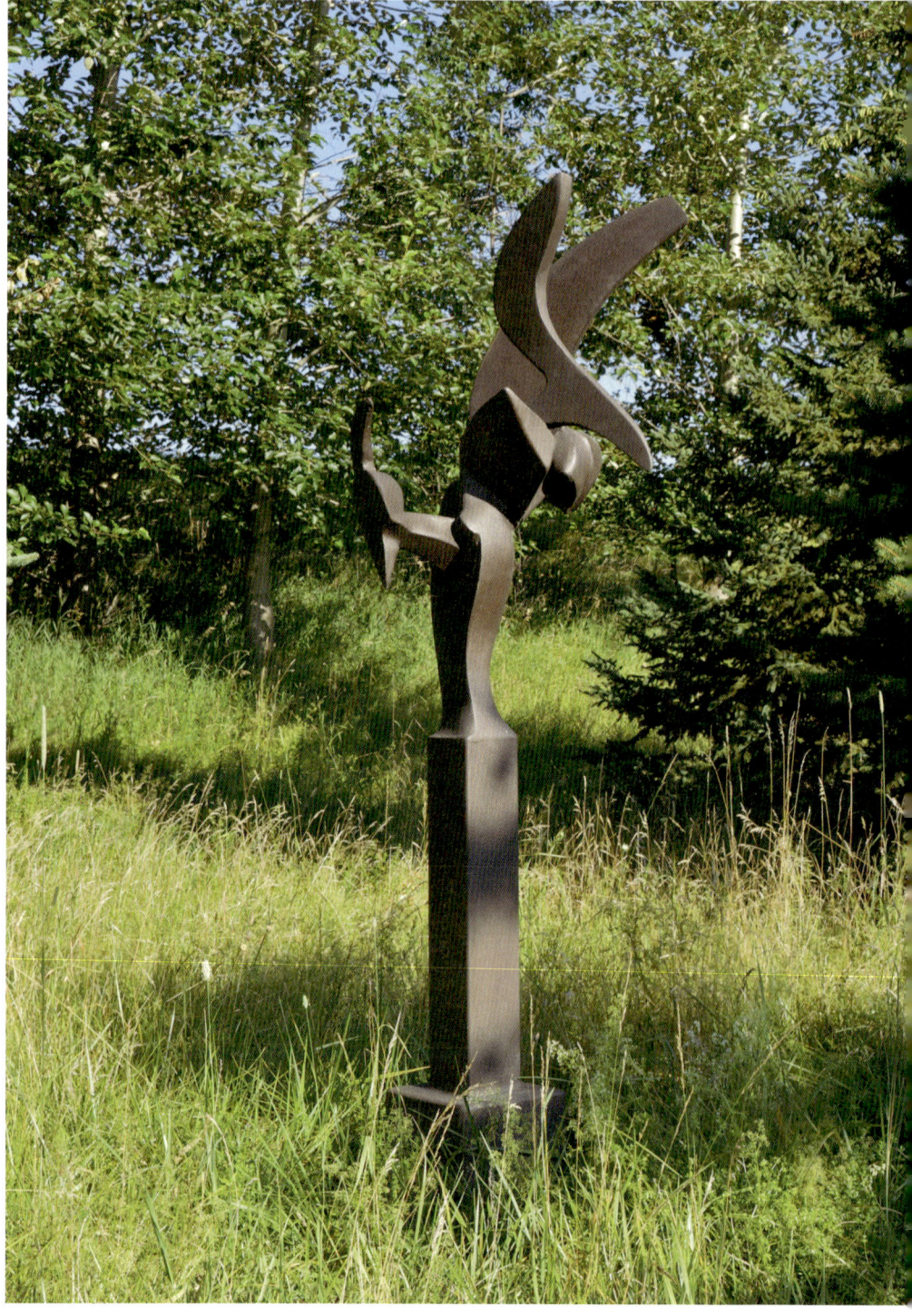

RICHARD HUNT

AMERICAN, BORN 1935

EXPANSIVE CONSTRUCTION, 1974
WEATHERING STEEL
7' 6" x 22½" x 26"
GIFT OF MR. AND MRS. SAMUEL DORSKY

Richard Hunt is best known for dynamic sculptures in which individual industrial forms are combined and metamorphosed to evoke biomorphic entities or forces of nature, and sometimes the forms of plants and animals. Hunt calls his sculptures "hybrid figures" and considers them to be "a kind of bridge between what we experience in nature and what we experience from the urban, industrial, technology-driven society we live in." Some of Hunt's sculptures summon ideas of growth or aspiration. In the aptly named *Expansive Construction*, the upward thrust of the curving projected elements suggests outward movement or a kind of organic growth process. Wings and images of flight also reverberate throughout Hunt's work.

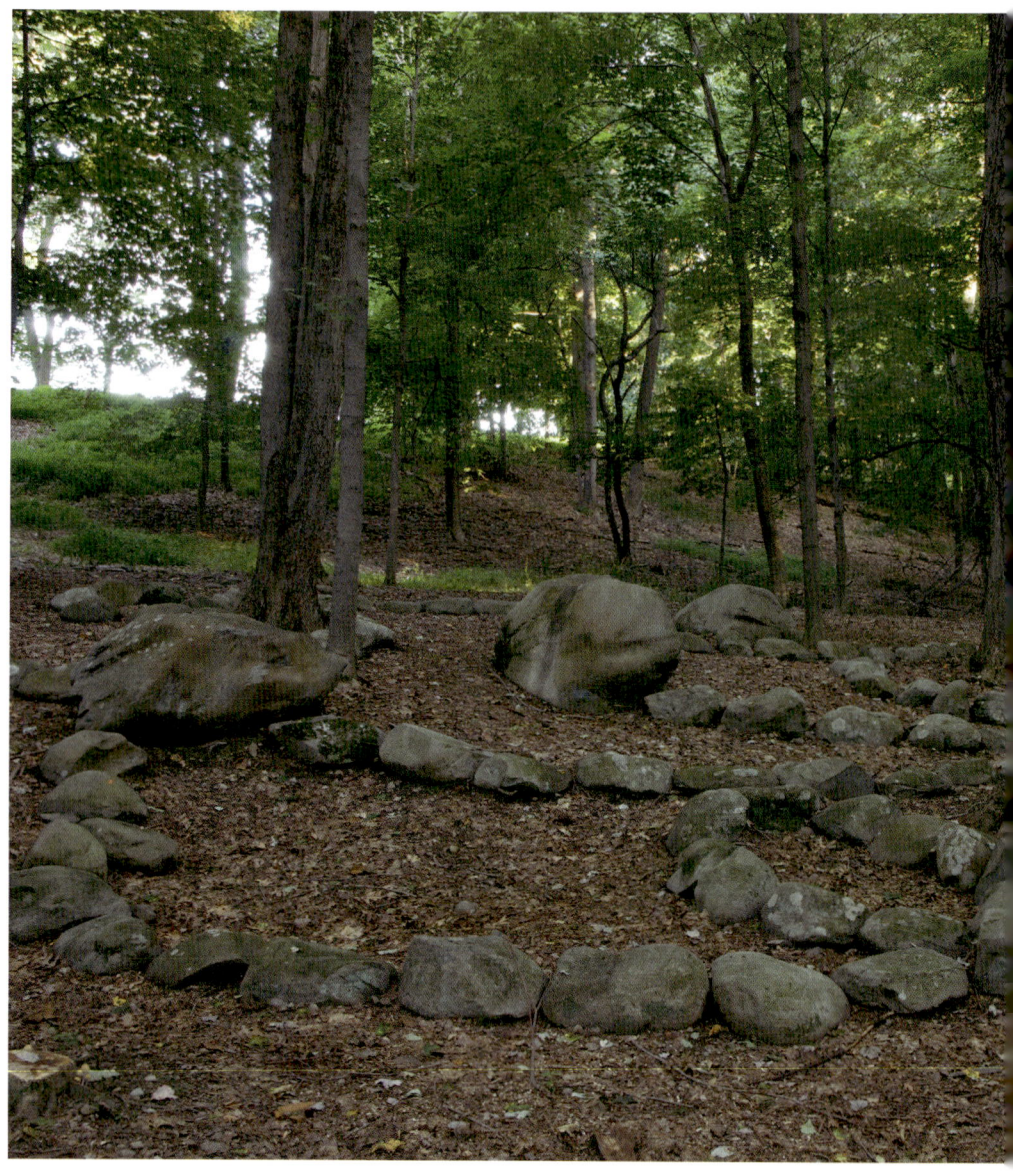

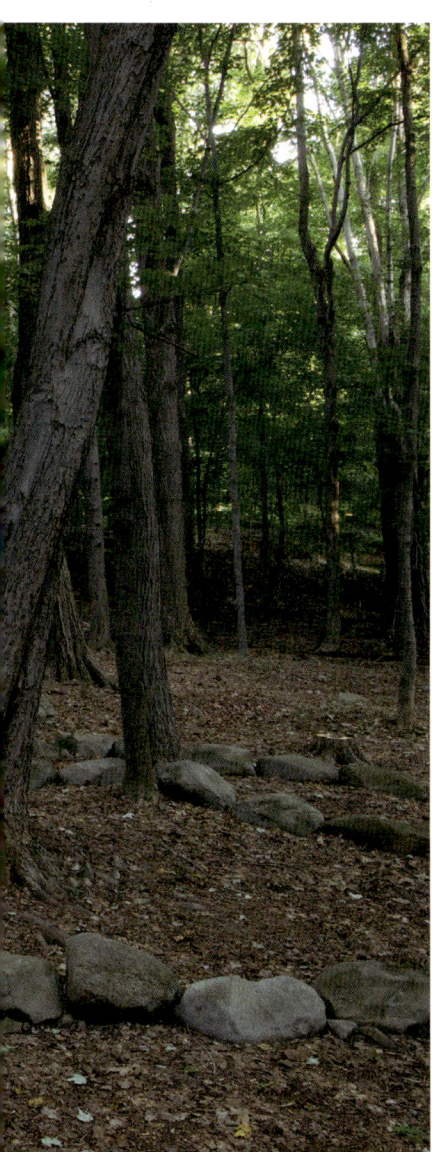

PATRICIA JOHANSON

AMERICAN, BORN 1940

NOSTOC II, 1975
STONE
30" x 49' 3" x 40' 9"
GIFT OF THE RALPH E. OGDEN FOUNDATION

Nostoc II is nestled in the woods at the northeast edge of the Storm King grounds, accessible by a narrow path off the Moodna Creek Trail. Set on a slightly downward slope, it does not immediately distinguish itself from its surroundings. Rather, *Nostoc II* emerges gradually in time and space, revealing its form as the viewer follows roughly circular paths of about 148 boulders and large rocks set on the ground in a 350-square-foot area punctuated by tall trees. Rejecting the single focus of traditional sculpture, Patricia Johanson creates space to be walked through and discovered; an overall scheme emerges only through physical interaction with the sculpture. The artist thus brings people to nature through art and to art through nature.

Nostoc II was the first commissioned work to be created entirely on-site with materials exclusively from Storm King's property. Its overall form is based on the molecular structure of nostoc, a blue-green algae that appears as a chain of irregular circular elements. The environmentally sensitive arrangement stems directly from Johanson's exploration of the relationship between plant forms and buildable structures and marks the first instance in which she was able to transpose the image of a plant form to a full-scale sculpture.

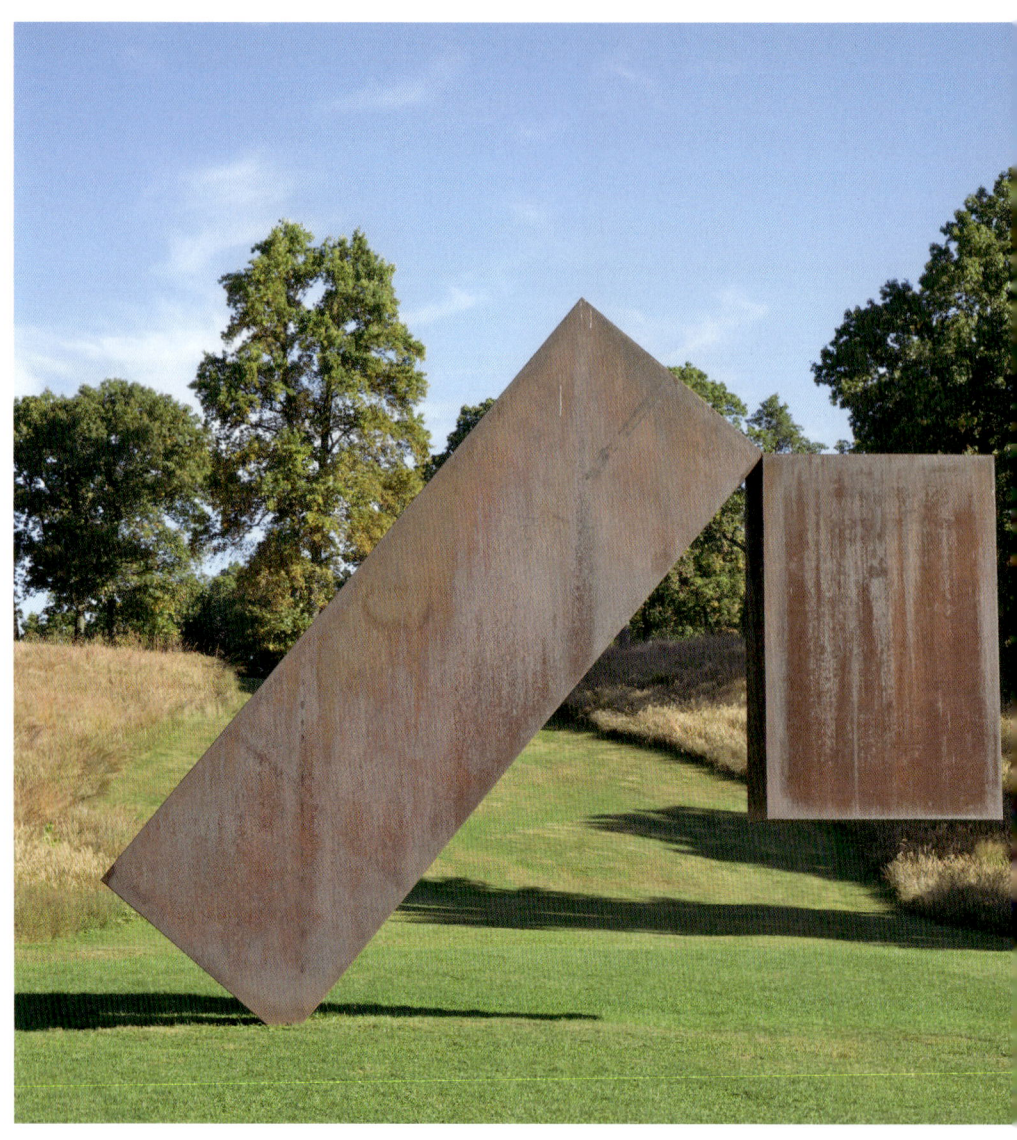

Suspended, 1977

MENASHE KADISHMAN

ISRAELI, 1932–2015

SUSPENDED, 1977
WEATHERING STEEL
23' x 33' x 48"
GIFT OF MURIEL AND PHILIP I. BERMAN

EIGHT POSITIVE TREES, 1977
WEATHERING STEEL
14' 5⅜" x 46' x 25' 3" OVERALL
GIFT OF MURIEL AND PHILIP I. BERMAN

The two simple forms of Menashe Kadishman's *Suspended* engage in a gravity-defying balance that belies expectation. Seen from a distance, atop one of two adjacent hilltops, the sculpture's balancing act is surprising. Viewed up close, the massive scale of the steel work becomes apparent and its structural viability even more difficult to comprehend. With no visible evidence of the engineering holding the sculpture up, *Suspended* prompts contemplation of the relationship between its two conjoined, towering masses, coupled with questions about what lies below ground. Rich and rusted, the patina of the weathered steel wraps the stark geometric shapes in a skin-like sheath.

After working with sculptors in his native Israel, Kadishman went to London in 1959, where he came under the influence of Anthony Caro at Saint Martin's School of Art. By the mid-1960s, he had established an international reputation for suspended sculptures that were gestural and full of dynamic tension. In some of his best-known works from this period, Kadishman attached glass or plastic sheets to wood or metal forms so that the mass seemed to float freely in space. *Suspended* represents his interest in such perceptual ambiguities. It is also a transitional work; by the late 1970s Kadishman began to focus on nature, particularly on tree and forest themes, and worked on an environmental scale. *Eight Positive Trees* reveals this ongoing fascination, which harkens back to his youth, when, like many other Israeli children, he planted trees throughout the new country. Kadishman's "negative" forms of stylized trees cut out from sheets of weathering steel were exhibited in the Venice Biennale in 1978. The viewer could see through the empty tree-shaped spaces, as well as walk through them to encounter the landscape. The steel silhouettes of Storm King's *Eight Positive Trees* are the shapes cut out from the trees exhibited in Venice. In contrast to their negative counterparts, the silhouetted shapes suggest both solid trees and shadows.

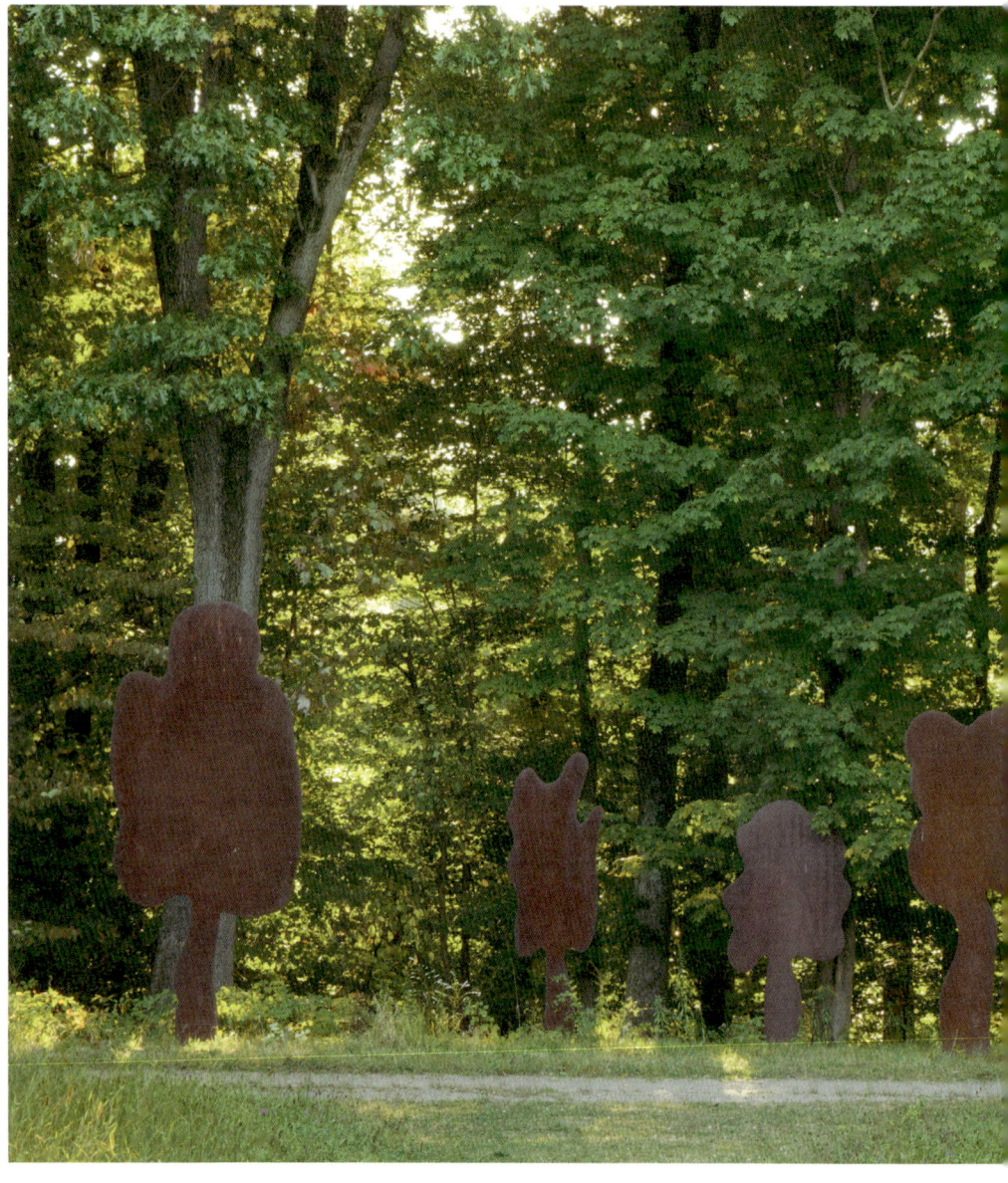

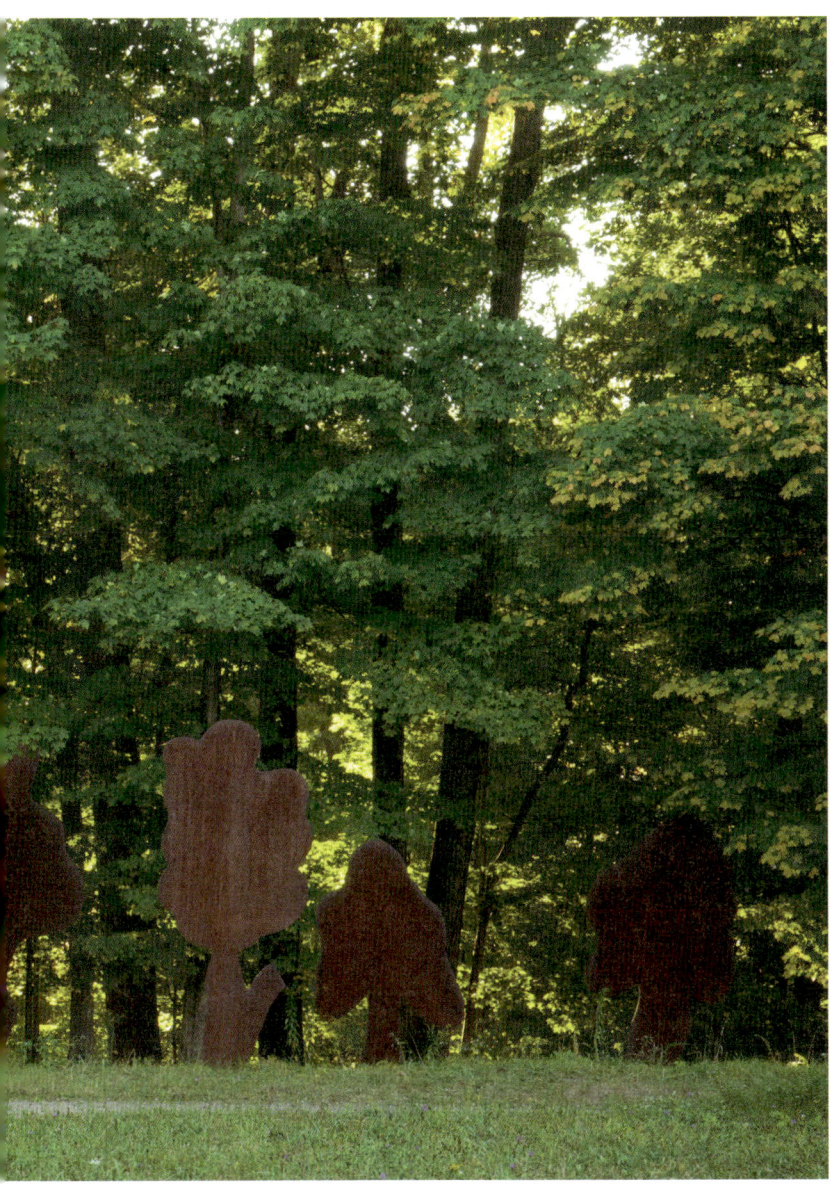

Eight Positive Trees, 1977

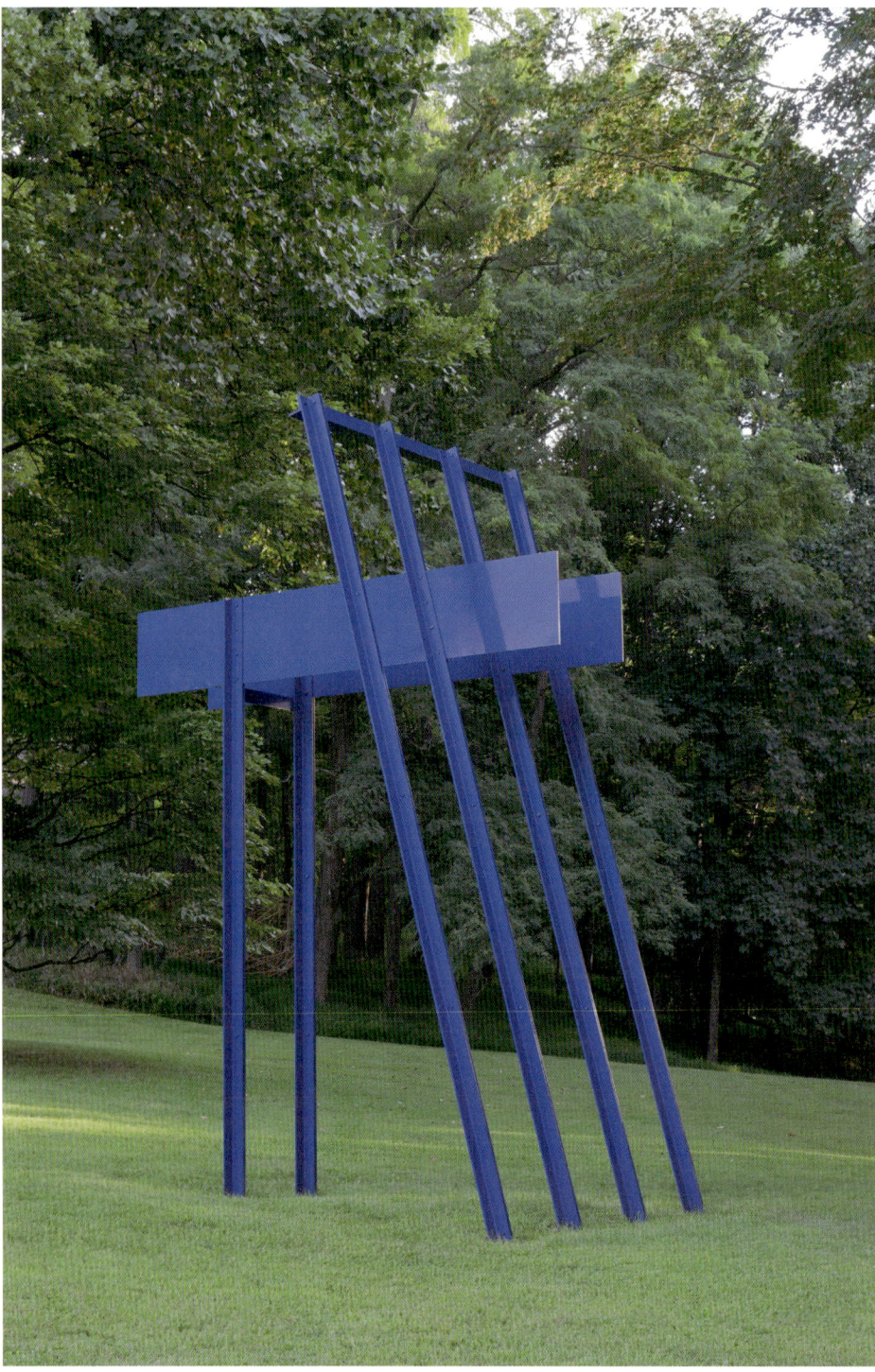

LYMAN KIPP

AMERICAN, 1929–2014

LOCKPORT, 1977
PAINTED ALUMINUM
17' 2" x 12' x 8' 11"
PURCHASED WITH THE AID OF FUNDS FROM THE NATIONAL ENDOWMENT
FOR THE ARTS AND GIFT OF THE RALPH E. OGDEN FOUNDATION

Lockport is among the most distinguished of Lyman Kipp's post and lintel assemblages. Post and lintel refers to the ancient Greek architectural innovation in which a horizontal element rests above two supporting vertical elements. Inspired in part by the shadows of half-completed buildings on construction sites, Kipp first conceived his sculptures by manipulating small wood blocks. By the late 1970s he had begun to experiment with aluminum. *Lockport*'s aluminum surfaces are painted bright blue, reflecting the artist's use of bright primary colors almost from the beginning of his career as well as his interest in the relationship between color and form. Kipp's commitment to large-scale sculpture led him to co-found ConStruct, a Chicago gallery devoted to monumental sculpture and collaboratively owned by its exhibiting artists, who include Mark di Suvero and Kenneth Snelson, both represented in Storm King's collection.

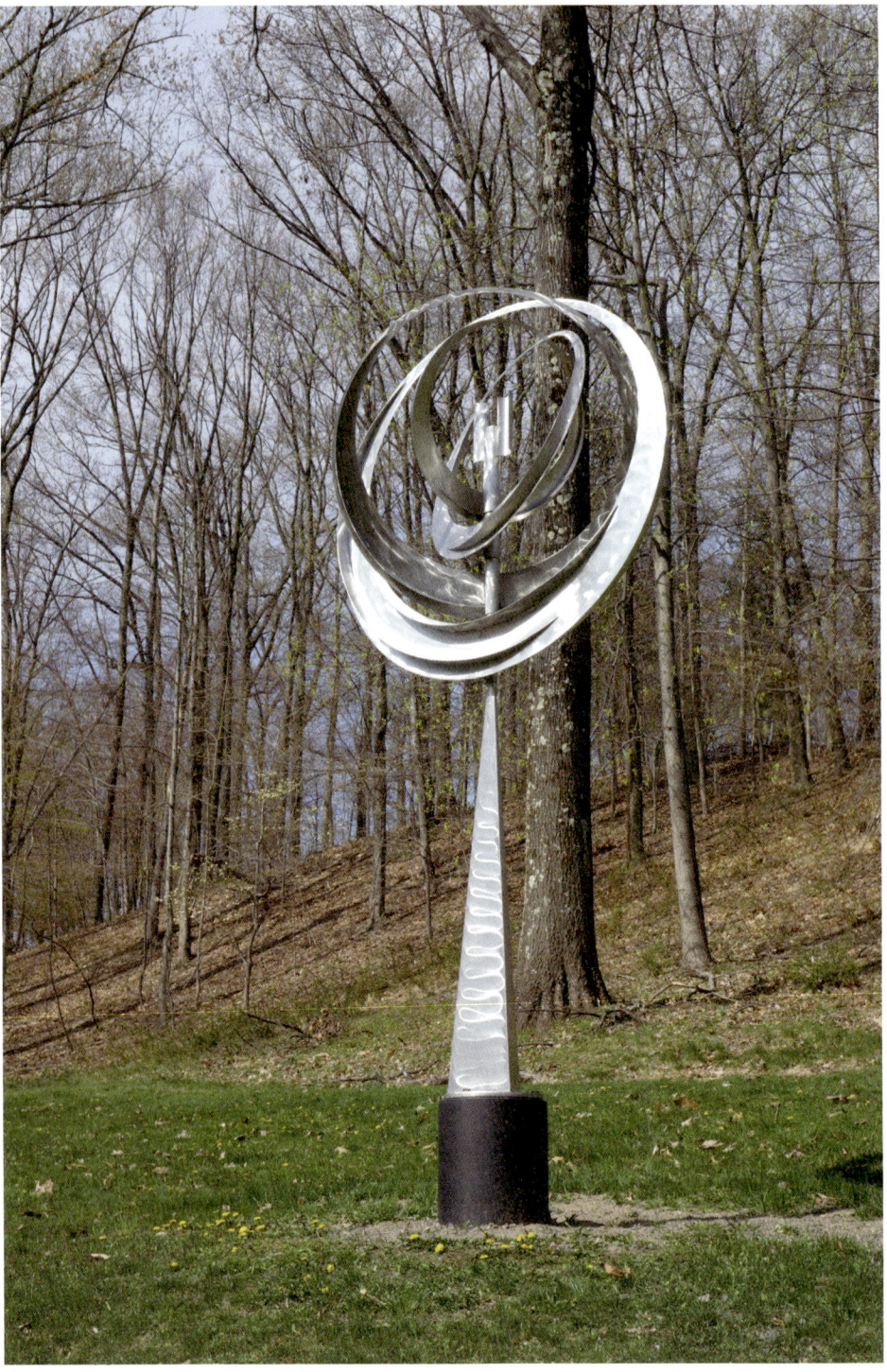

JEROME KIRK

AMERICAN, BORN 1923

SELECTED WORK:
ORBIT, 1972
STAINLESS STEEL
12 x 6 x 6'
PURCHASED WITH THE AID OF FUNDS FROM THE NATIONAL ENDOWMENT
FOR THE ARTS AND GIFT OF THE RALPH E. OGDEN FOUNDATION

While studying mechanical engineering at the Massachusetts Institute
of Technology, Jerome Kirk was deeply impressed by an exhibition of
Alexander Calder's sculpture held in Cambridge, Massachusetts. Kirk's
own first mobiles, which date from after his graduation in 1951, bear the
influence of the elder artist's work. *Orbit*, one of two works by Kirk in the
collection, was commissioned specifically for Storm King, and its highly
polished and reflective surfaces are characteristic of his work. The form
of *Orbit* resembles a planet with orbiting suns, its concentric circular
forms spinning gently and easily in the wind. Kirk has in fact imagined the
sculpture's movement out in the universe: "Natural forces provide fixed
parameters within which I have to work, but the forms and shapes are
largely intellectually and emotionally derived. A static sculpture would
not change if moved from the face of the earth, however, kinetic sculpture
would behave very differently on the moon or [in] outer space."

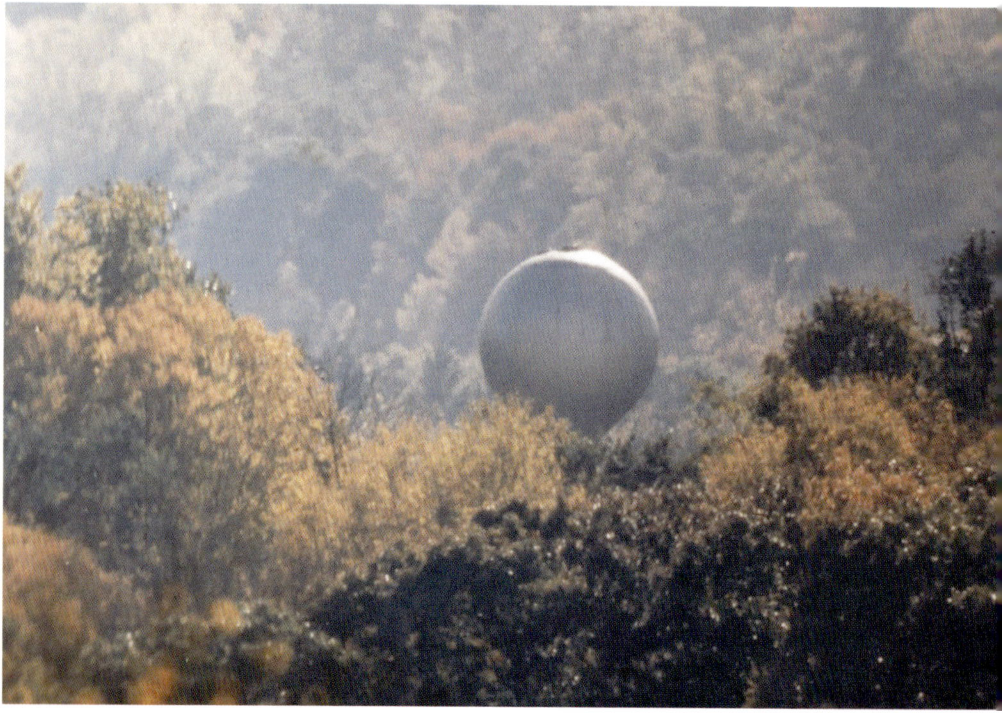

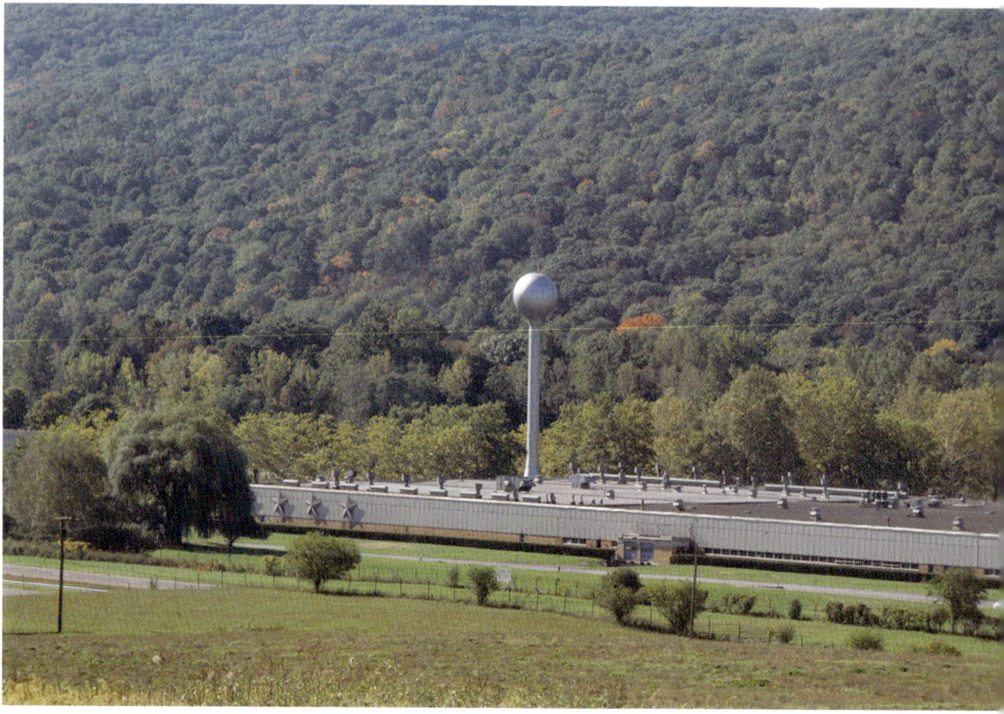

JOHN KNIGHT

AMERICAN, BORN 1945

87°, 1997–99
TELESCOPE AND VIEW
GIFT OF THE RALPH E. OGDEN FOUNDATION

John Knight's *87°* is precisely site specific. Installed on Storm King's Museum Hill, it is comprised of a telescope—similar to those used by tourists at scenic overlooks—and the view through the telescope's lens. When directed toward the 87 degrees of the work's title, the telescope focuses in on a rounded water tower, erected by the former Star Expansion Company in 1958, just south of Storm King's property. In prioritizing this viewpoint, Knight conceptually connects Storm King's pastoral hills with the industrial production just beyond them. Star Expansion Company, which manufactured industrial fasteners, was owned and operated by the family that founded Storm King. The water tower's sleek, steel design was a purposeful aesthetic choice for the company, and it was created at great expense—suggesting another connection between industry and artistic design highlighted by *87°*.

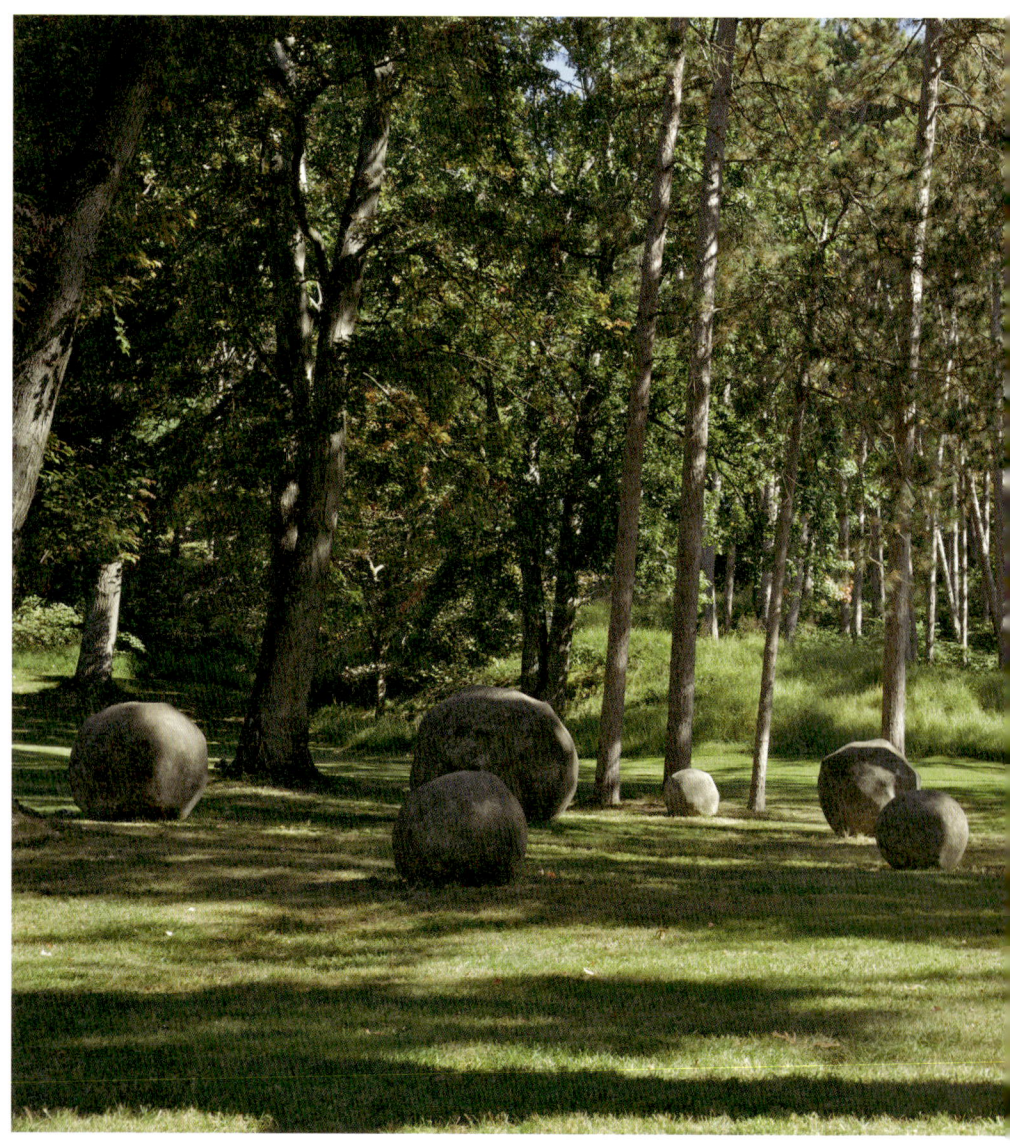

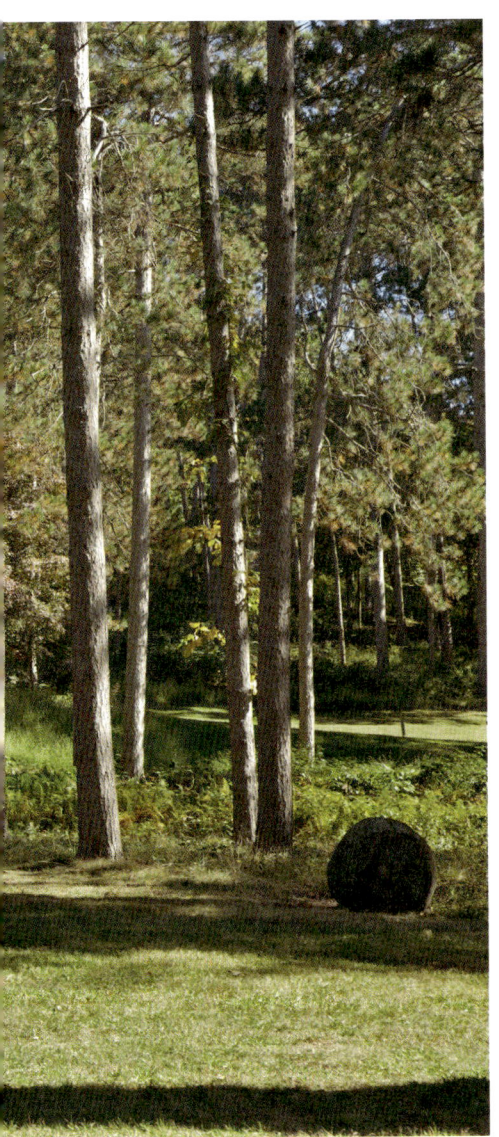

GRACE KNOWLTON

AMERICAN, BORN 1932

SPHERES, 1973–75/1985
CONCRETE, FIBERGLASS, AND TERRACOTTA
TEN ELEMENTS; OVERALL DIMENSIONS
VARIABLE
GIFT OF THE ARTIST AND THE RALPH E.
OGDEN FOUNDATION

Grace Knowlton creates spheres out of materials including concrete, clay, copper, steel, and iron. All bear subtle and unique imperfections that evidence their hand-crafted origins. The spheres—of widely varied scale—seem to walk a fine line between natural object and work of art when placed in Storm King's environment. Knowlton has referred to the process of their creation as "an ancient technique involving the laying on of hands." She initially set out to make ceramic pots, until, as she has said, "I got so interested in closing the pots, in making a secret space closed off forever, that it caught me and I never went back."

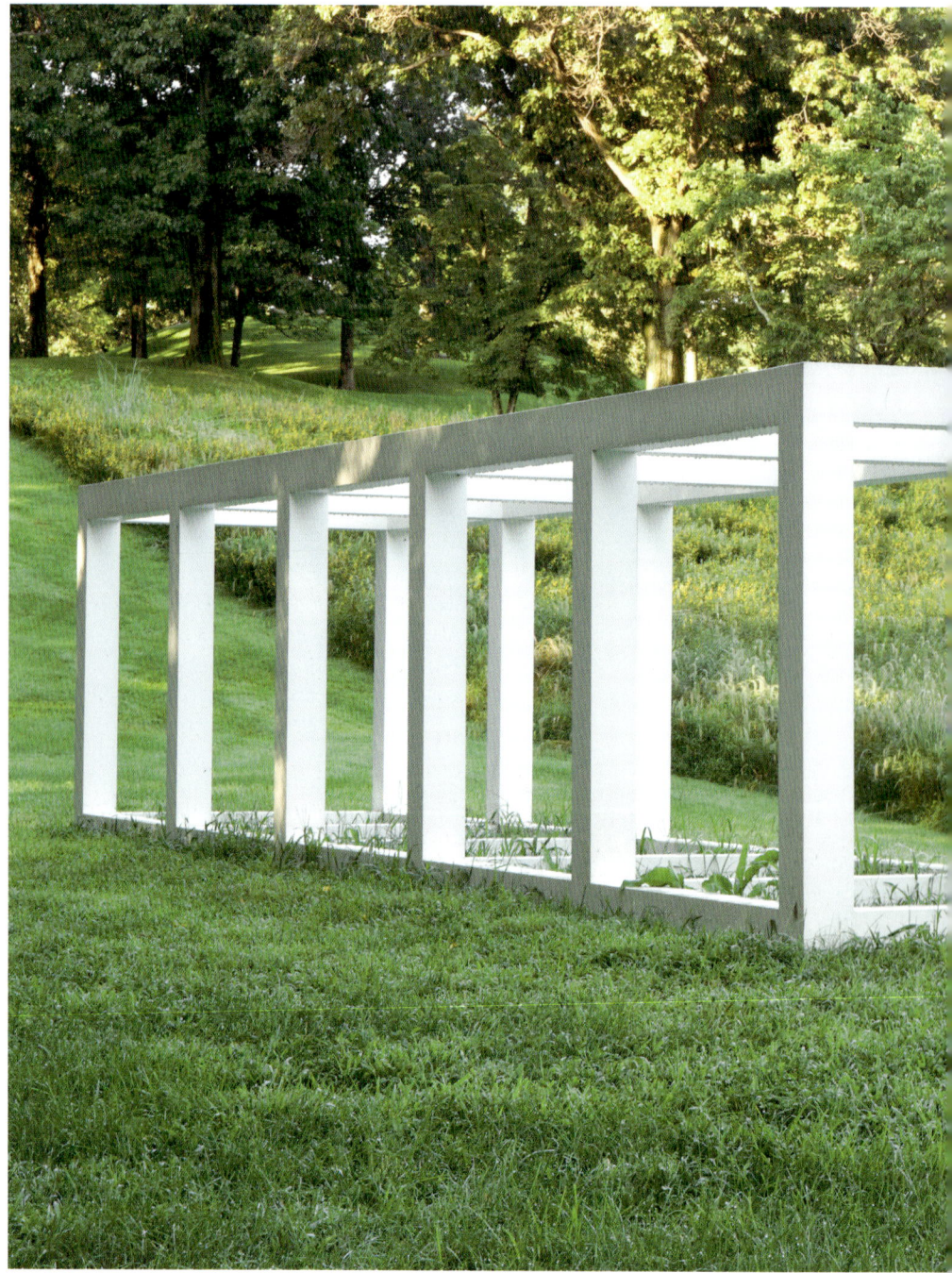

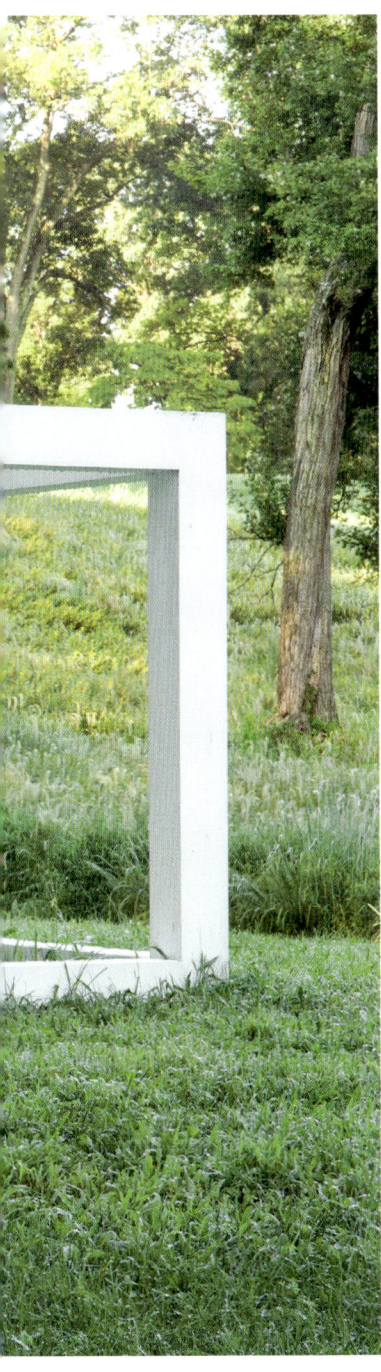

SOL LEWITT

AMERICAN, 1928–2007

FIVE MODULAR UNITS, 1971 (REFABRICATED 2008)
PAINTED ALUMINUM
63" x 63" x 24' 3½"
GIFT OF THE RALPH E. OGDEN FOUNDATION

Sol LeWitt once described his artistic process this way: "The idea becomes the machine that makes the art." Finding creative possibilities within tight instructional parameters, he often remarked that many of his works would be equally powerful had they been made by others (and in fact many of them were). LeWitt restricted his sculptural output to austere materials, wood or steel, and employed neutral colors, usually white enamel, to achieve a cool, impersonal, industrial look. Throughout the 1960s and early 1970s, he designed elaborate units of cubes, exploring all possible combinations and permutations, usually by means of mathematical calculations, and frequently repeating identical forms in a serial format. As he noted, "The most interesting characteristic of the cube is that it is relatively uninteresting…. It is best used as a basic unit for any more elaborate function, the grammatical device from which the work may proceed." *Five Modular Units* occupies a decisive position within his oeuvre. The simple units were a starting point for LeWitt to conceive increasingly complex aggregate structures. And while its cubes are reductive in format, their size and scale—sixty-three inches high, approximately eye-level for many—presaged a new direction in his work, toward more monumental forms.

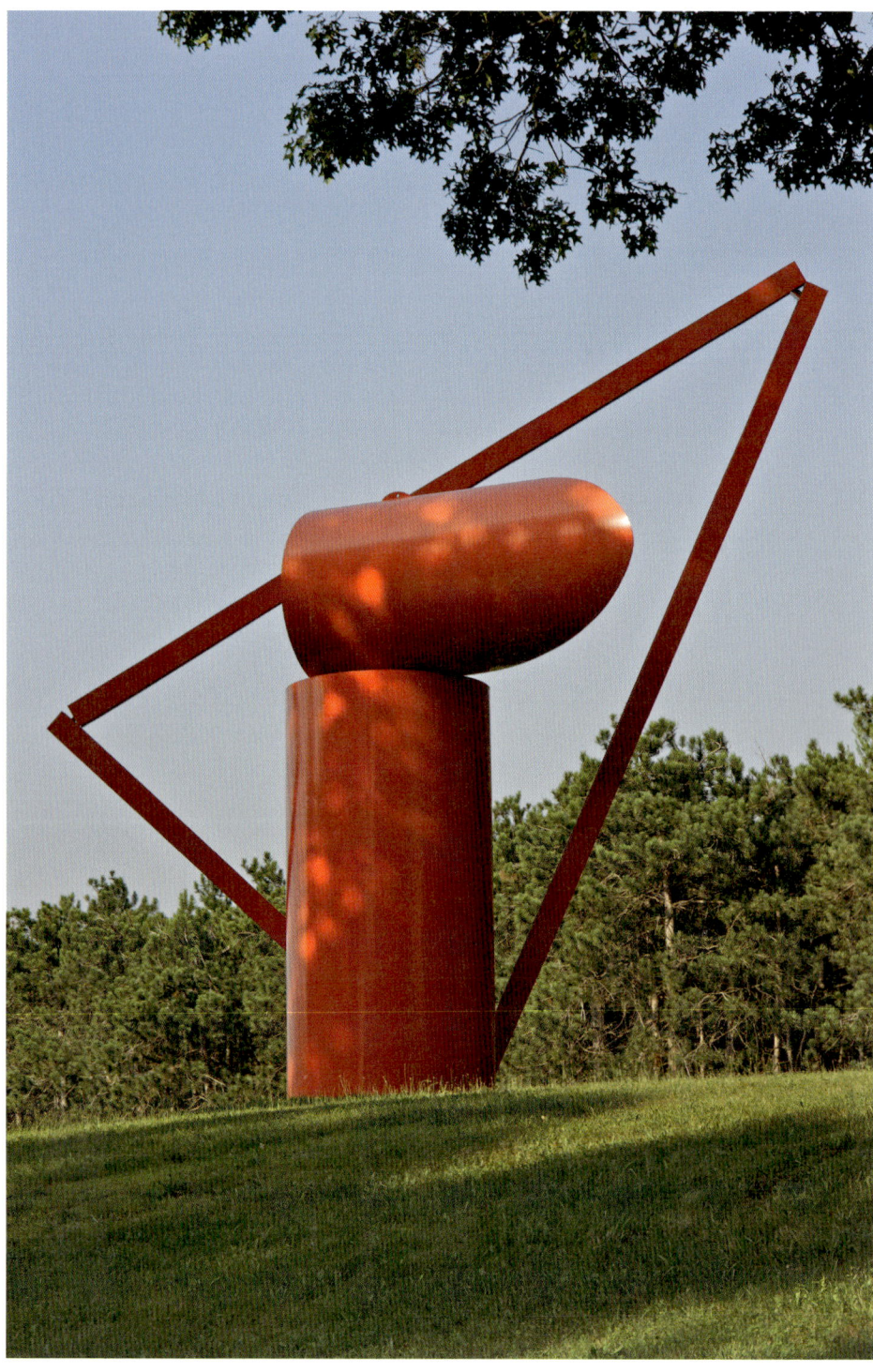

ALEXANDER LIBERMAN

AMERICAN, BORN RUSSIA, 1912–1999

ADAM, 1970
PAINTED STEEL
28' 6" x 24' x 29' 6"
GIFT OF THE RALPH E. OGDEN FOUNDATION

ADONAI, 1970–71 (REFABRICATED 2000)
STEEL
29' 6" x 63' x 52' 8"
GIFT OF THE RALPH E. OGDEN FOUNDATION

ILIAD, 1974–76
PAINTED STEEL
36' x 54' 7" x 19' 7"
GIFT OF THE RALPH E. OGDEN FOUNDATION

Alexander Liberman's three large-scale sculptures at Storm King reflect his studies in architecture, painting, and photography, along with his exploration of readymade, industrial forms. They also recall his early childhood memories of stage sets from Russia's State Children's Theater—founded by his mother—and towering forests that he toured with his father, the forestry minister under Lenin. Throughout his life Liberman sustained parallel commercial and artistic careers. In 1960 he had his first solo exhibition at the Betty Parsons Gallery, New York. Two years later he was appointed editor-in-chief of all Condé Nast magazines, a position he held for more than thirty years.

Adonai was one of a few sculptures Liberman made using six-foot-long gas storage tanks. "I use cheap materials for economic reasons," he noted. "But also, there's an odd, maybe a romantic longing to contact the earth. I like rust. I like earth. I like rocks. The quality of a primitive forge anchors a modern mind to the earth." The work was one of the last major sculptures acquired for the collection by Ralph E. Ogden, Storm King's co-founder, who enjoyed solving the installation challenges it presented. Over time, the rusted steel gas storage tanks physically deteriorated, and the massive sculpture was refabricated in 2000. While suggesting a number of visual analogies, from fallen columns to trees, Liberman cited his inspiration in the renowned medieval cathedral Chartres:

> I had gone to Chartres. I was trying to analyze why cathedrals started with the basic portal. So I started with the basic portal, the two vertical cylinders of *Adonai*. Then there's a nave. If you look at the long horizontal cylinder of *Adonai*, that's my imaginary nave.

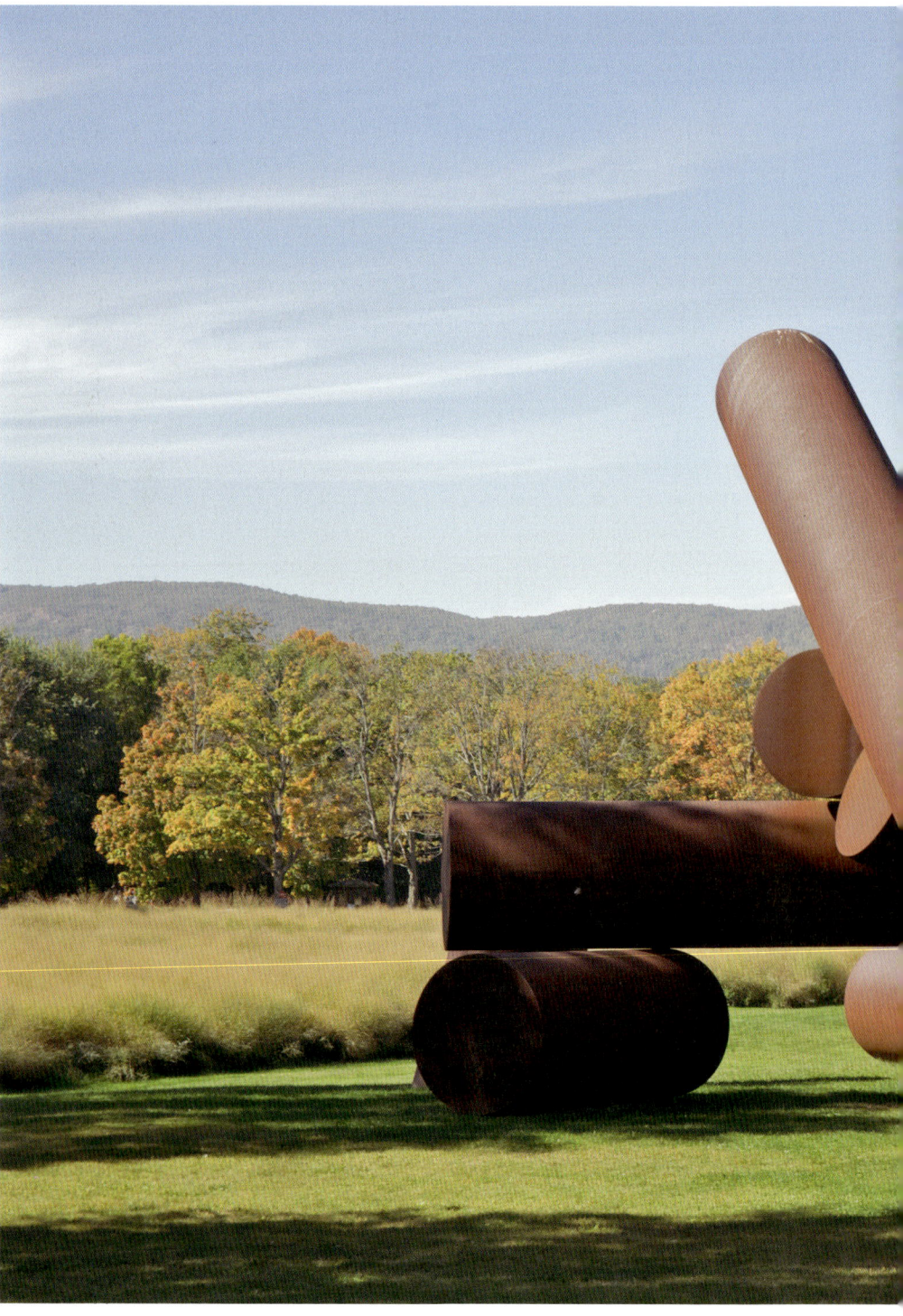

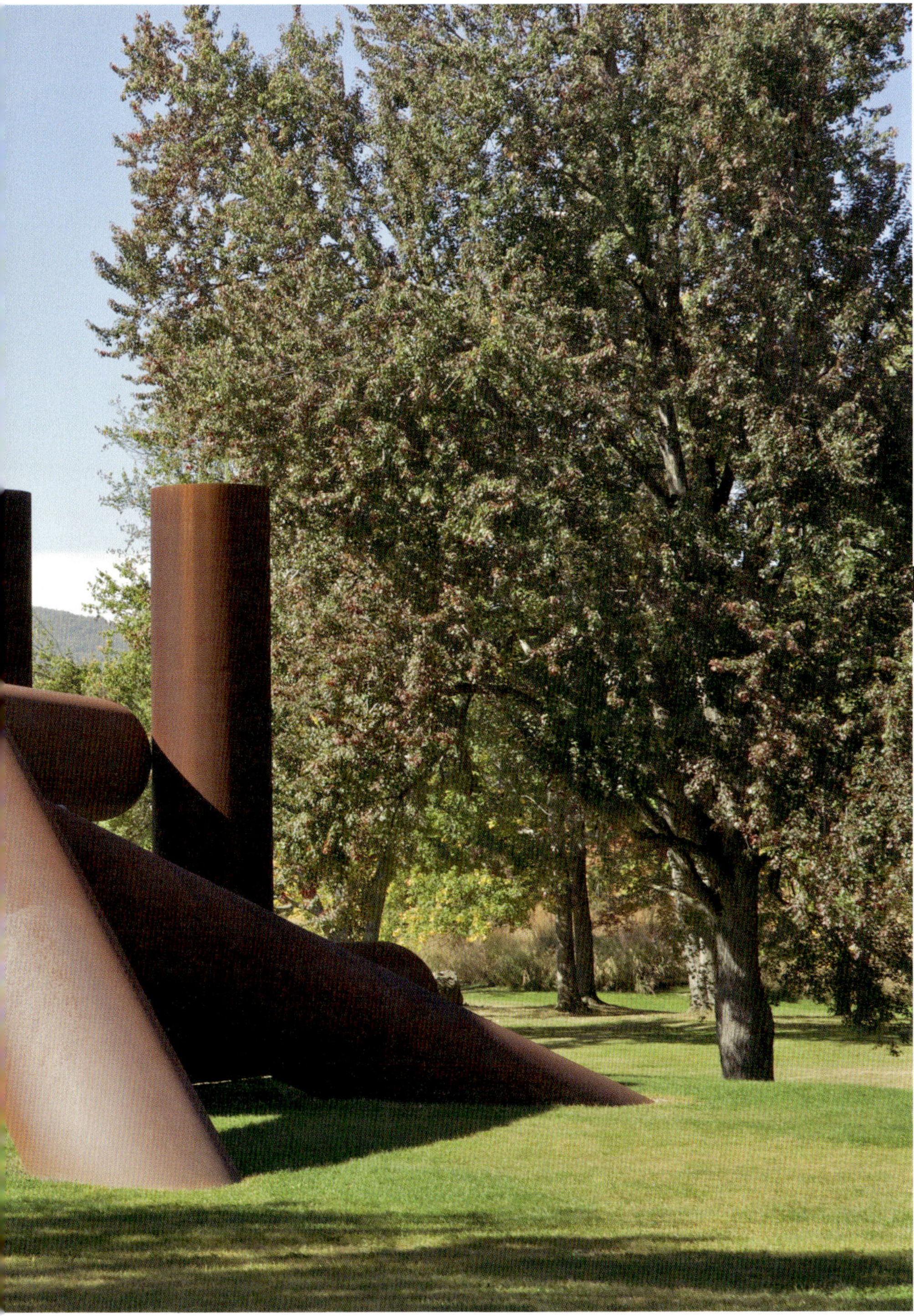

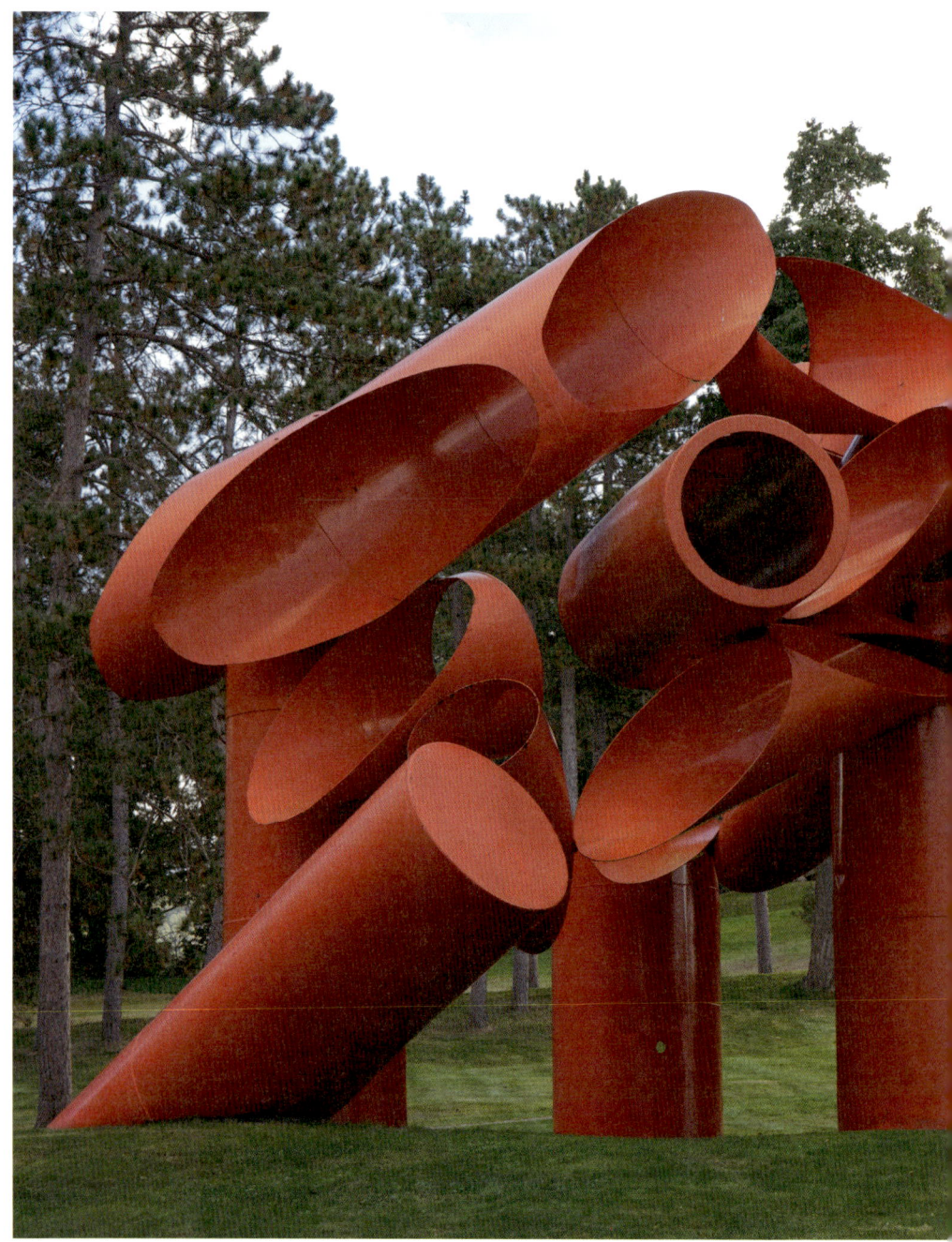

PREVIOUS SPREAD: *Adonai*, 1970–71; ABOVE: *Iliad*, 1974–76

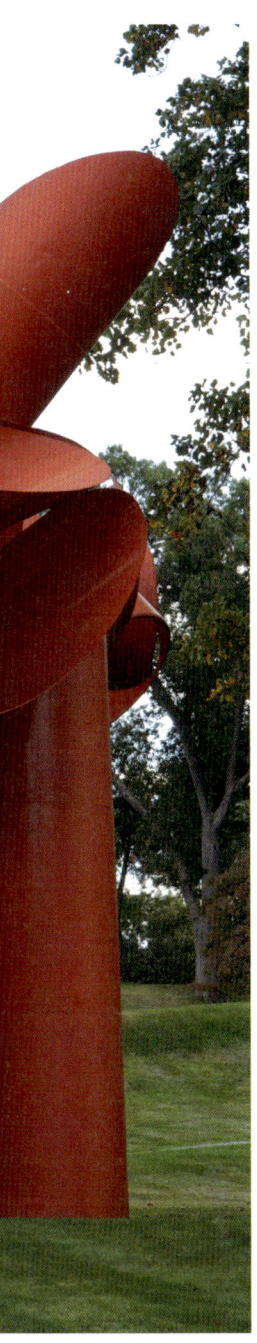

The flat circle of the cylinder, which is frontal, is held by the two uprights. You build your own imaginary cathedral.

Liberman chose an unexpected title—*Adonai*, the Hebrew word for god—for this cathedral-inspired work. Many of his other sculptures, such as *Adam* and *Iliad* at Storm King, bear similar biblical and mythical references. When asked years later about his interest in heroic titles, Liberman claimed his close friend Barnett Newman, the artist, had been influential in this regard, but that he had come to dislike titles. "They mean nothing to me," he stated, "and today everybody wants titles. It's like attaching a wooden handle to something that hopefully cannot be pinned down."

In contrast to *Adonai*, the cylindrical shapes of *Iliad* and *Adam*, each painted bright red, have been sliced to make elliptical and circular forms. *Iliad*, with its dramatically cantilevered elements, forms a dynamic architectural space through which to walk. Liberman spoke about creating the work's "extreme overhang, because I want to achieve a certain sense of awe." *Adam* was created using Liberman's unique approach to making large sculptures. An assistant driving a crane would position the various elements and weld them together temporarily; Liberman then photographed the assembled sculpture, printed and cut the elements, and repositioned and pasted them in varying positions until the composition seemed right. Using grease pencil, he then drew the composition on a photograph, mirroring the manner in which layout pages in magazines are created.

First exhibited in 1970 outside the Corcoran Gallery in Washington, DC, *Adam* incited outrage on the part of President Richard Nixon, who demanded the sculpture be relocated to the less visible venue of Haines Point. The work arrived at Storm King a few years later. Liberman did not create site-specific sculpture, arguing instead that his work had the strength to create its own environment.

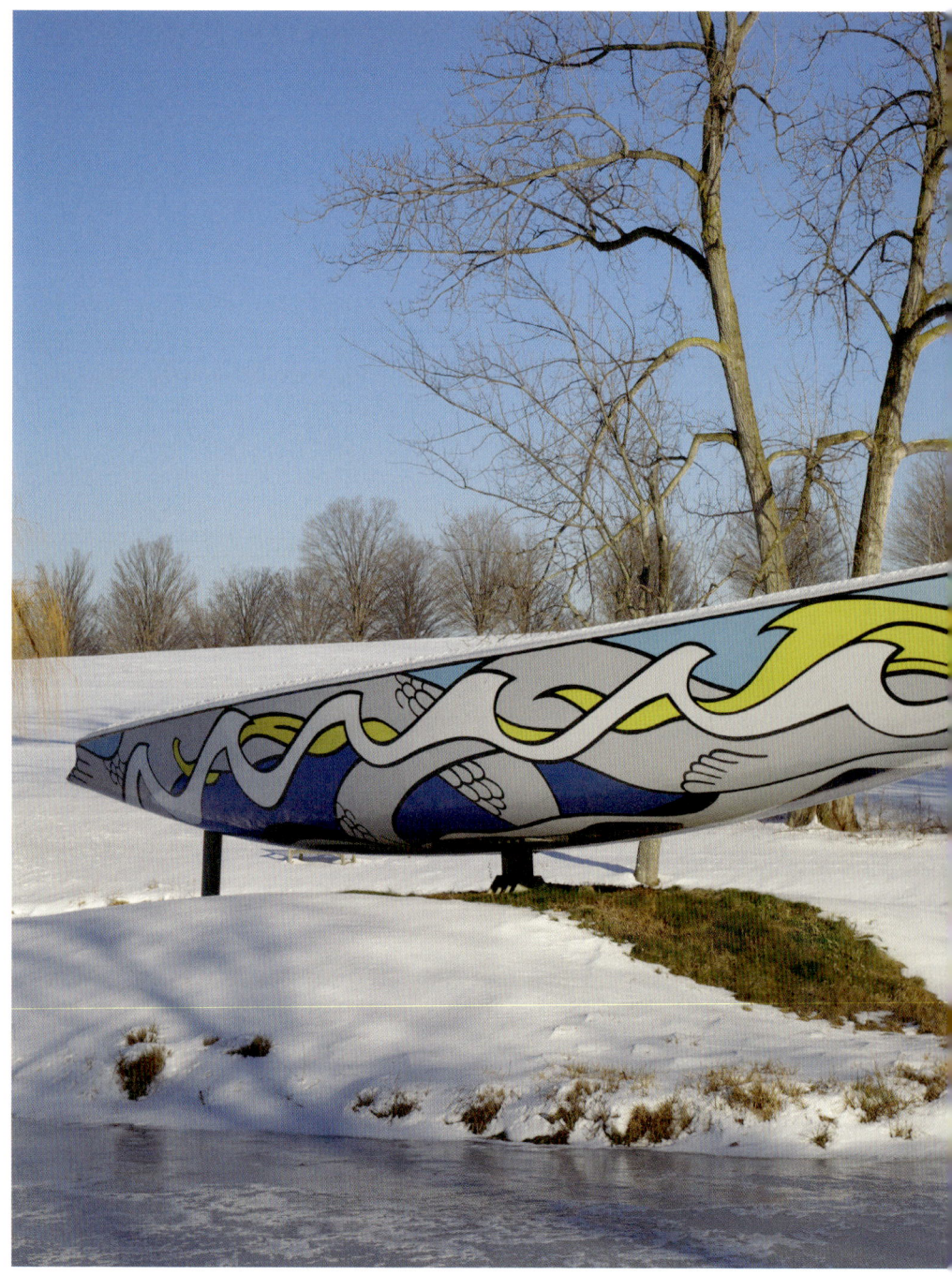

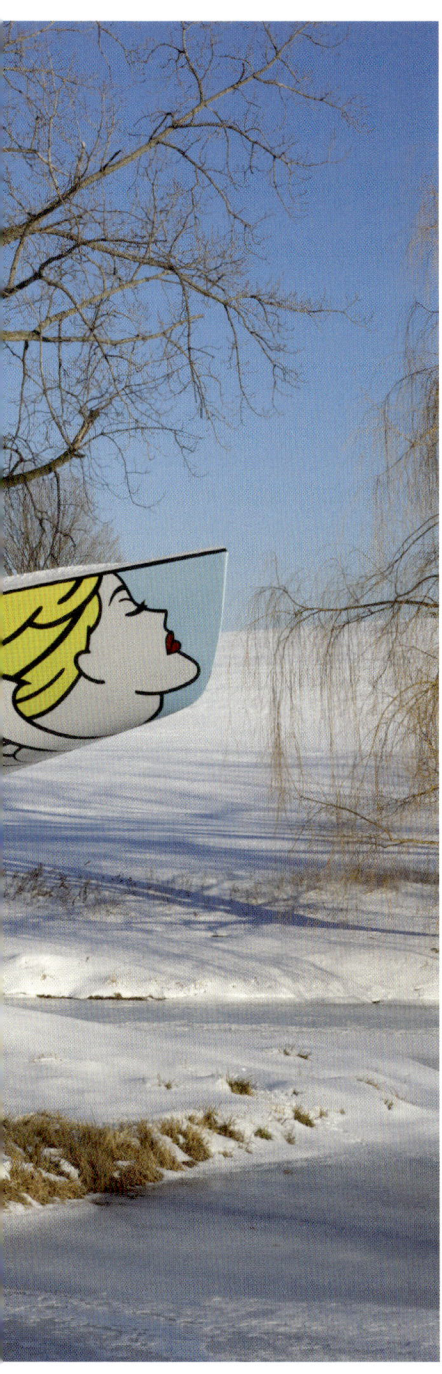

ROY LICHTENSTEIN

AMERICAN, 1923–1997

MERMAID, 1994
PAINTED CARBON FIBER AND EPOXY OVER
ALUMINUM HONEYCOMB CORE
8 x 77 x 14'
MAJOR FUNDING PROVIDED BY: FORD MOTOR
COMPANY FUND, THE RALPH E. OGDEN
FOUNDATION, THE YOUNG AMERICA FOUNDATION;
ADDITIONAL GENEROUS SUPPORT PROVIDED BY:
MR. AND MRS. ROBERT M. BASS, MR. C. THOMAS
CLAGETT, JR., THE HORACE W. GOLDSMITH
FOUNDATION, MR. AND MRS. THOMAS H.
GOSNELL, MR. BERNARD H. GUSTIN, THE
CHARLOTTE AND WALTER KOHLER CHARITABLE
TRUST, ANN & JOHN MARSHALL, MARGARET T.
MORRIS FOUNDATION, MR. AND MRS. JAMES X.
MULLEN, MR. AND MRS. THOMAS L. STARK,
MR. ROBERT G. STONE, JR., AND MR. AND MRS.
KENNETH WEG

L

LICHTENSTEIN, ROY

Roy Lichtenstein, whose flat, bold paintings derived from comic strips became some of the best-known works of Pop art in the 1960s, designed a painting of a mermaid to grace the side of a functioning sailboat. Following Lichtenstein's plan, students from the Rhode Island School of Design painted the boat, *Young America*, which then raced in the 1995 America's Cup. The late J. Carter Brown, former director of the National Gallery of Art in Washington, DC, and long-time Storm King board member, was an enthusiastic sailor, and facilitated the donation of the vessel to Storm King after it was retired from competition. The mound on which the boat rests, in the middle of the north pond, was enhanced for the purpose of this display.

MAYA LIN

AMERICAN, BORN 1959

STORM KING WAVEFIELD, 2007–2008
EARTH AND GRASS
240,000 SQUARE FEET (11-ACRE SITE)
GIFT OF THE RALPH E. OGDEN FOUNDATION, JANET INSKEEP BENTON, THE PHILIP
AND MURIEL BERMAN FOUNDATION, THE BROWN FOUNDATION INC. OF HOUSTON,
TEXAS, AMB. AND MRS. W. L. LYONS BROWN, JR., CALLAHAN AND NANNINI QUARRY
PRODUCTS, CHARINA ENDOWMENT FUND, THE DONOHUE FAMILY FOUNDATION,
EDMUND G. GLASS, THE HAZEN POLSKY FUND, PAUL AND BARBARA JENKEL, THE KAUTZ
FAMILY FOUNDATION, THE LIPMAN FAMILY FOUNDATION, MARTIN Z. MARGULIES, THE
MARGARET T. MORRIS FOUNDATION, ROY R. AND MARIE S. NEUBERGER FOUNDATION,
INC., PECKHAM FAMILY FOUNDATION, JEANNETTE AND DAVID REDDEN, GABRIELLE H. REEM,
M.D. AND HERBERT J. KAYDEN, M.D., THE RICHARD SALOMON FAMILY FOUNDATION,
INC., SARA LEE AND ALEX H. SCHUPF, ANNE AND CONSTANTINE SIDAMON-ERISTOFF,
AND MR. AND MRS. THOMAS W. SMITH

Viewed from above, the undulating swells of earth forming *Storm King Wavefield* appear to naturally rise from and roll along the grassy terrain. Set against a backdrop formed by Schunnemunk Mountain to the west and the Hudson Highlands to the south and east, Maya Lin's earthwork inspires a broad perspective on the landscape from which it emerges and entices deep exploration of the grassy alleys between the cresting peaks. The seven nearly four-hundred-foot-long waves, ranging in height from ten to fifteen feet high, proceed at the same scale as a series of mid-ocean waves. The resulting effect recalls the experience of being at sea, where sight of adjacent waves and land is lost between the swells.

Storm King Wavefield is the largest and last in a series of three of Lin's wavefields. (The other two are located in Ann Arbor, Michigan, and Miami, Florida.) Lin selected the eleven-acre site as an environmental reclamation project, a sustainable reworking of the former gravel pit that supplied material for the New York State Thruway. When Storm King was founded in 1960, a significant portion of its grounds consisted of large stores of gravel in surrounding fields. The ravaged landscape was in turn landscaped and shaped anew by the very same gravel. This compelling, untold story excited Lin. "I've tended to create works on the edges and boundaries of places…. I always knew that I wanted to culminate the series with a field that literally, when you were in it, you became lost inside it." Working with the New York State Department of Environmental Conservation, which sanctioned and supported the reclamation of the site, Lin collaborated with landscape architects to utilize the existing gravel and topsoil at the site. The low-impact grasses and natural drainage system she introduced make *Wavefield* an organic, living work that continues to evolve.

Lin's biography provides some insights into *Wavefield*'s origins and imagery. Growing up in rural Ohio, she visited the earthen mounds of the Hopewell and Adena Indians. She learned about Japanese gardens and architecture from her father, a ceramist and dean of the College of Fine Arts at Ohio University, Athens, who had grown up in a Japanese-style house in China. These early experiences, along with the influential innovations of earthwork artists in the 1960s and '70s, helped shape what has become Lin's lifelong interest in working with the landscape.

Lin earned great prominence early on, while still a student at Yale University, for her Vietnam Veterans Memorial in Washington, DC. Breaking from typical memorial form, Lin's striking design features a deep cut into the earth and is at once profoundly minimal and metaphorical. Such qualities have threaded throughout her prolific career in art and architecture, along with a sustained commitment to environmentalism. *What is Missing?*, a multi-sited, ongoing project that Lin considers her final memorial, focuses on bringing awareness to the current crisis surrounding biodiversity and habitat loss. "Whether it's art, architecture, or memorials," she notes, "I realize now that all my work is intrinsically tied to the natural landscape around us."

L

LIN, MAYA

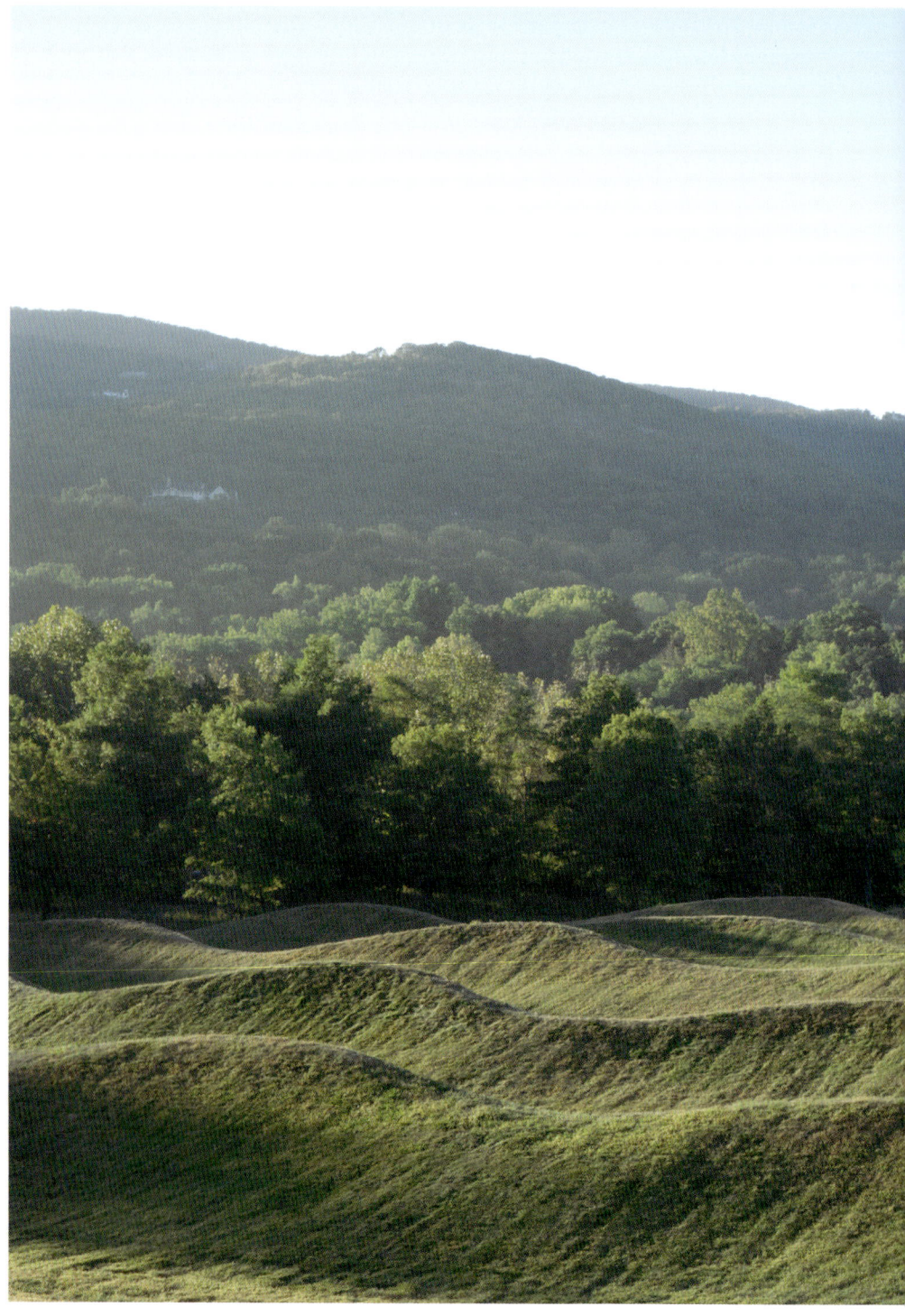

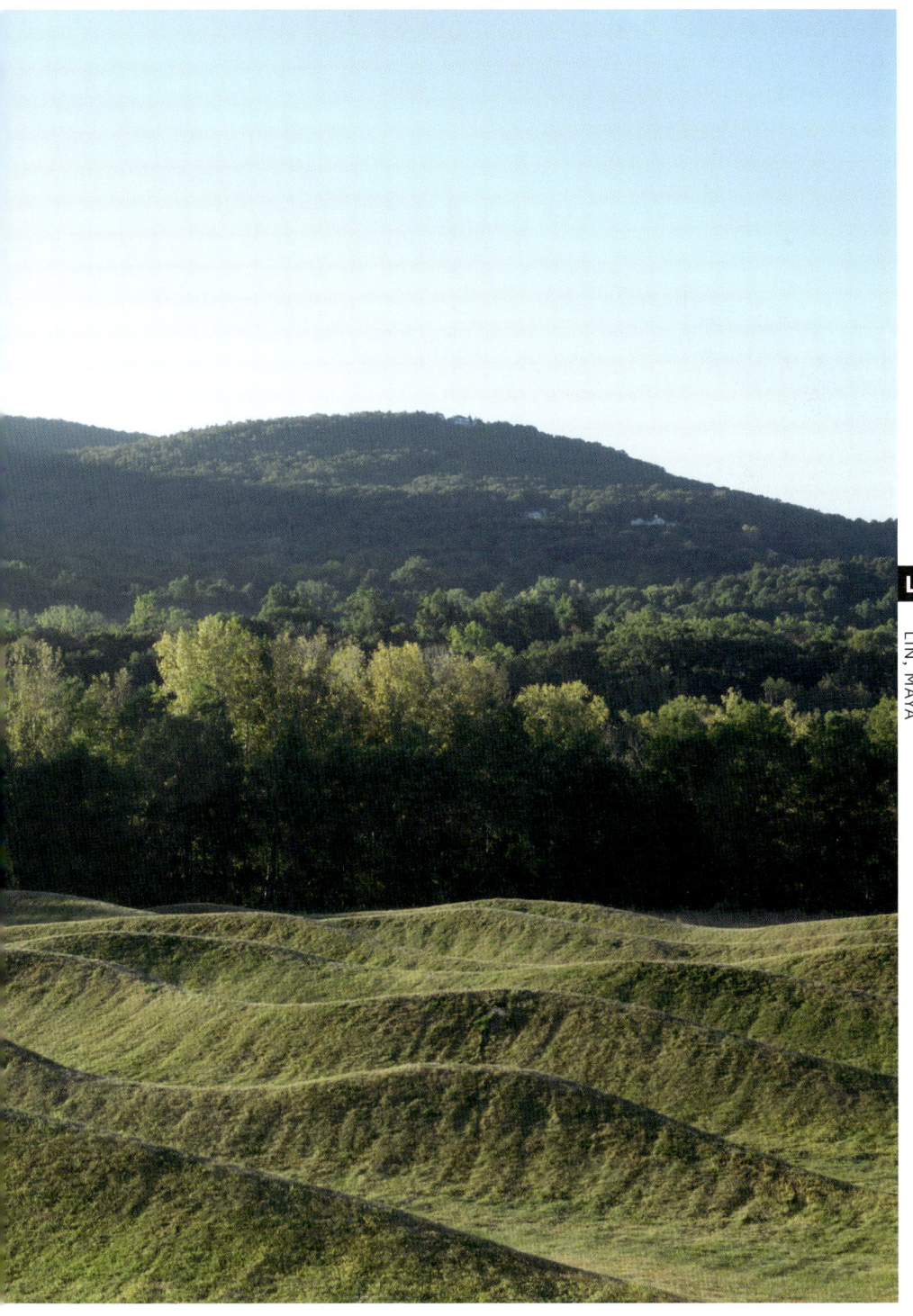

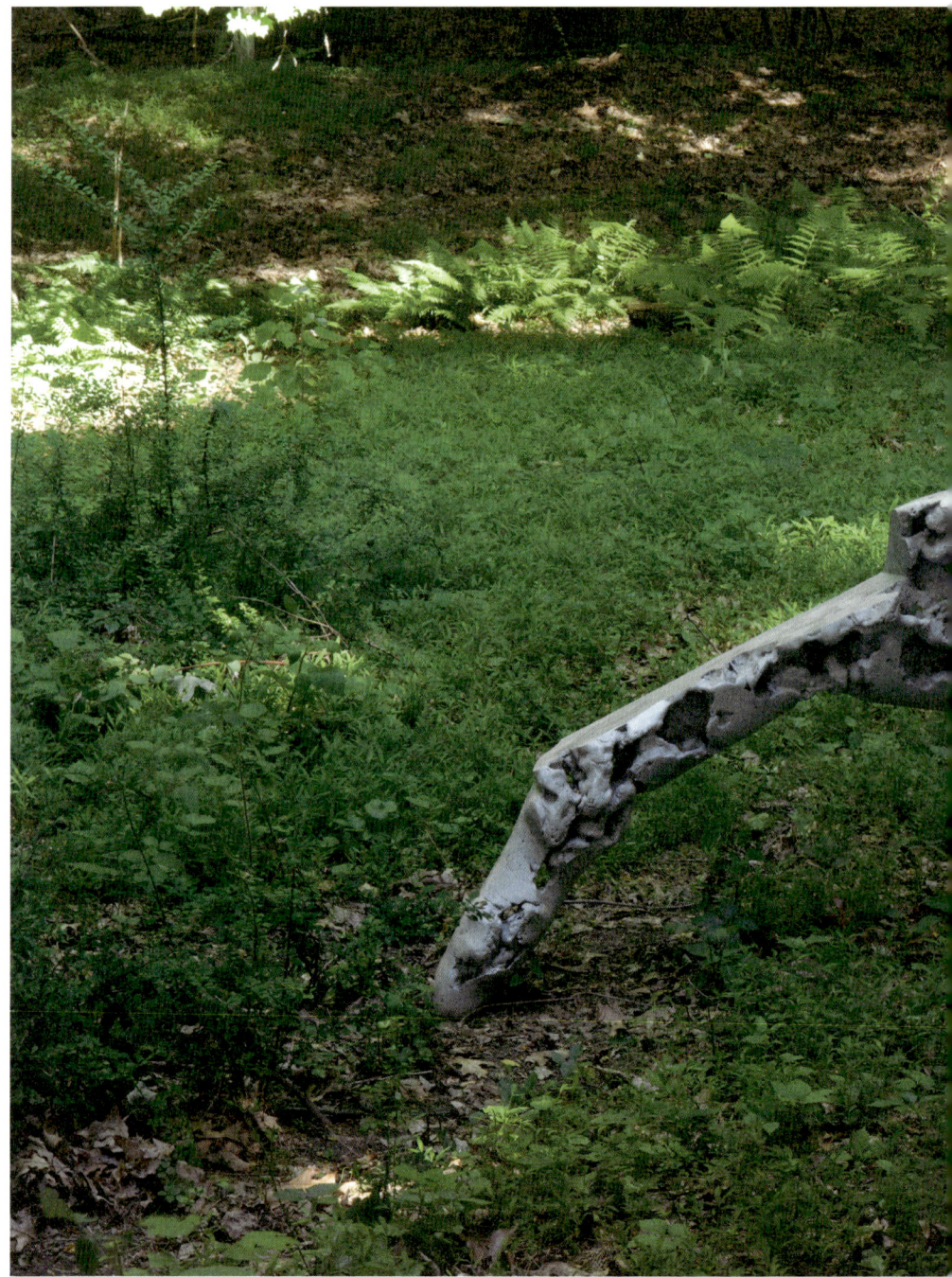

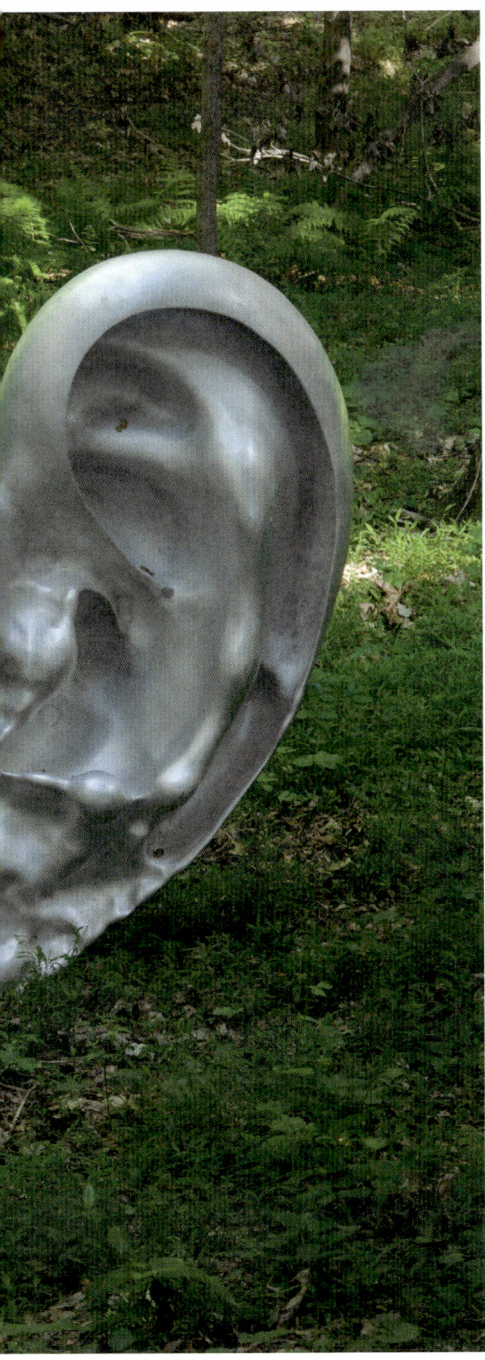

TOMIO MIKI

JAPANESE, 1937–1978

EAR, 1965
ALUMINUM
65½" x 8' 11" x 17"
GIFT OF THE ARTIST AND MINORU NIIZUMA

Tomio Miki, who exhibited among a group of avant-garde, politically active artists in Tokyo in the late 1950s and early 1960s, settled in 1963 on the human ear as his primary sculptural subject for the next several years. He often depicted them individually, on a giant scale, as represented in the work at Storm King. Sometimes he combined ears with other elements, such as spoons or colored lights, or made series of them set in rows or in boxes. Miki spoke quixotically about his choice of the ear, saying that it originated in an "experience in a train, when, for no reason, I suddenly felt myself surrounded by hundreds of ears trying to assault me. This personal episode, however, wouldn't be any precise answer to why I make ears. I can hardly say I chose the ear. More precisely, isn't it that the ear chose me?"

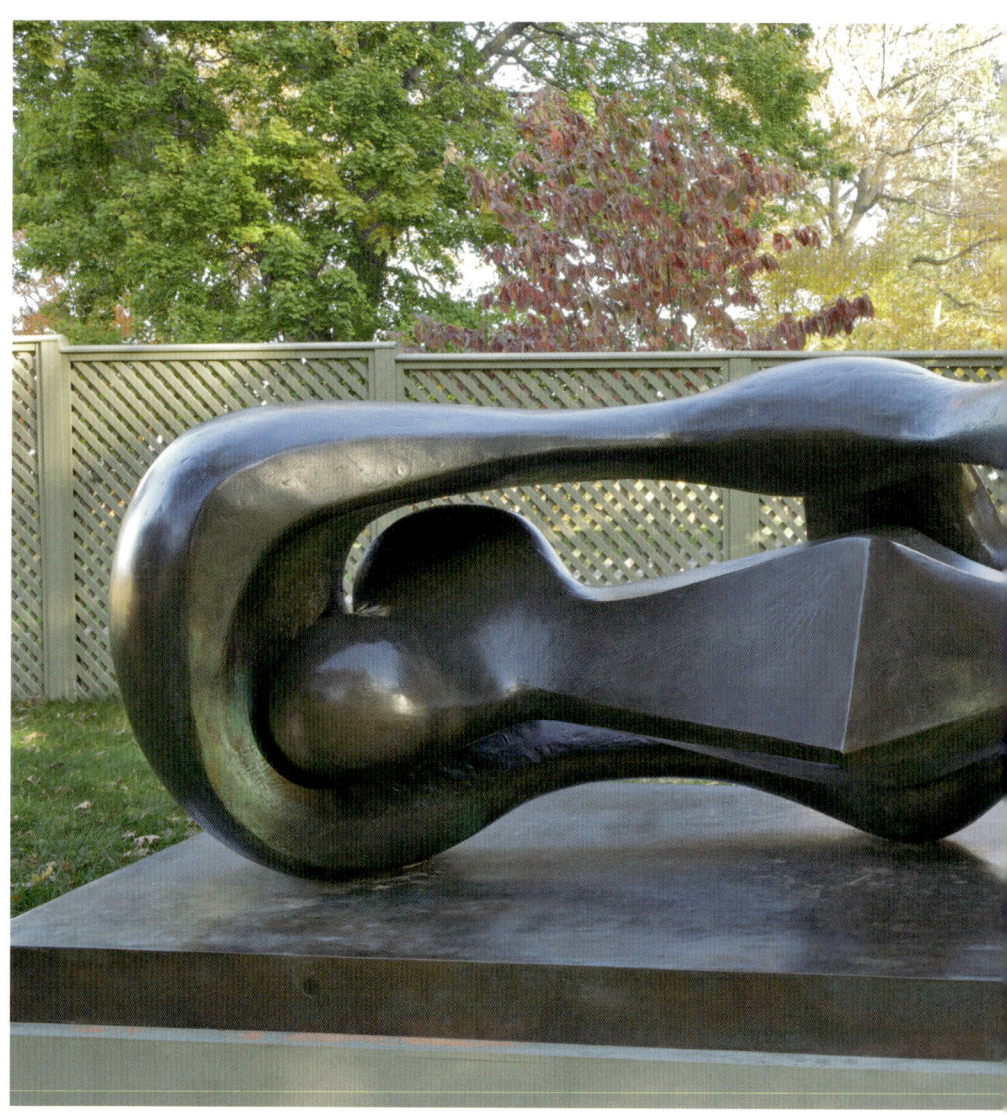

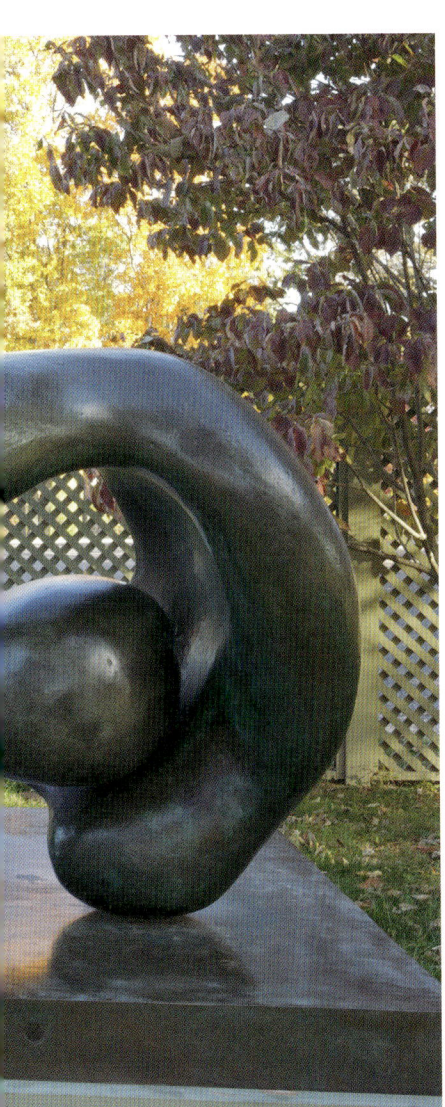

HENRY MOORE

BRITISH, 1898–1986

RECLINING CONNECTED FORMS, 1969
BRONZE
36¼" x 7' 4" x 52"
GIFT OF THE RALPH E. OGDEN FOUNDATION

The abstracted shapes of *Reclining Connected Forms* allude to two enduring themes within the art of Henry Moore, one of Britain's leading twentieth-century sculptors: the reclining figure and the mother and child. Here, undulating organic forms evoke a recumbent human figure, a mother embracing a child, or perhaps an infant in the womb. Henry Moore once associated the motif of the mother and child in his work to his discovery of and interest in armor: "Armor is an outside shell like the shell of a snail which is there to protect the more vulnerable forms inside.... This has led sometimes to the idea of the Mother and Child where the outer form, the mother, is protecting the inner form, the child." Moore began his life-long exploration of reclining figures in the 1930s, sometimes separating the figures into two or three pieces. In addition, he began to experiment with the inclusion of holes that penetrate the biomorphic shapes of his carvings, and beginning in the 1950s, often treated the open spaces within his sculpture as significantly as he did the solid forms.

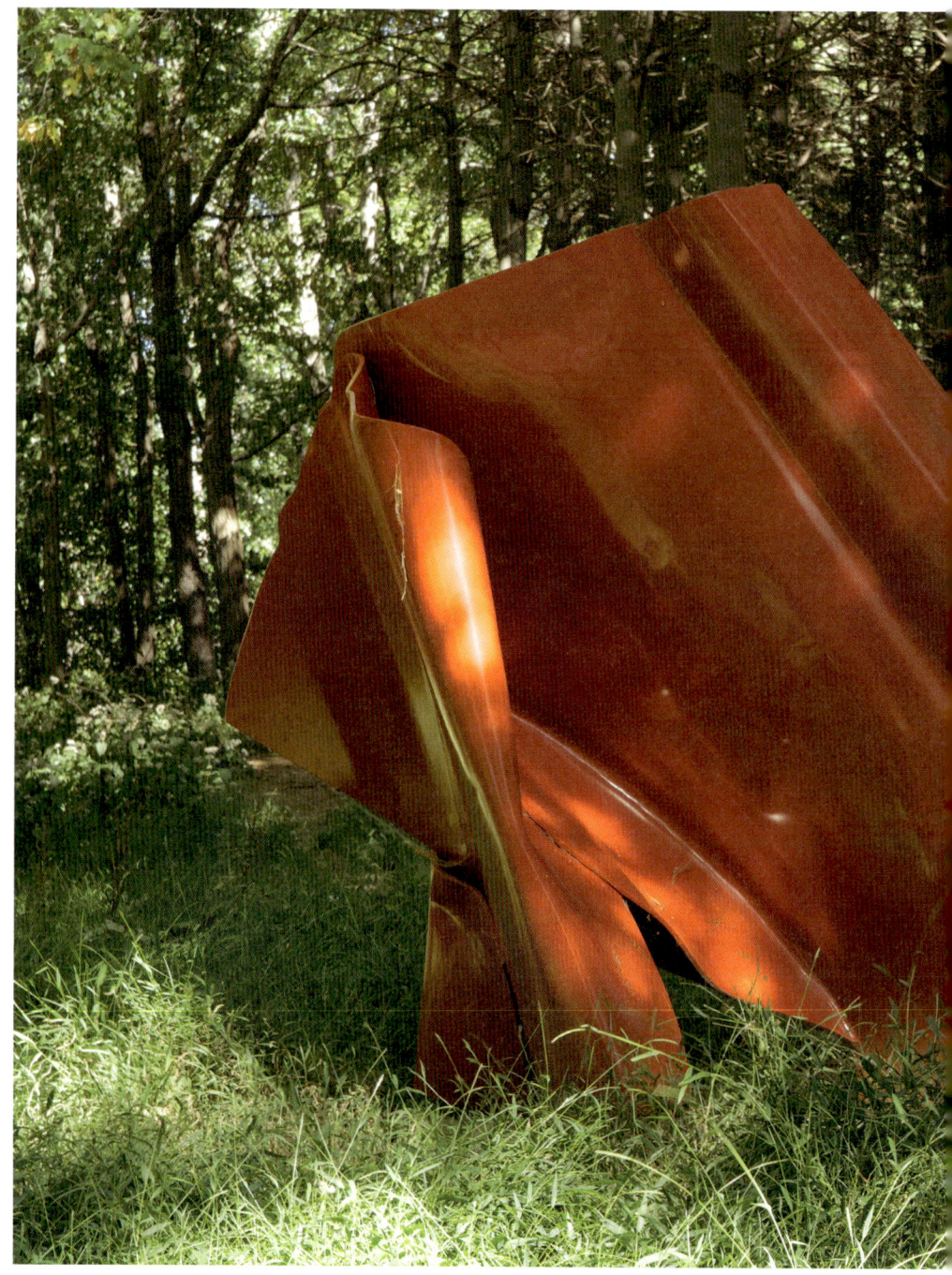

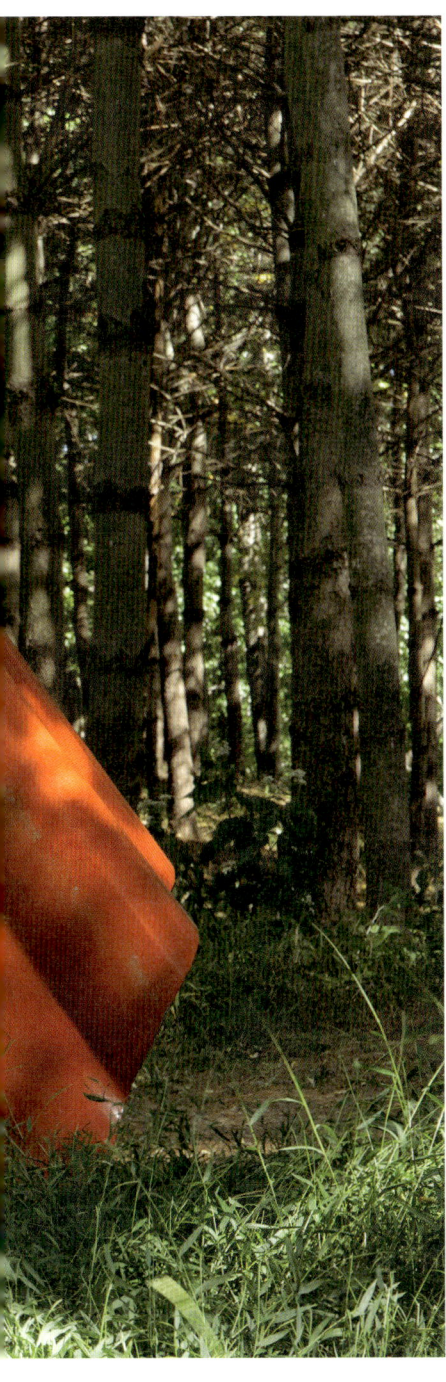

ROBERT MURRAY

CANADIAN/AMERICAN, BORN 1936

KIANA, 1978
PAINTED ALUMINUM
6'2" x 57" x 7'5"
PURCHASED WITH THE AID OF FUNDS FROM THE
NATIONAL ENDOWMENT FOR THE ARTS AND GIFT
OF THE RALPH E. OGDEN FOUNDATION

Robert Murray developed his signature method of folding and bending a sheet of metal in the early 1960s, working with foundries to achieve his artistic vision. *Kiana*'s deep curves were wrought by steel rollers, while its bent or folded parts were created with a hydraulic press brake. Murray always starts with a flat, single plate of steel, which, he has noted, he "tend[s] to look at…like a big piece of canvas." The paint of *Kiana* is bright and shiny, similar to the exterior of a car, however, the deep bends of the sculpture form extreme ripples never seen in automobile design. As Murray has commented, "In a nutshell, and it's probably hedonistic, these works are really an attempt to get sensuous responses out of metal without it becoming playful."

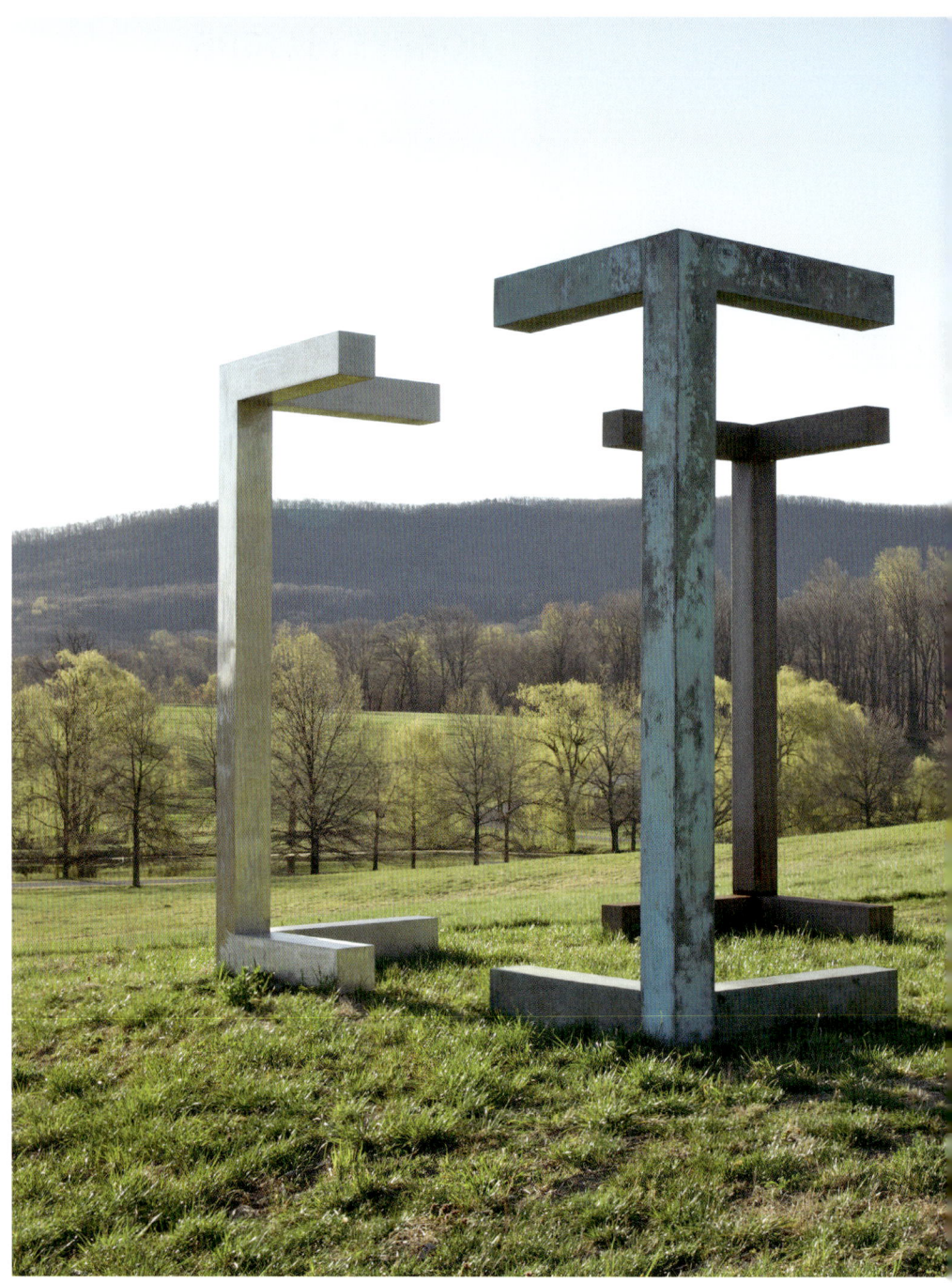

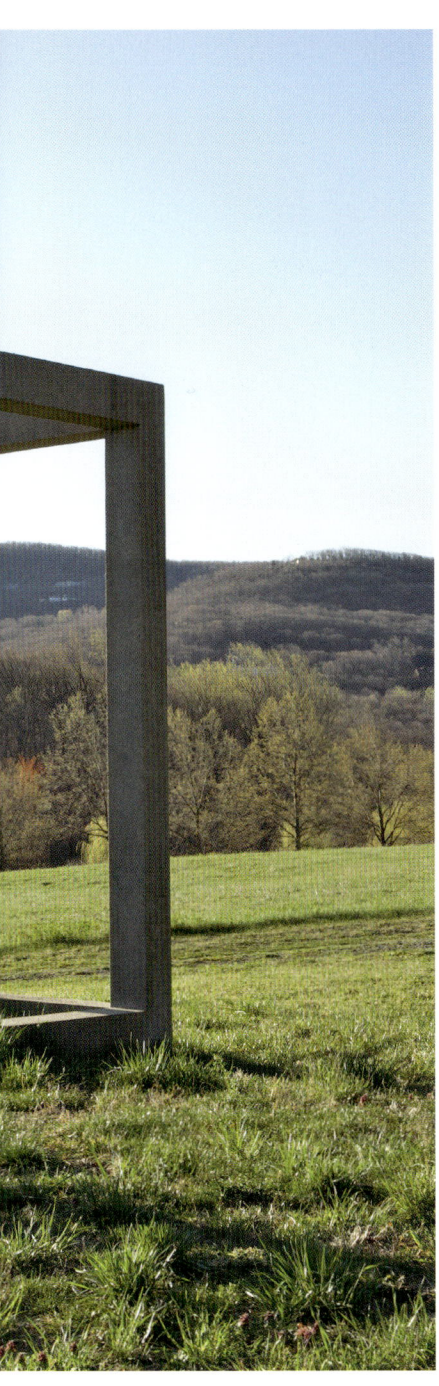

FORREST MYERS

AMERICAN, BORN 1941

SELECTED WORK:
FOUR CORNERS, 1969–70
WEATHERING STEEL, STAINLESS STEEL,
BRONZE, AND CONCRETE
10 x 10 x 10'
GIFT OF THE RALPH E. OGDEN FOUNDATION

Forrest Myers's *Four Corners*, a visually complex, open, incomplete cube, is composed of four different materials: bronze, stainless steel, weathering steel, and concrete. It exemplifies an interest held by many sculptors in the 1960s and 1970s in physically and mentally engaging the viewer and playing with perception. In *Four Corners*, the viewer is invited to enter the sculpture's space and mentally complete its known Platonic form. The work activates additional layers of meaning in its title, which refers not only to the four corners of a cube but also to the four materials used to create the sculpture and perhaps to the far reaches of the globe.

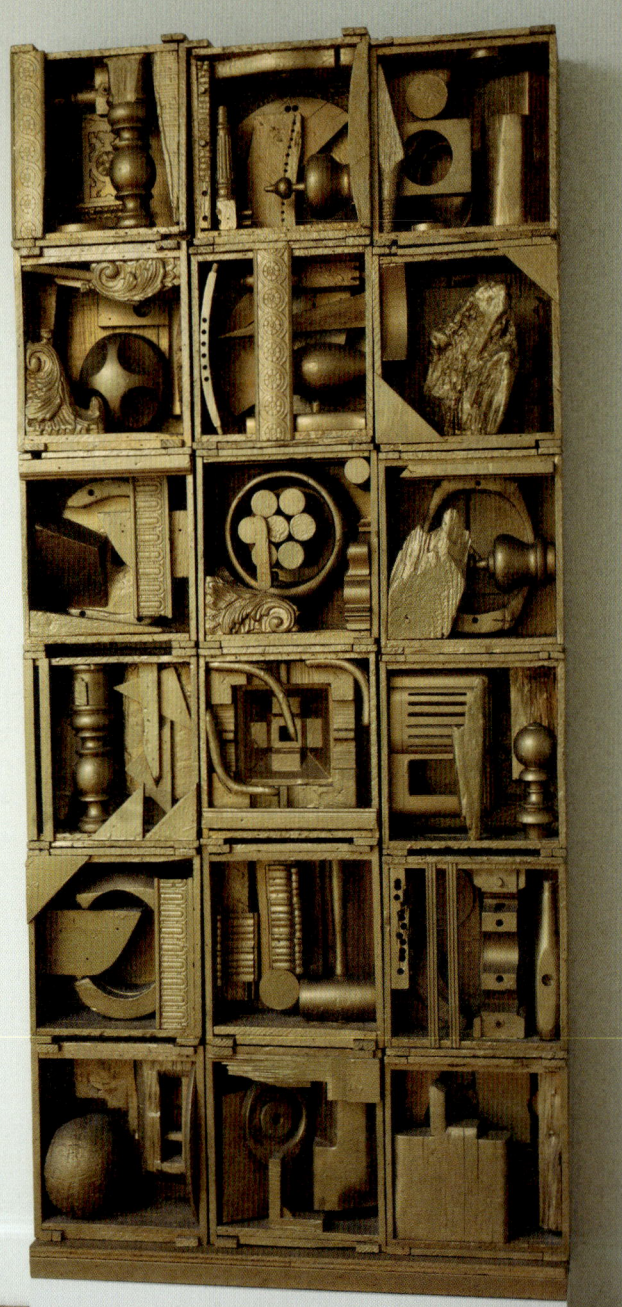

LOUISE NEVELSON

AMERICAN, BORN RUSSIA, 1899–1988

ROYAL TIDE I, 1960
PAINTED WOOD
86 x 40 x 8"
COLLECTION OF PETER AND BEVERLY LIPMAN

DIMINISHING REFLECTION XXV, 1966
PAINTED WOOD AND PLEXIGLAS
17 5/8 x 17 1/2 x 6"
GIFT OF CYNTHIA HAZEN POLSKY

CITY ON THE HIGH MOUNTAIN, 1983
PAINTED STEEL
20' 6" x 23' x 13' 6"
PURCHASE FUND

Louise Nevelson's *City on the High Mountain*, sited just outside Storm King's Museum Building, is a playful and complex assemblage of black-painted steel. Nevelson frequently combined elements from existing works to create new compositions, and *City on a High Mountain* is sourced from models for different sculptures she had created several years earlier. Conjoining the elements with large curvilinear shapes, she eventually enlarged what was a ten-foot model to the sculpture's current height of more than twenty feet. Additional pieces added to create the final composition include the grill-like "lace," which reminded her of lace doilies from her childhood, and a gong-like, suspended element. Of the ball of railroad spikes, created several years earlier and placed at the very top, Nevelson noted, "Sometimes it's only a period that really finishes the sentence, and that was the period that finished that sentence." The entire assemblage is painted black, a signature color Nevelson used extensively for three decades. "In the academic world, they used to say black and white were no colors," Nevelson observed, "but I'm twisting that to tell you that for me it is the total color. It means totality. It means: contains all."

Diminishing Reflection XXV, a small-scale, black, wood relief enclosed in a box, typifies Nevelson's evocative wall pieces of the 1950s and '60s and follows on her earliest abstract wood constructions from the mid-1940s, which incorporated found objects. Reflecting on her process of constructing such works, Nevelson said, "Sometimes it's the material that takes over; sometimes it's me that takes over. I permit them to play, like a seesaw. I use action and counteraction, like in music, all the time. Action and counteraction. It was always a relationship—my speaking to the wood and the wood speaking back to me." While typically black, Nevelson's sculptures are occasionally white or gold; their monochromatic surfaces lend a sense of order and unity to the varied parts. Among Nevelson's first gold-painted sculptures, *Royal Tide I* was included in the historic *Art of Assemblage* exhibition at New York's Museum of Modern Art in 1961. Nevelson cited a religious resonance in the color gold, as well as a natural and spiritual connection to the sun. She was also interested in its timeless quality: "Gold has been the staple of the world for ages; it is universal."

Nevelson's unique, distinctive sculpture reflects her rich and varied career. Born in 1899 in Kiev, Russia, she emigrated with her family to Rockland, Maine, in 1905 and married and moved to New York in 1920. Hungry for new artistic experiences, she took classes at the Art Students League in New York and with Hans Hoffman in Munich. In 1933 she assisted Diego Rivera on his *Portrait of America* mural for the New Workers School in New York City. By this time Nevelson had also embarked upon a decades-long dedication to dance and modern movement techniques. Finally, after a 1941 one-woman gallery exhibition, Nevelson's work began to receive notice. Her first experiments with weathering steel date from 1966; the material enabled her to work with new, large-scale forms, matching her visions for what her art could be, and would become. During the 1970s, when Nevelson was in her seventies, commissions and demand for her monumentally scaled work expanded dramatically. She retained great ambition and vision throughout her career. "Humans really are heir to every possibility within themselves, and it is only up to us to admit it and accept it," Nevelson stated. "You see, you can buy the whole world and you are empty, but when you create the whole world, you are full."

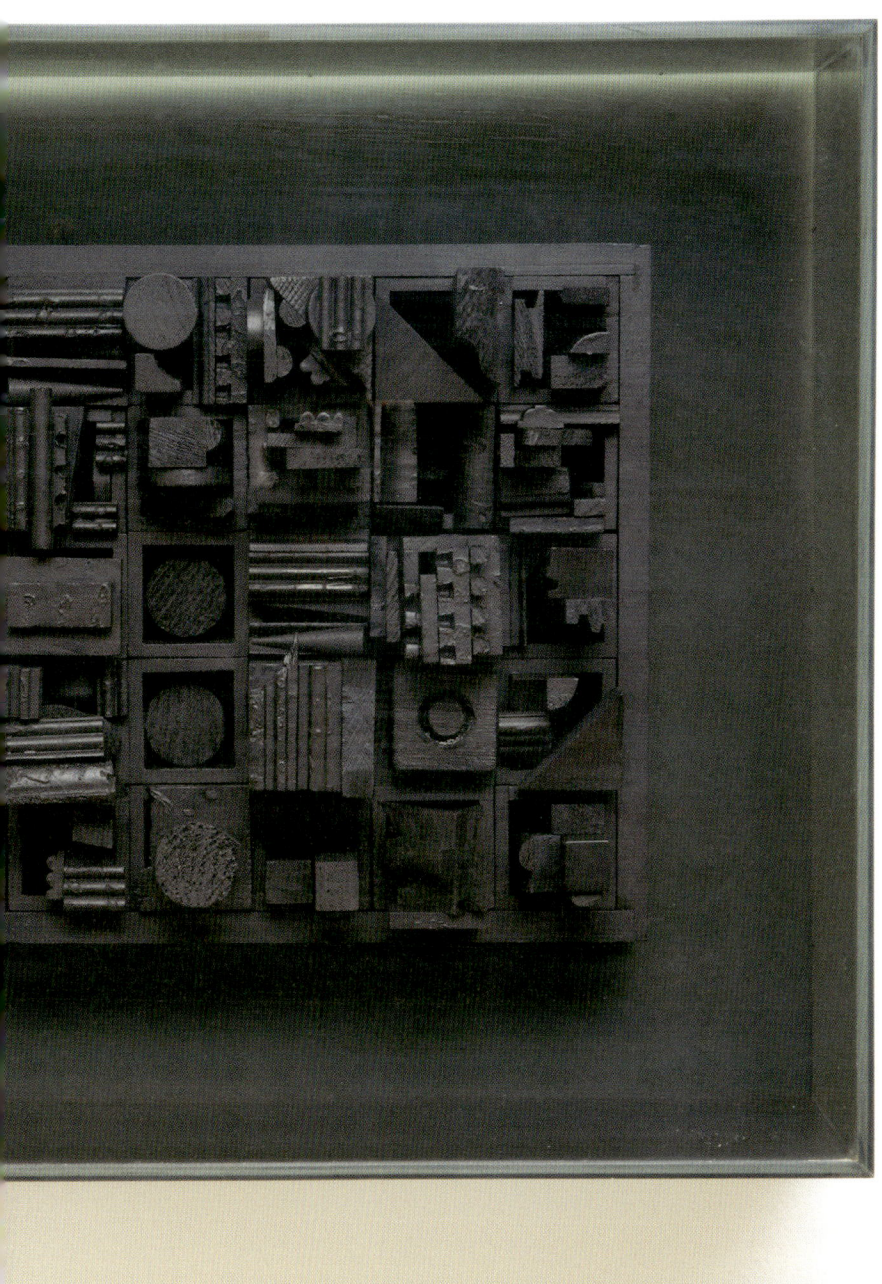

ABOVE: *Diminishing Reflection XXV*, 1966; FOLLOWING SPREAD: *City on the High Mountain*, 1983

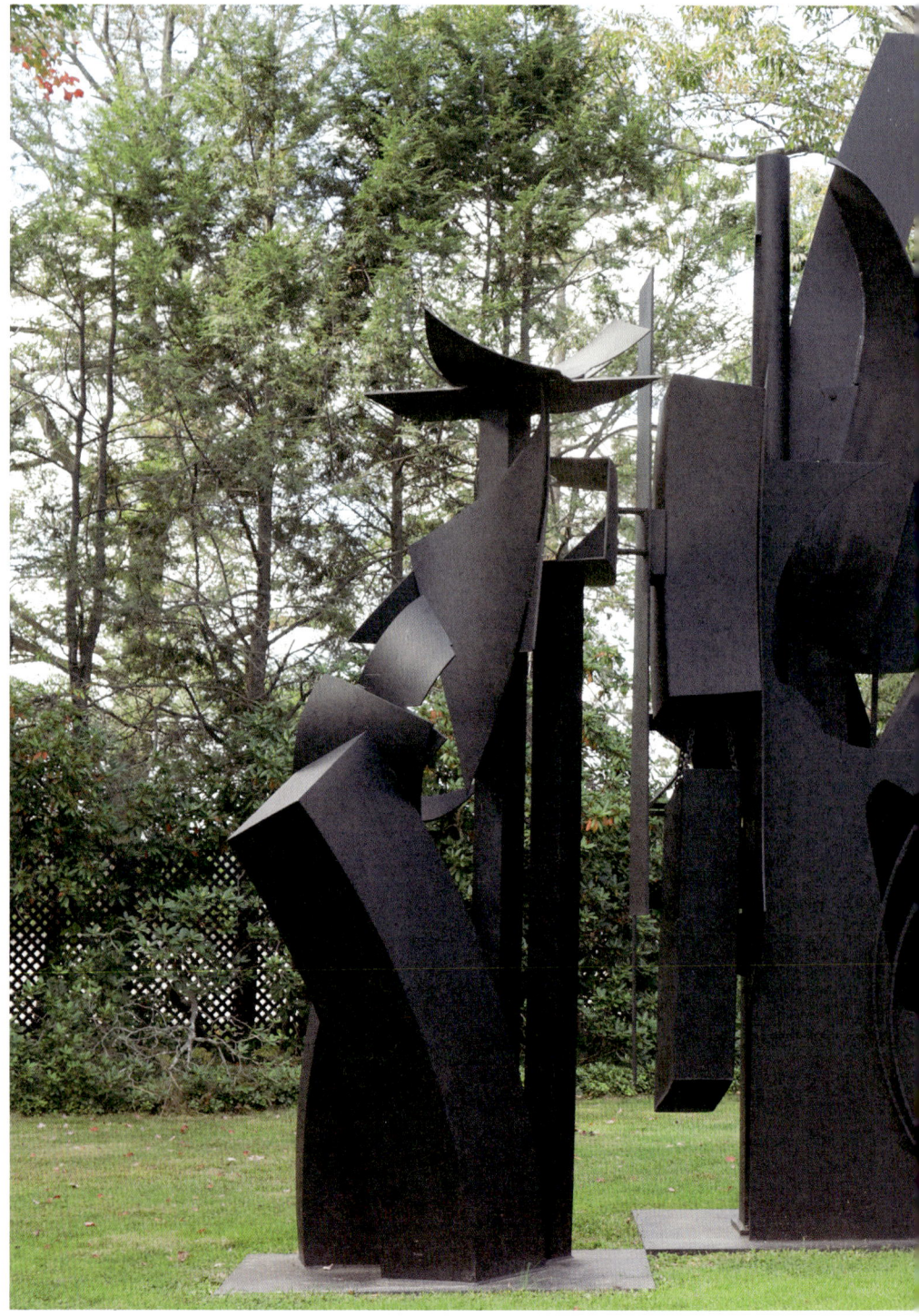

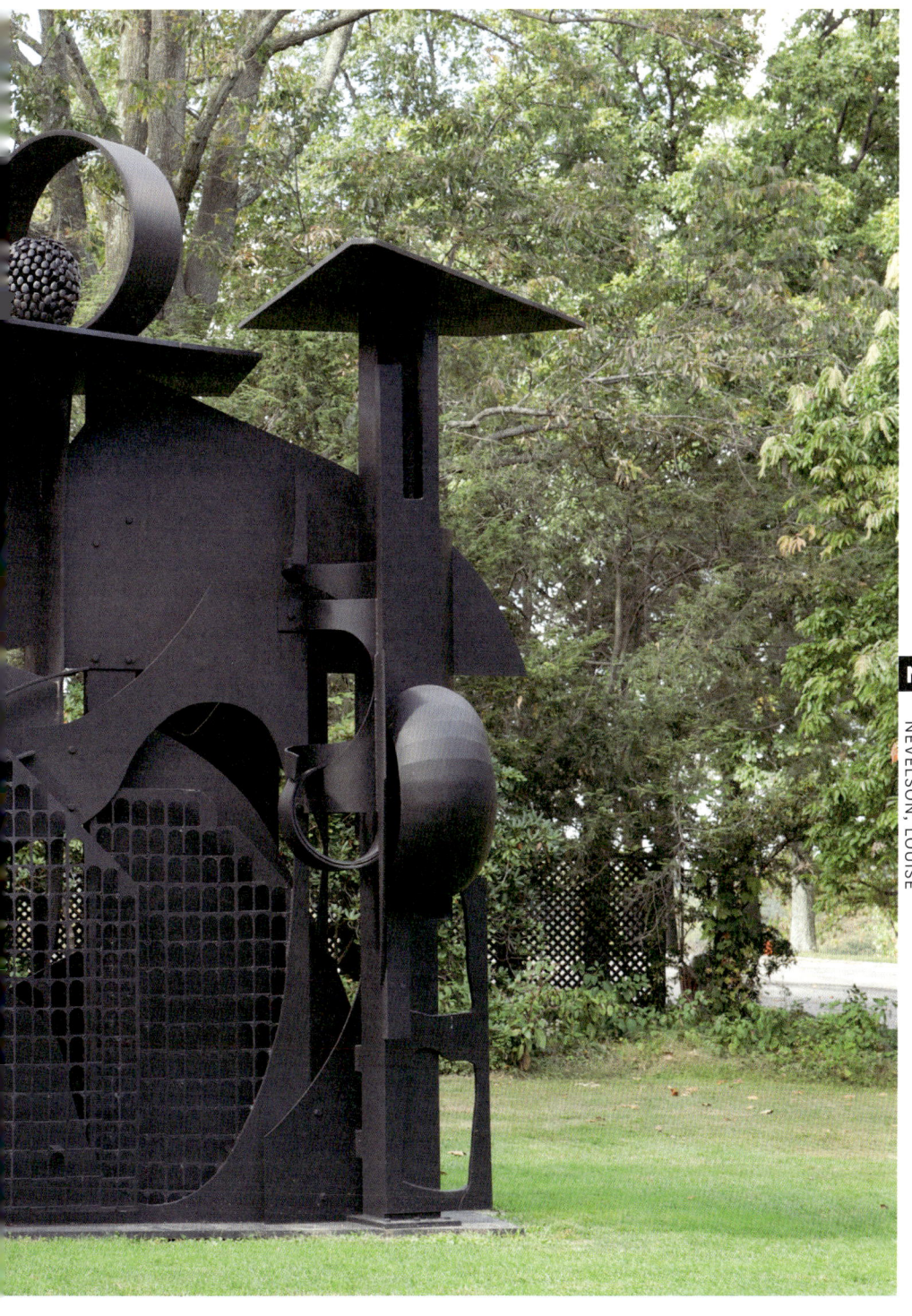

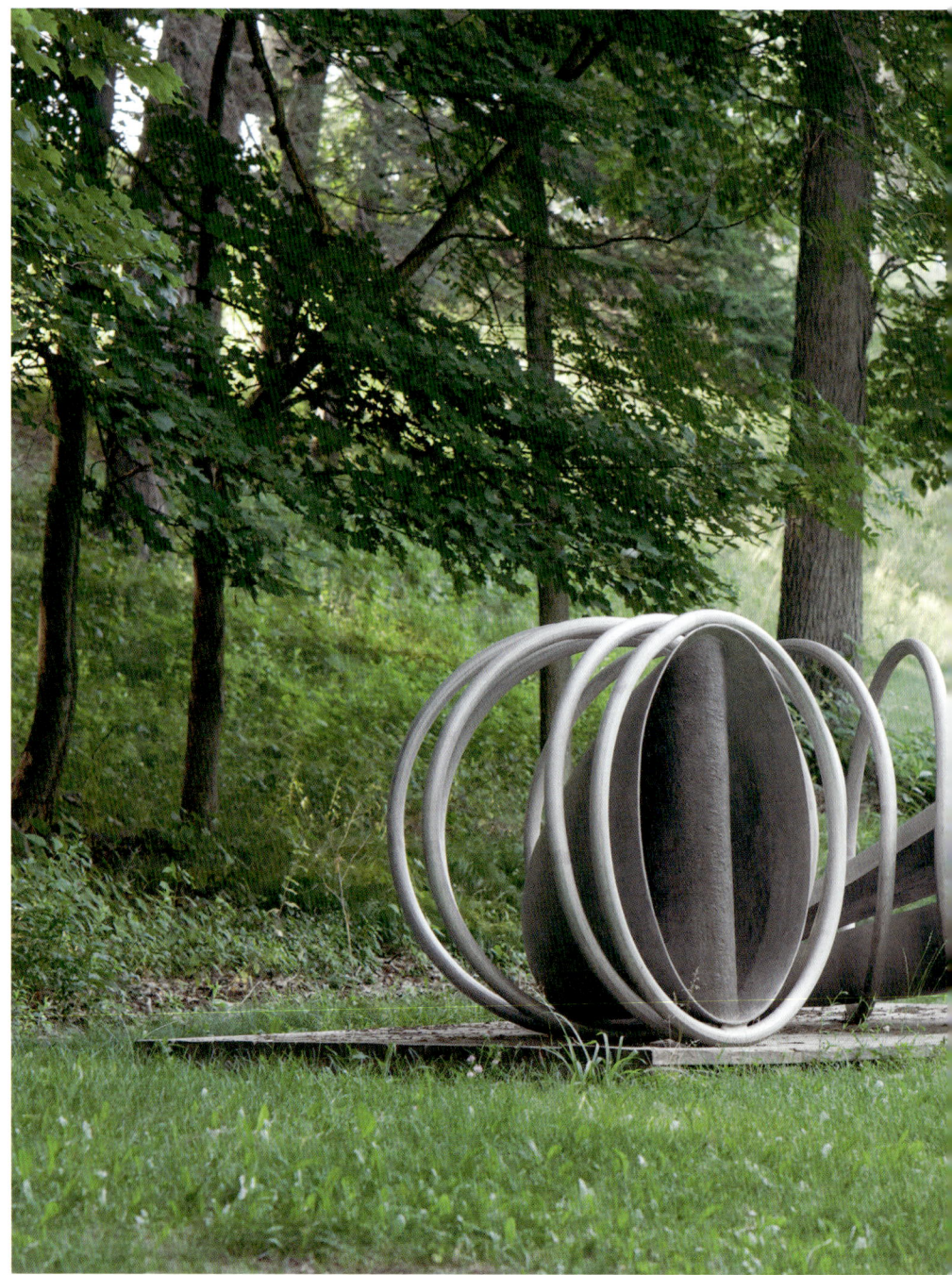

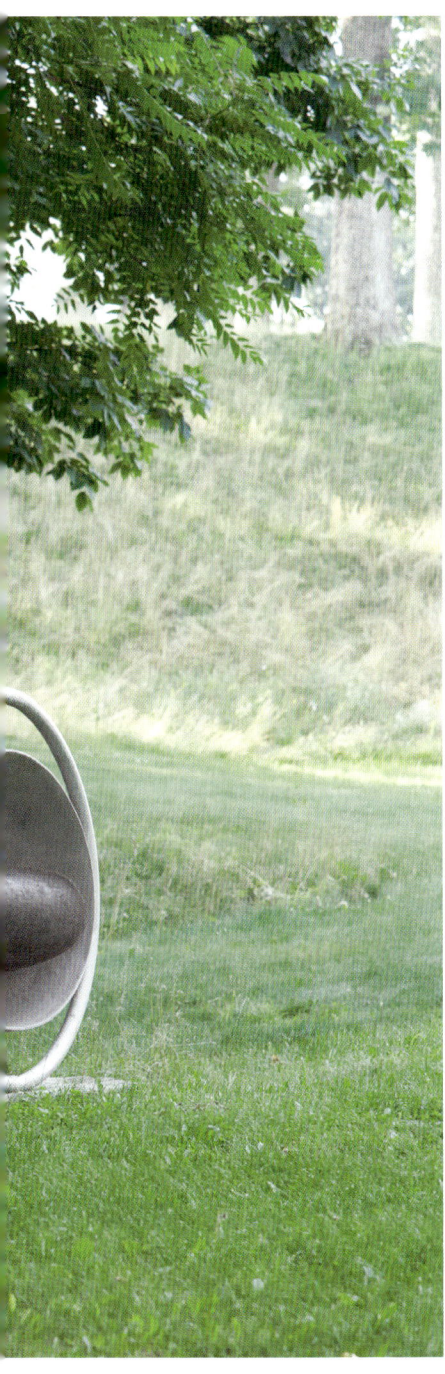

JOHN NEWMAN

AMERICAN, BORN 1952

WIT'S END, 1988–89
ALUMINUM
46½" x 10' 9" x 64"
GIFT OF THE FAMILY OF JOSEPH H. HAZEN
IN HONOR OF HIS 90TH BIRTHDAY

Wit's End, a work that was commissioned
for Storm King, evokes organic shapes
and at the same time feels somewhat
mechanistic, due in part to being constructed of cast aluminum. Its form melds
John Newman's interests in exoskeletons
and topology (the study of objects that
can be stretched into other shapes without changing their essential nature).
Newman's interests extend to medieval
armor and Japanese samurai helmets, and
he integrates them into his sculpture in
unexpected and perhaps unprecedented
ways. As he has described, "I want to
expand the spectrum of sculpture's vocabulary…to make something I've never seen
before. I realize that there is a certain level
of grandiosity in this statement, because
there's nothing new under the sun. But as
a goal, as a method for working, it is something I like thinking about."

ISAMU NOGUCHI

AMERICAN, 1904–1988

MOMO TARO, 1977–78
GRANITE
9' x 34'7" x 21'7" OVERALL
GIFT OF THE RALPH E. OGDEN FOUNDATION

After Storm King's co-founder H. Peter Stern invited Isamu Noguchi to build a sculpture for the collection, Noguchi visited in 1977, surveyed the landscape, selected a site, then returned to his studio on the Japanese island of Shikoku to work on *Momo Taro*. Keeping Storm King's topography in mind, he consulted many site photographs and measurements gathered during his visit. Noguchi, admired for his unparalleled ability to blend aesthetic achievement with function, made a model for a stone work that included two split boulders. After he began working with the stones, however, the design changed significantly. One of his assistants searched for boulders on the nearby island of Shodoshima, in the Seto Inland Sea, and found one too large to move; it had to be split. The rock's appearance after being split reminded his assistants of Momo Taro, an ancient folk hero who emerged from a peach pit to become the son of an elderly couple. The work was finished within a year and was installed in the spring of 1978.

The nine-part, forty-ton granite sculpture, hugging the earth and anchored to a concrete base underground, sits atop a specially landscaped hill, with commanding views of the surrounding area. The dramatic setting on a high mound was created at the artist's request by former Storm King landscape architect William A. Rutherford, Sr. The hill is integral to the work. Noguchi noted, "The sculpture lives as part of a hill. It was the hill that got me going, which inspired me." While Noguchi is known for creating fully orchestrated environments, on this occasion he set his carved stones into surroundings whose ultimate evolution would be out of his control.

The full realization of *Momo Taro* depends on the interaction of visitors, who are invited to not just touch, but to enter, to sit, and to unite their bodies with the work—to participate in its existence. Noguchi's flat bench provides a welcome site for rest and contemplation. The "center" of the piece—the hollowed-out granite "peach pit"—serves as a peaceful retreat. Even on the hottest summer days this interior remains cool. Noguchi expressed his wish that visitors, especially children, would not only climb into the cavity but also sing inside it and enjoy its special aural resonance. The reflective "mirror," a highly polished surface, is angled to fully reflect the sun in summer. The theatrical aspect of the work as a place for action or social gathering reflects Noguchi's extensive history of designing stage sets, primarily for Martha Graham between 1935 and 1966, as well as public plazas and playgrounds.

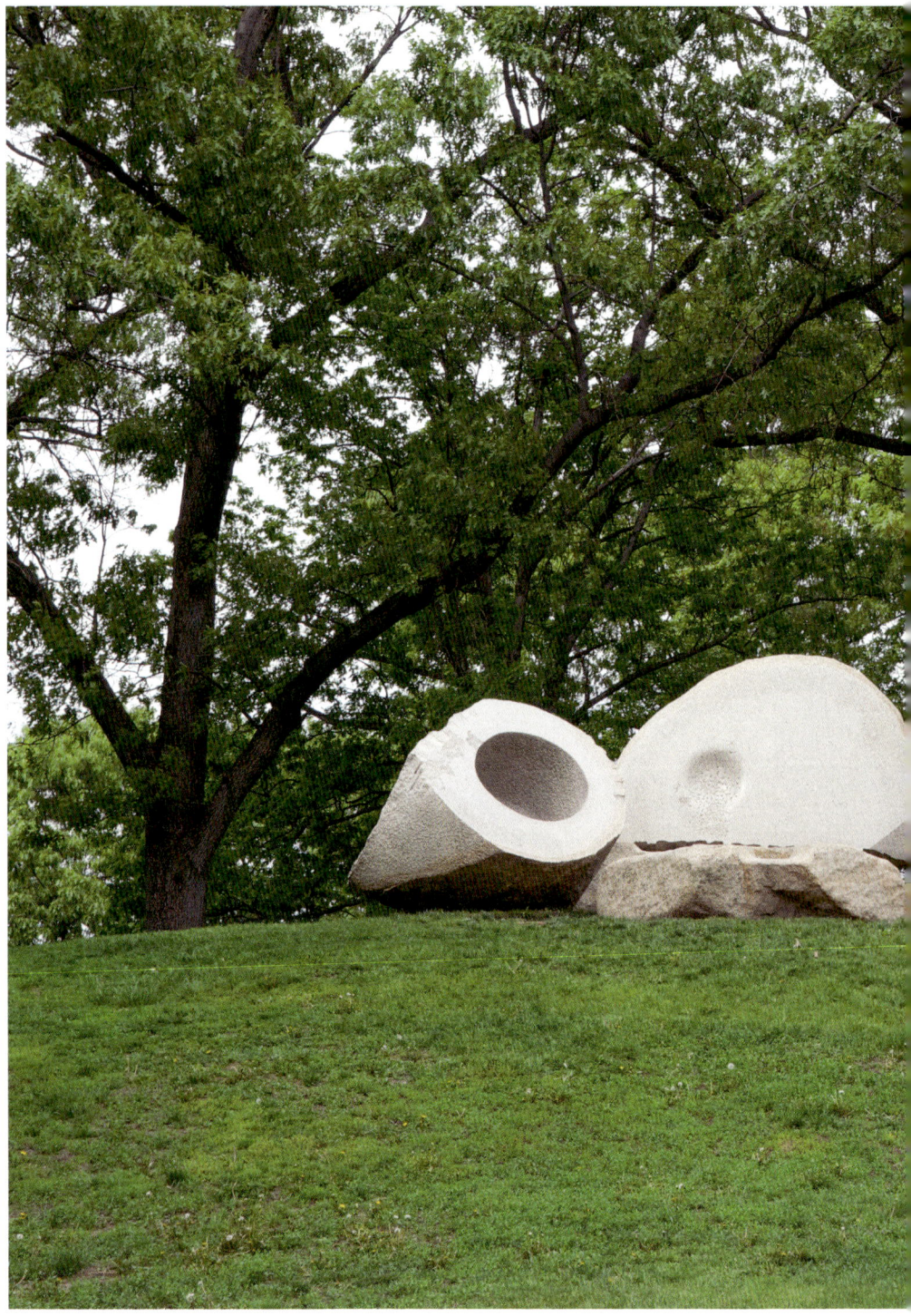

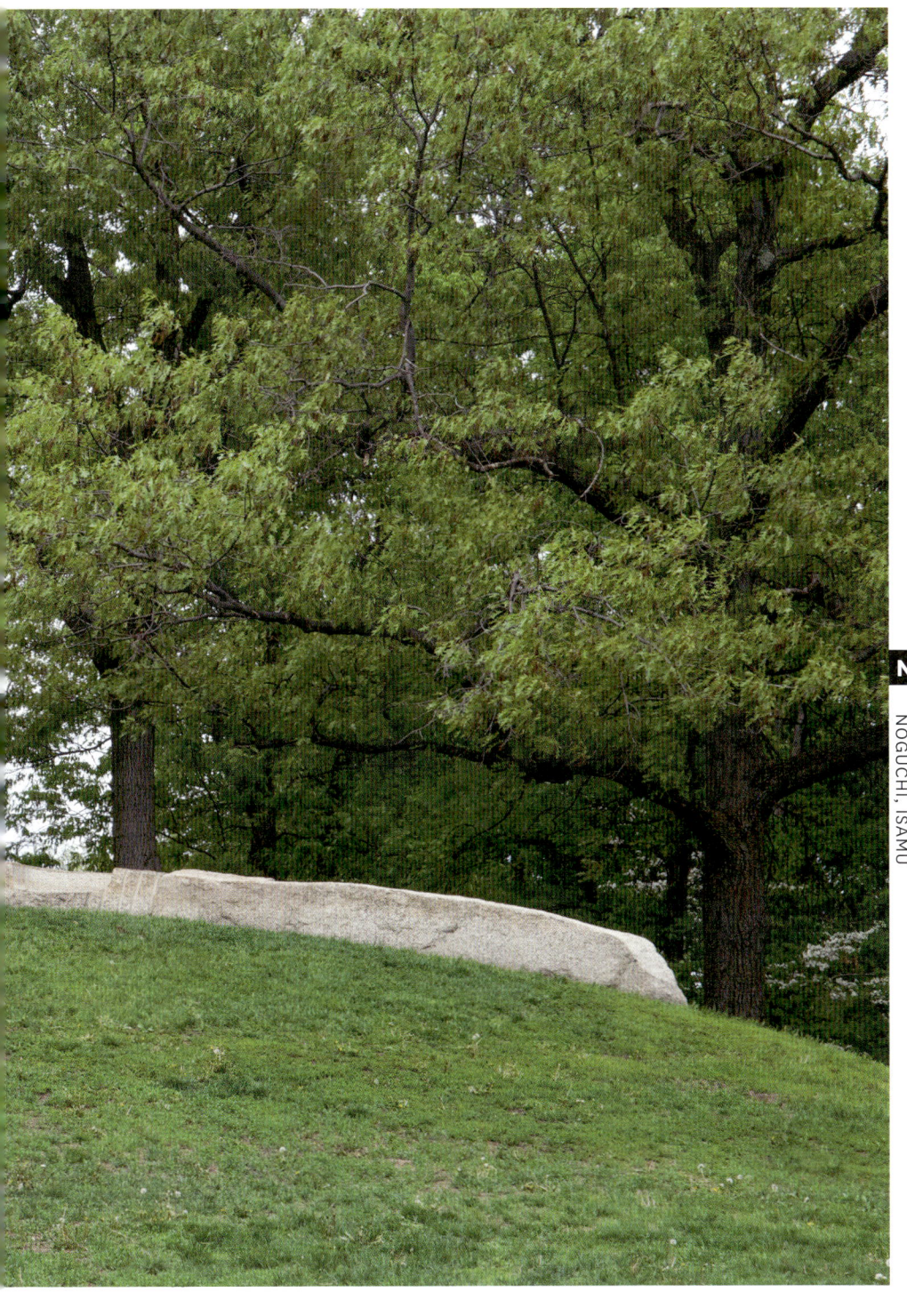

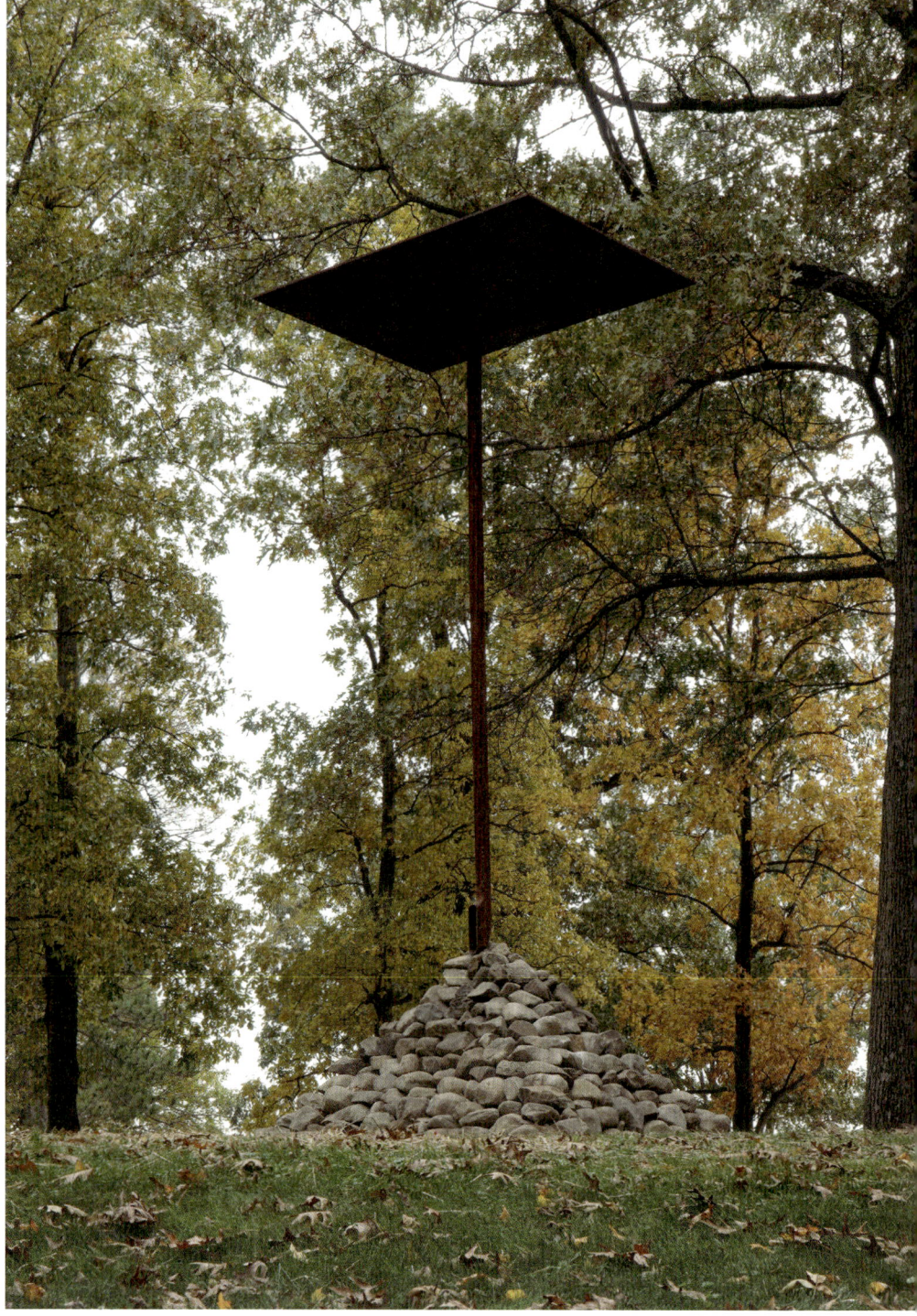

CLAES OLDENBURG AND COOSJE VAN BRUGGEN

AMERICAN, BORN SWEDEN, 1929; AMERICAN, BORN NETHERLANDS, 1942–2009

WAYSIDE DRAINPIPE, 1979
WEATHERING STEEL AND FIELDSTONE
19' 8 ¼" x 8' 1" x 6'
GIFT OF DONALD AND ALFRED LIPPINCOTT AND THE RALPH E. OGDEN FOUNDATION

Wayside Drainpipe is inspired by advertisements that Claes Oldenburg saw for drainpipes in a Swedish newspaper. The stones that form a pyramid around its base were collected from Storm King's property; water flows through the drainpipe positioned above, and is improbably channeled onto the stones. Oldenburg, who has created—with his late wife, Coosje van Bruggen—well-known, inventive public art projects for cities around the world, had several ideas for this drainpipe shape, many fantastical and ultimately unrealized. He envisioned the drainpipe as a grand waterfall erected in the city of Toronto, with the T shape at the drainpipe's top signaling the city's name. In this version, Oldenburg noted, "The drainpipe has a pool at the top. The water runs down through the pipe, and then out into this waterfall at the bottom. And actually, the top is a landing strip for planes; so that you land on a hard surface over the water. People are swimming in the water, so they can look up at the planes landing on top of them and see the passengers get out." In another proposal, Oldenburg envisioned an underground drainpipe in which "the green part [above] is just a park, and the park consists of pure grass except at the center there's a little hole. You look down into that hole, and you look far, far down into the earth, and into the illuminated interior of a vast underground drainpipe." Storm King's *Wayside Drainpipe* joins a few completed indoor sculptures of drainpipes, as well as drawings of these other public monuments, and is the largest version of a drainpipe that Oldenburg and van Bruggen completed.

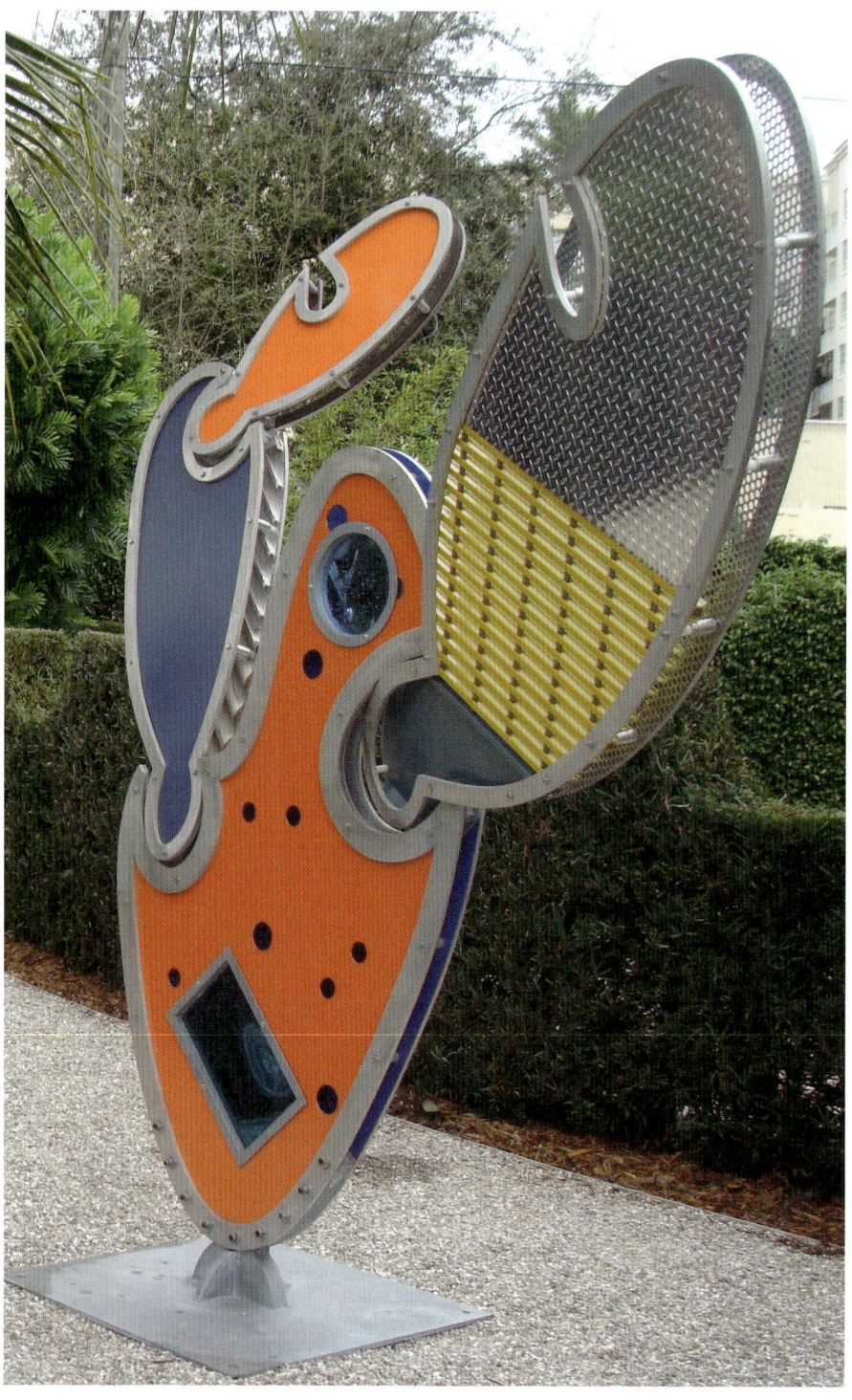

DENNIS OPPENHEIM

AMERICAN, 1938–2011

ARCHITECTURAL CACTUS #6, 2008
ALUMINUM SHEET, COMPOSITE ALUMINUM, DIAMOND PLATE ALUMINUM,
COLORED CORRUGATED ALUMINUM, ACRYLIC, FIBERGLASS GRATING,
GALVANIZED STEEL BASE, STAINLESS STEEL HARDWARE
9 x 6 x 8'
GIFT OF THE WATERMILL CENTER, NEW YORK, NY

As evidenced in this work's title, Dennis Oppenheim had a deep interest in both architecture and cacti. He once noted that he liked that cacti were both soft and hard, he liked the unpredictable shapes into which they grow, and he liked their prickly nature. Oppenheim created eighteen sculptures in his "Architectural Cactus" series, in six different shapes. The surface of each is designed in various colors and materials, so each sculpture is unique. The series was first produced as a public artwork for a location in the desert landscape of Scottsdale, Arizona. Its site across from a police station led Oppenheim—an artist whose work was frequently offbeat and humorous—to design these cactuses to suggest puzzle pieces fit together, like the clues that detectives piece together in the process of solving a crime.

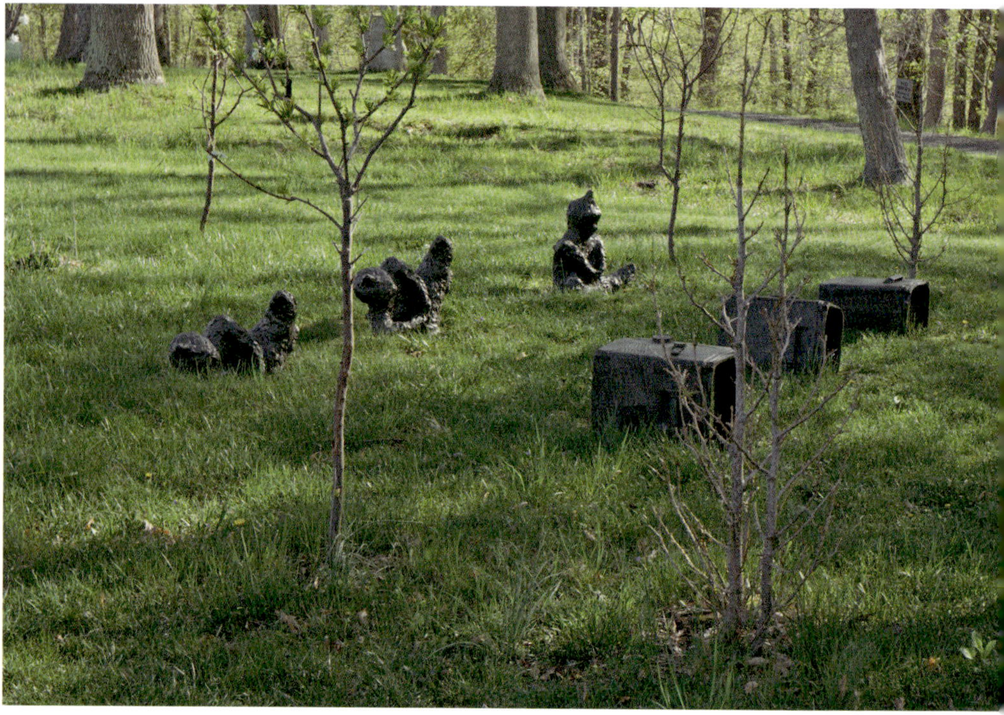

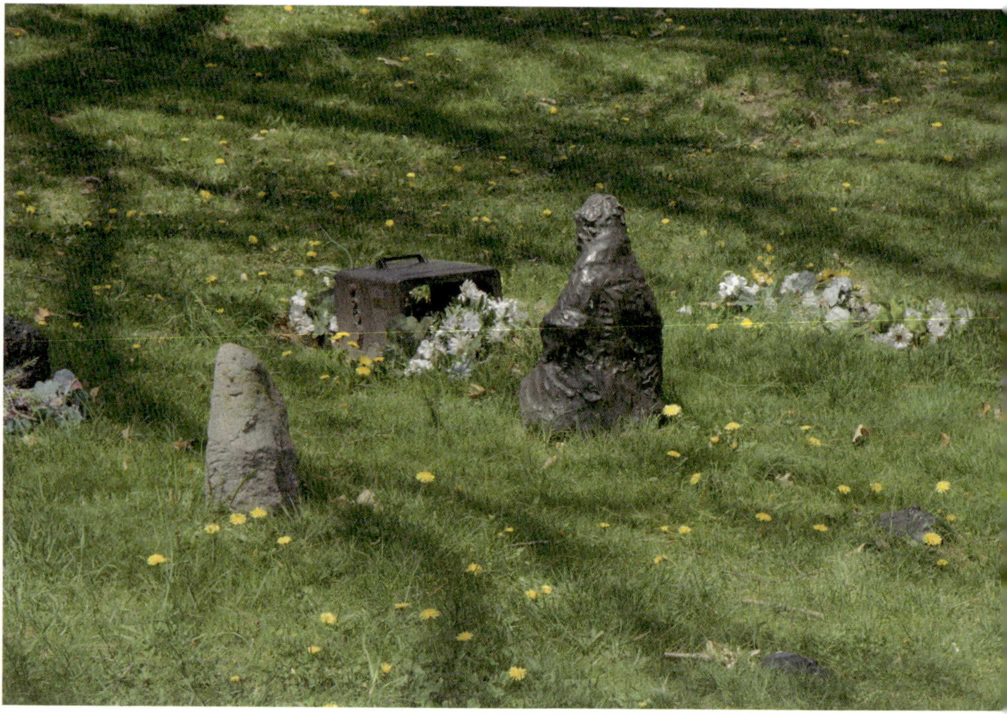

NAM JUNE PAIK

AMERICAN, BORN KOREA, 1932–2006

WAITING FOR UFO, 1992
BRONZE, STONE, PLASTIC, AND CONCRETE (IN THREE PARTS)
A) 24" x 10'7" x 15'
B) 6' x 20'2" x 20'2"
C) 41 x 28 x 30"
GIFT OF CYNTHIA HAZEN POLSKY, THE JOSEPH H. HAZEN FOUNDATION,
AND THE RALPH E. OGDEN FOUNDATION

Nam June Paik's *Waiting for UFO* is a three-part work installed in three locations on and near Storm King's Museum Hill. The sculpture has no single focus or narrative; it is discovered gradually throughout the viewer's encounters with its three distinctly sited parts. While it features some of the elements typical of Paik's interior artificial landscapes—scattered televisions, castings of TV consoles, and representations of Buddha—*Waiting for UFO* is one of very few pieces of outdoor sculpture the artist created. A commissioned gift to Storm King, the sculpture was sited according to the artist's choice, but it can be moved to other locations.

Paik was a pioneer video and performance artist who became world-renowned for his experiments with technology. He began to exploit televisions in his art in the early 1960s, exhibiting his earliest "electronic paintings"—television sets with scrambled images—in 1963. His interactive video works of the period presented the spectator with unprecedented visual experiences. In subsequent decades Paik was known for his installations of television sets filled with assorted objects or stacked video monitors displaying witty or dazzling abstract imagery. In Paik's work, television often represents a landscape of contemporary America, assuming a shrine-like role as it does in modern society.

Installed outdoors, *Waiting for UFO* takes on additional significance, suggesting unanswerable questions about the relationship between technology and nature. Old, empty television consoles, dropped haphazardly onto the ground, appear like technological ruins. Paik also included artificial flowers, bronze and stone Buddhas, and solemn bronze masks of himself staring blankly up toward the heavens. Does the work suggest that technology (or its detritus) has overtaken nature, or merged with it? What do Paik's own self-portrait masks signify? This evocative work lends itself to a variety of interpretations.

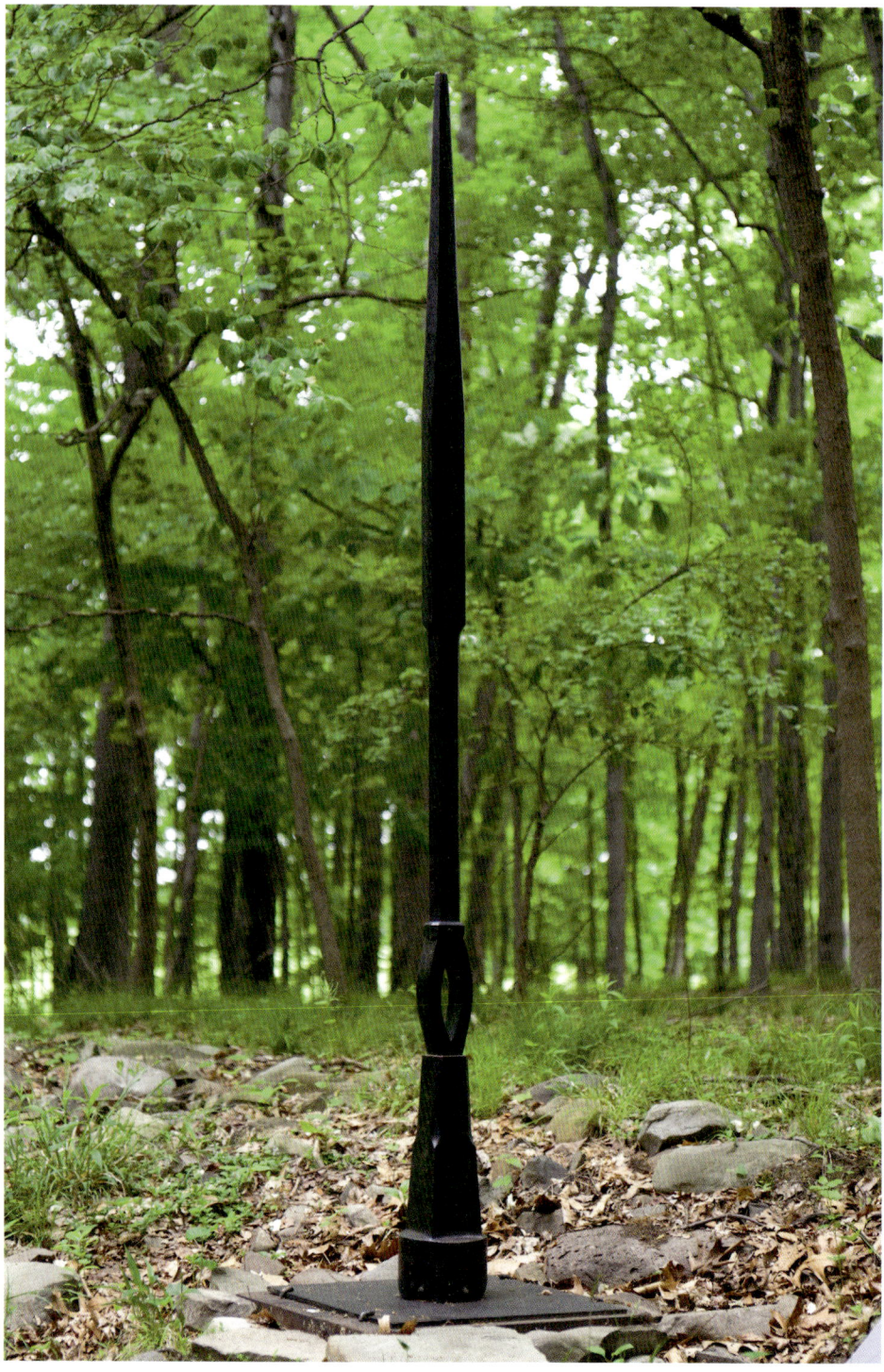

BEVERLY PEPPER

AMERICAN, BORN 1922

KING RITUAL, 1983
BRONZE
8' 6 ½" x 21 ¾" x 21 ¾"
GIFT OF PHILIP M. STERN, WASHINGTON, DC

Several of Beverly Pepper's sculptures include the word "ritual" in their title, an indicator of the way in which she perceives their meaning. She has stated that for her, the meaning of any one sculpture is not pre-determined, but is created by any viewer's face-to-face experience with it. *King Ritual* has precedents in Pepper's small-scale forged and cast-iron sculptures from the late 1970s, whose hieratic forms suggest ancient totemic figures. These eventually increased in size, and by 1982–83, had become tall and attenuated. She has explained, "My work both responds to and tries to rein-force the human capacity for wonder, for reorienting ourselves in relation to powers or fields of force (whether internal or external), which are greater than our merely biographical or social selves. Obviously we can't rebuild the monuments of the ancient world, but we can aspire to re-evoke, in how-ever modern a world, some of the enduring and perhaps renewable sensa-tions of amazement, even awe." Born in Brooklyn, Pepper has spent most of her adult life working in central Italy, and her work has been inspired by obelisks and other ancient artifacts of the Mediterranean region.

P

PEPPER, BEVERLY

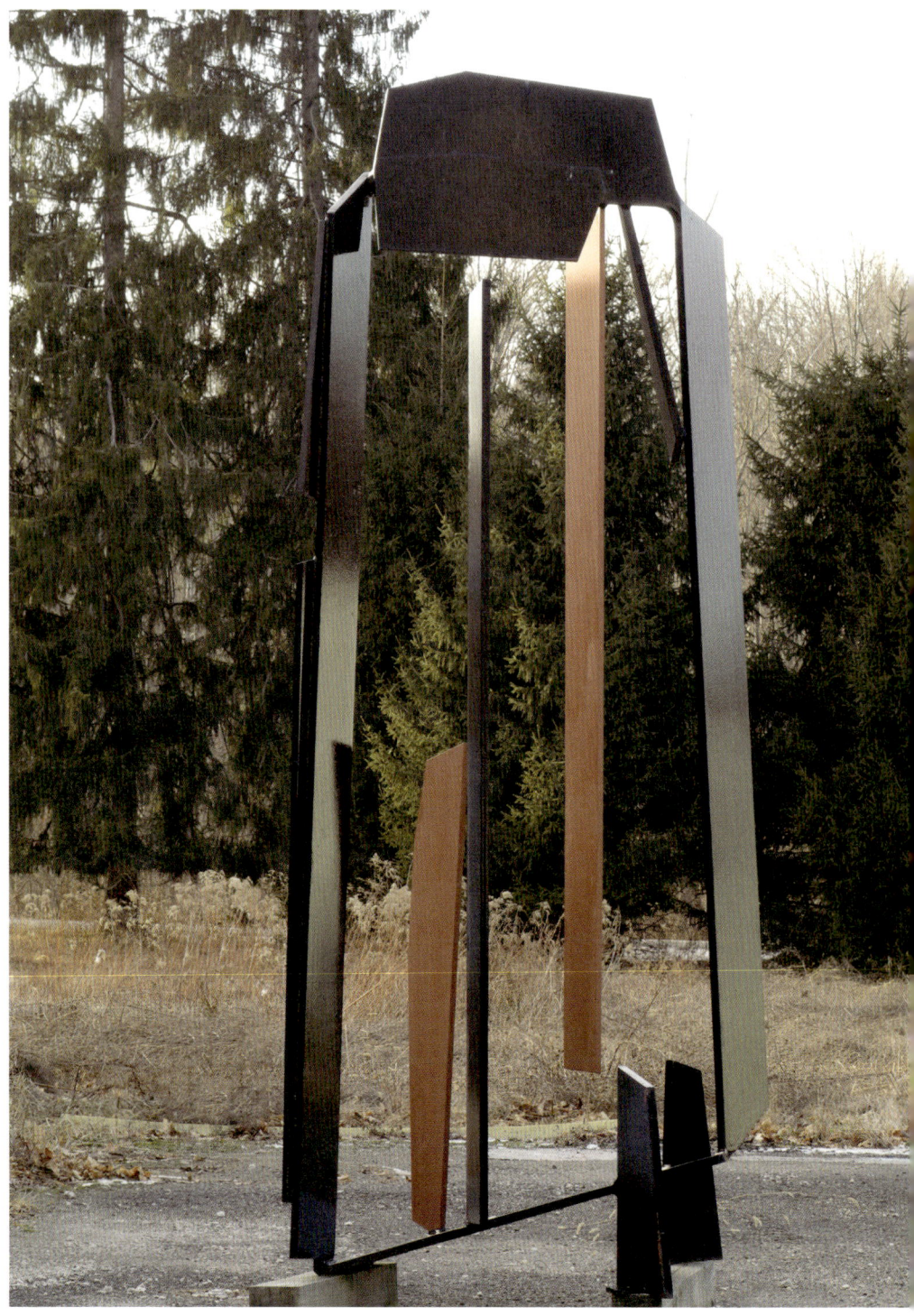

JOEL PERLMAN

AMERICAN, BORN 1943

NIGHT TRAVELER, 1977
PAINTED STEEL
10'11" x 47" x 47"
PURCHASED WITH THE AID OF FUNDS FROM THE NATIONAL ENDOWMENT
FOR THE ARTS AND GIFT OF THE RALPH E. OGDEN FOUNDATION

Night Traveler's fragmented post-and-lintel gateway is characteristic of
Joel Perlman's sculptures of the late 1970s. The visually shifting planes
in a shallow space, combined with muted coloration, suggest his interest
in applying the painterly innovations of Cubism to the real space of
sculpture. The monumental, vertical construction evokes the forms of
skyscrapers, doorways, or ancient temples. "Architecture is a definite
influence," Perlman has stated. "If I were not a sculptor, I would want to be
an architect." *Night Traveler* was commissioned by Storm King. According
to the artist, when he conceived the work he was interested in certain
colors receding and others moving forward. Indeed, the close color
contrast of brown and black creates a spatial tension, as do the work's
positive and negative spaces.

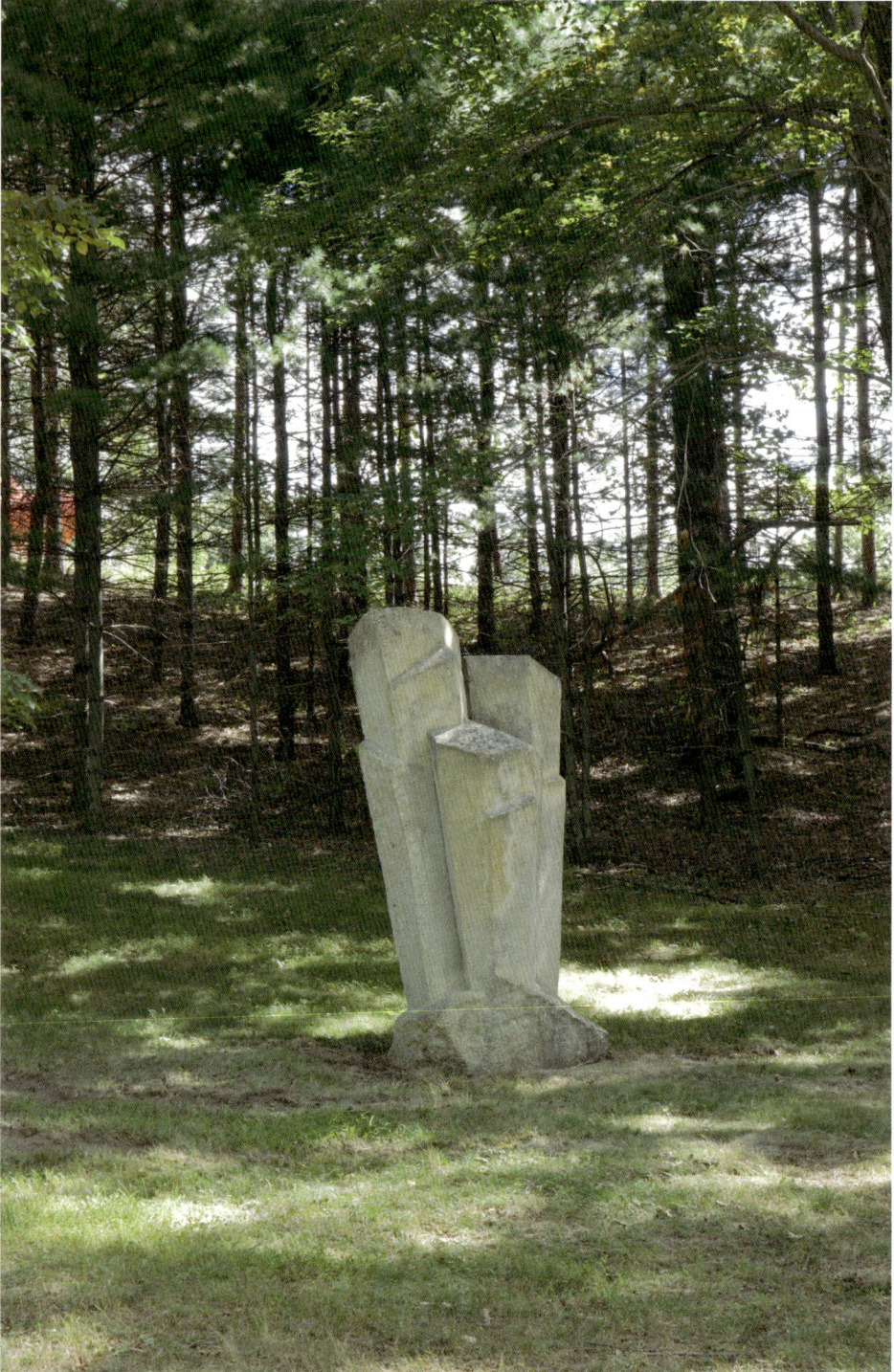

KARL PFANN

AUSTRIAN, BORN 1921

TRINITY, 1960
LIMESTONE
8' 10" x 58" x 49"
GIFT OF THE RALPH E. OGDEN FOUNDATION

Karl Pfann's *Trinity* arrived at Storm King in 1961 without a title. In 1993, in response to an inquiry from Storm King, Pfann recalled an earlier working title, *Dreieinigkeit*, which translates to *Trinity*. Pfann remarked that he intended the title to resonate "not as much in a sacred sense, much more in a sense concerning the human being and his three parts: body, spirit, and soul." *Trinity* became the sculpture's new title. Pfann created *Trinity* at the 1960 Symposium of European Sculptors at St. Margarethen Quarry, Burgenland, in eastern Austria near the Hungarian border. The quarry goes back to the Roman era, and is the site of Austria's oldest sculptors' guild, founded in 1653. Its limestone is composed of clay and calcareous deposits from petrified algae, corals, and other crustaceous freshwater animals, fragments of which are sometimes embedded in the stone.

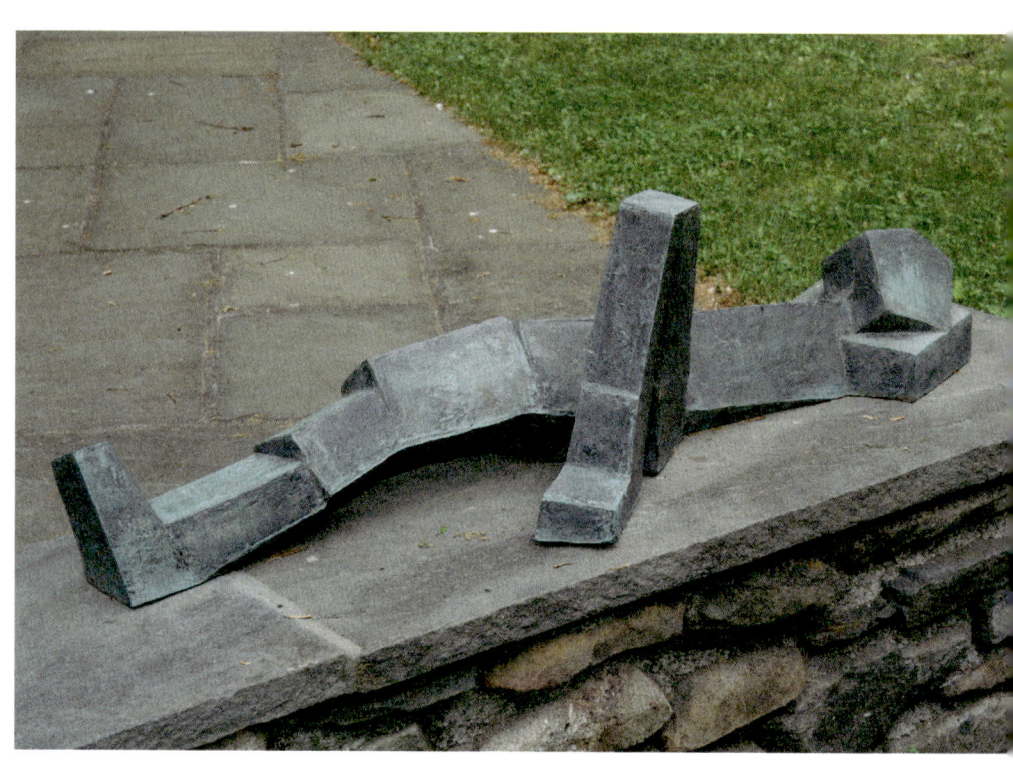

JOSEF PILLHOFER

AUSTRIAN, 1921–2010

SELECTED WORK:
RECLINING MAN (LIEGENDER MANN), 1964
BRONZE
13 x 46 x 15"
EDITION 1 OF 6
GIFT OF JOAN O. STERN

Josef Pillhofer's sculptures, while primarily cubic, nonetheless suggest human forms, not only in their formal arrangement but in their scale. His work expresses both discipline and tension. The prostrate pose of *Reclining Man* suggests a completely relaxed figure with one knee pulled up for stability, seemingly daydreaming or contemplating the sky. Head, torso, and the extended leg comprise one continuous, elongated, hard-edged form. Anatomical partitions are indicated by horizontal and diagonal accents recalling the shifting facets of Cubist painting.

As an early student at the Academy of Fine Arts in Vienna, Pillhofer witnessed and absorbed the conflict between traditional and new formal vocabulary in the work of his teacher, Fritz Wotruba, another artist in Storm King's collection. Dissecting Wotruba's architectonic anatomy into its components, he rooted his images in nature while vacillating between naturalistic and abstract form.

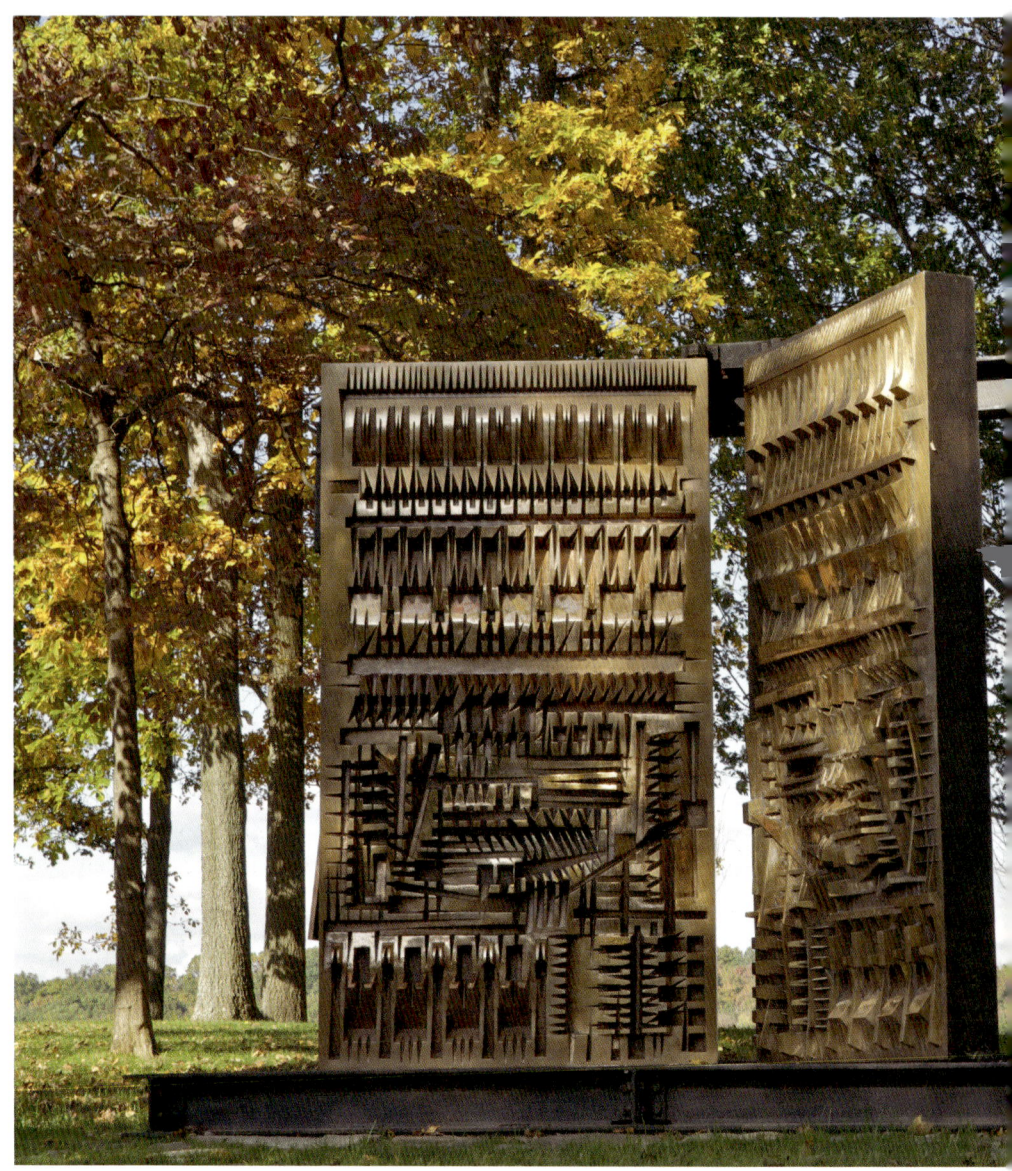

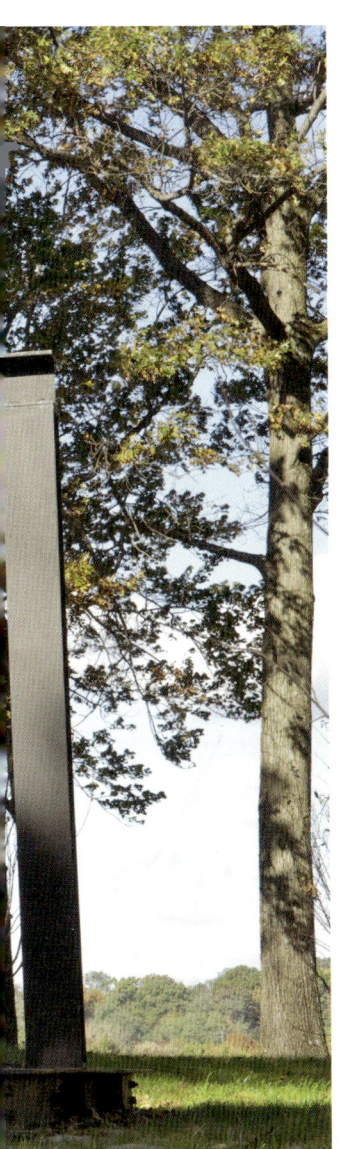

ARNALDO POMODORO

ITALIAN, BORN 1926

THE PIETRARUBBIA GROUP: IL FONDAMENTO, L'USO,
IL RAPPORTO, 1975–76
BRONZE, STEEL, FIBERGLASS, AND MARBLE
9' 2 ¼" x 17' 4 ⅝" x 11' 9 ¼"
EDITION 2 OF 2
GIVEN IN LOVING MEMORY OF GABRIELLE H. REEM, M.D. BY
HER HUSBAND, HERBERT J. KAYDEN, M.D. ON JULY 8, 2011

Arnaldo Pomodoro created *The Pietrarubbia Group*
to commemorate Pietrarubbia, a dilapidated Italian
village near his hometown. As he has explained,
"I felt duty bound to deal with my memories,
and I wanted to make sense out of that situation,
those fragments of a culture that were being
destroyed." Pomodoro has called this work both
a "village-sculpture" and "a vision of an archaic
settlement." The sculpture itself, which visitors can
enter through its grand, slab-like doors, stands in
for the village; the scratched, jagged writing on the
walls attests to life within this forgotten society, a
memento of time past.

   A great power of Pomodoro's art lies in his
juxtapositions of divergent textures and materials
and in the contrasts that he creates between interior
and exterior surfaces. He works back and forth,
as he has put it, "between lucidity and obscurity."
Metaphors for the earth and the universe are clearly
apparent within Pomodoro's production, and his
references stretch forward and backward in time.
His expressive surfaces seem to reference the hiero-
glyphic texts of pre-modern societies, while highly
polished areas seem to look forward into a utopian,
technological world. Pomodoro honed his skills
developing intricate patterns and designs in metals
while working in the 1950s as a jewelry designer.

P

POMODORO, ARNALDO

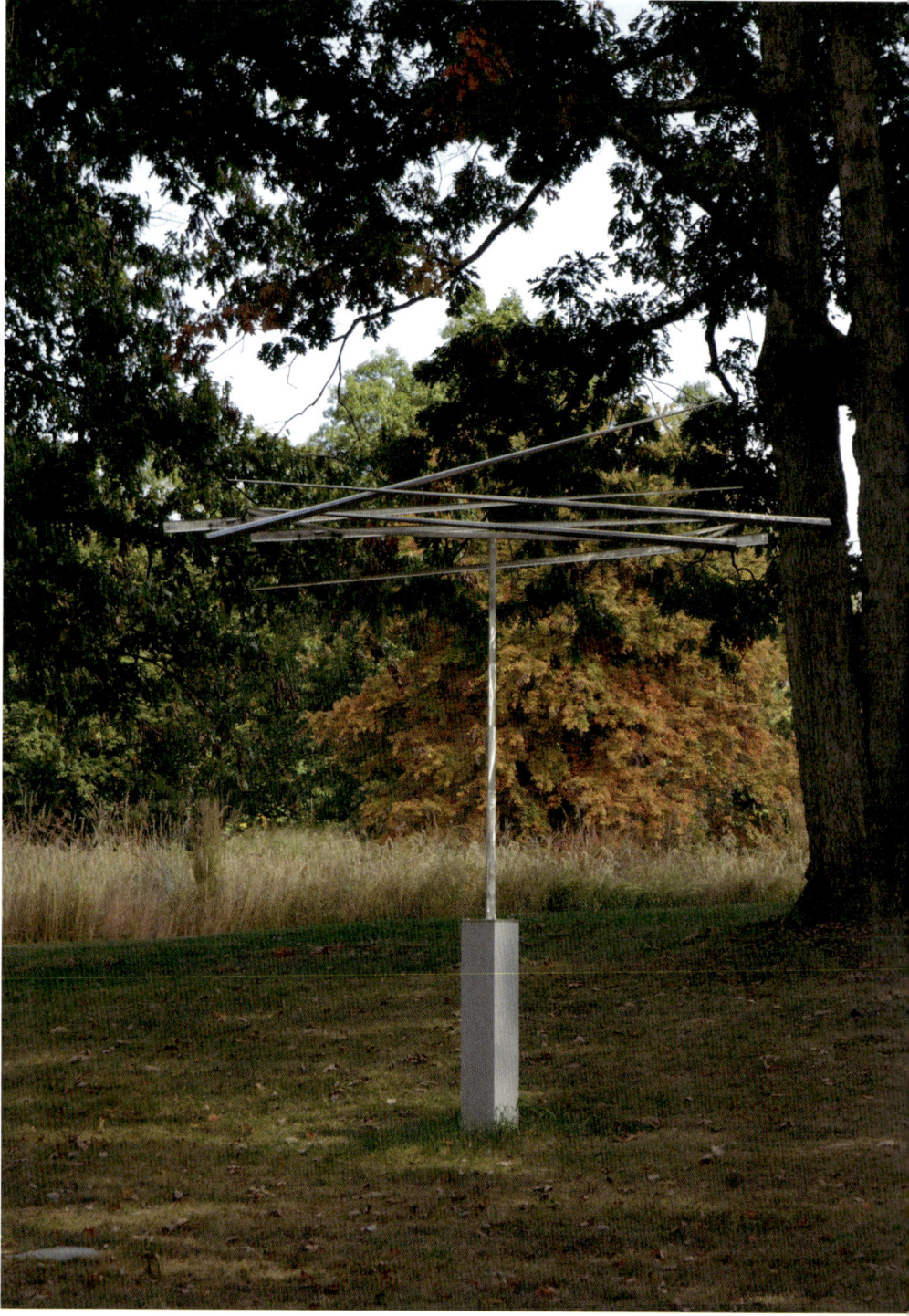

GEORGE RICKEY

AMERICAN, 1907–2002

SIX LINES IN A T, 1966–79
STAINLESS STEEL
10' 8" x 6' 6½" x 30½"
GIFT OF THE RALPH E. OGDEN FOUNDATION

TWO PLANES VERTICAL-HORIZONTAL II, 1970
STAINLESS STEEL
14' 7⅝" x 10' 5" x 6' 3"
GIFT OF THE RALPH E. OGDEN FOUNDATION

FIVE OPEN SQUARES GYRATORY GYRATORY, 1981
STAINLESS STEEL
9' 4" x 6' x 42"
GIFT OF THE ARTIST AND JOAN O. STERN BY EXCHANGE

George Rickey is best known for what he called his "useless machines." Carefully crafted kinetic sculptures made of reflective stainless steel, these graceful, precisely calibrated sculptures move with the wind at unpredictable intervals, calling attention to the effects of wind, light, and the changing surroundings. Rickey is represented at Storm King by three sculptures tracing various trajectories of his mature work. The sculptures are sited in a glade, as Rickey's works are not intended for the strong gusts of open spaces.

Born in South Bend, Indiana, in 1907, Rickey was the son of an engineer with a degree from MIT and the grandson of a clockmaker. Both encouraged Rickey's early interest in engineering and tinkering, which he largely abandoned to pursue the study of art and work as a painter. Serving as an engineer in the Army Air Corps in World War II rekindled Rickey's childhood interests and he made his first simple mobiles at this time. By the late 1940s Rickey had abandoned painting and devoted himself to making kinetic sculpture, an art form that enabled him to join his natural facility for engineering with his poetic sensibility. From then on, his work evolved toward a vocabulary of simplified geometric forms set in carefully planned patterns of wind-driven movement.

In *Six Lines in a T*, among Rickey's first non-objective works, six hand-crafted, reflective, stainless steel blades are attached to a thin horizontal scaffold welded to a slender vertical pole. When at rest, the lines are roughly parallel to the ground, but the slightest breeze sets them in motion, each blade moving in its own predetermined arc, crisscrossing the paths of the others, without ever touching them. While never making a sound, the sculpture makes palpable the movement of the surrounding breeze, like leaves on a tree, its variegated surface changing with the ambient light.

In late 1965 Rickey extended his vocabulary from lines to planes to create enchanting and evocative drawings in space that would further focus on the motion of the work. *Two Planes Vertical-Horizontal II* is a visually simple, engaging work that takes the moving square as its subject. Two internally weighted shallow boxes made of burnished stainless steel pivot on either side of a similarly burnished round pole, to which they are attached. Like Rickey's *Lines*, the *Planes* are compound pendulums—objects with weights above and below the pivot point— that move in parallel paths. A small trap door allows for access to the internal ball bearings and supporting structure, counterweights for the compound-pendulum system. Styrofoam filling ensures the boxes move without making a sound.

Other kinds of movement, including gyratory, or a full rotation around a work's central stem, emerged in the early 1970s, along with a frame-like, elongated, open rectangle. The open square elements of *Five Open Squares Gyratory Gyratory* are sensitively calibrated so that they move with the slightest breeze, continually transforming the piece's configuration. While the squares rotate independently, they remain connected, creating an ongoing dialogue between unpredictable motion and prescribed order. Looking through the open squares, viewers will sense that the landscape itself is constantly shifting.

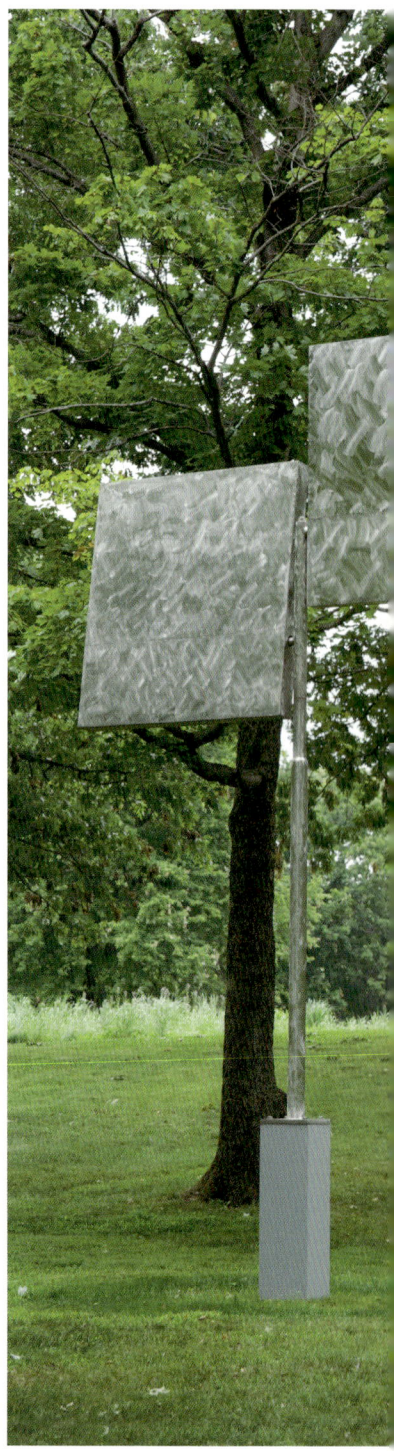

FROM LEFT: *Two Planes Vertical-Horizontal II*, 1970; *Five Open Squares Gyratory Gyratory*, 1981

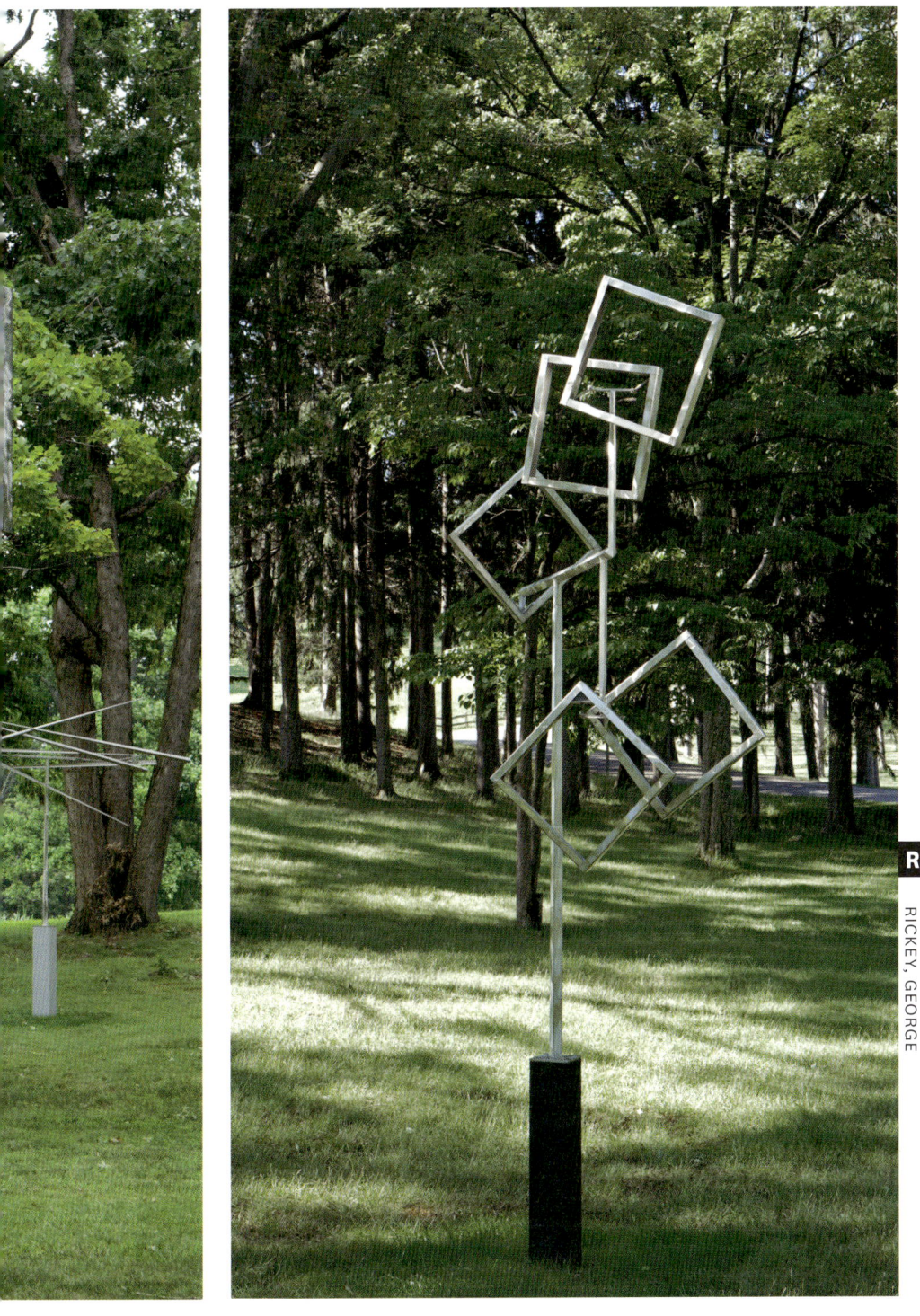

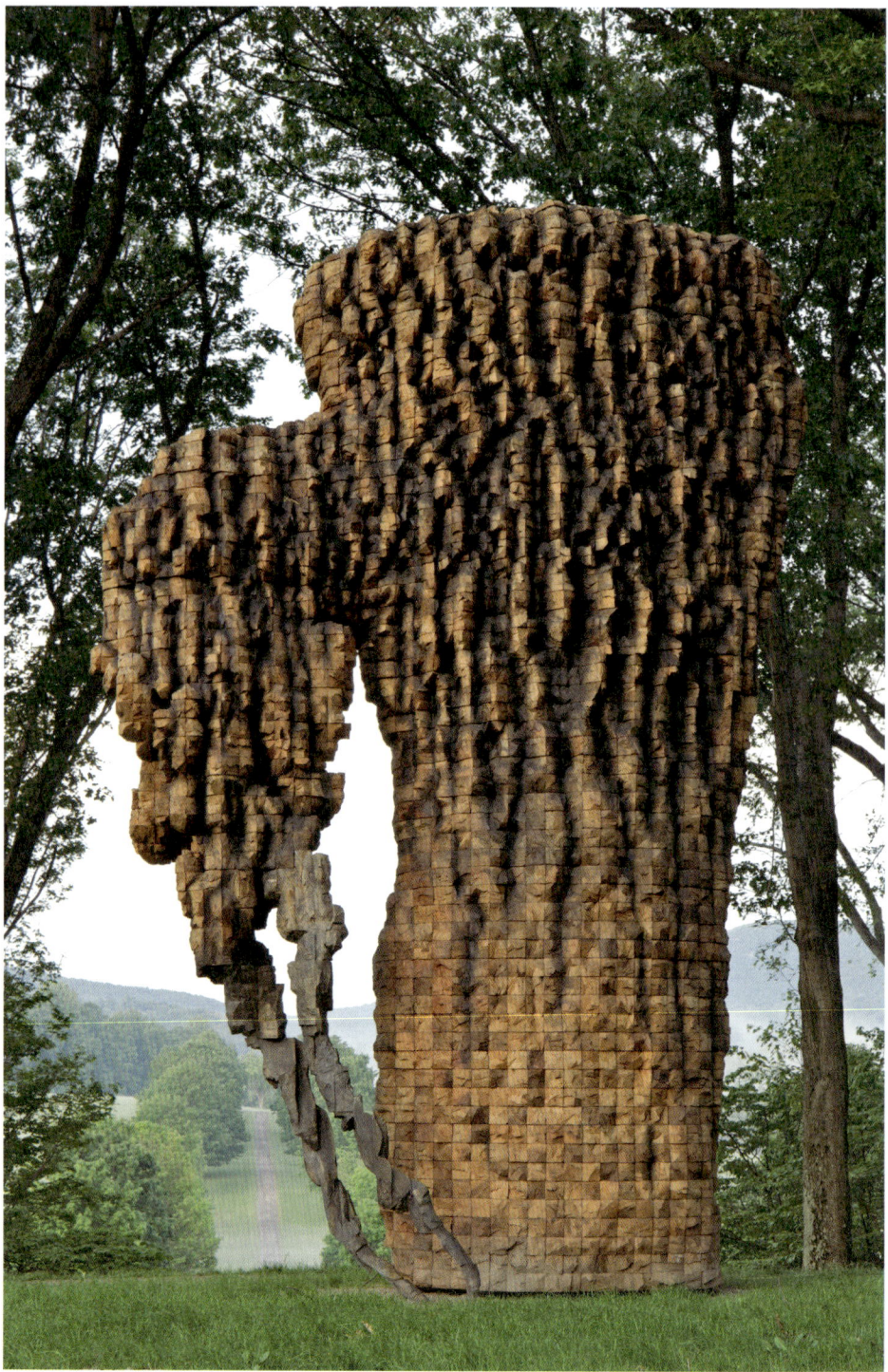

URSULA VON RYDINGSVARD

AMERICAN, BORN GERMANY, 1942

FOR PAUL, 1990-92/2001
CEDAR AND GRAPHITE
14' 4" x 9' x 13' 8"
GIFT OF SHERRY AND JOEL MALLIN, THE HORACE W. GOLDSMITH FOUNDATION,
VERA G. LIST, ANN M. HATCH, AND STEVEN AND NANCY OLIVER

LUBA, 2009-2010
CEDAR, CAST BRONZE, AND GRAPHITE
17' 6" x 59" x 59"
MADE POSSIBLE THROUGH GENEROUS LEAD SUPPORT FROM THE ARTIST, ROBERTA
AND STEVEN DENNING, GALERIE LELONG, NANCY BROWN NEGLEY AND THE BROWN
FOUNDATION, INC. OF HOUSTON, AND THOMAS A. AND GEORGINA T. RUSSO. ADDITIONAL
SUPPORT IS PROVIDED BY AN ANONYMOUS DONOR, THE HAZEN POLSKY FOUNDATION,
THE OHNELL FAMILY FOUNDATION, AND HUME R. STEYER. SPECIAL THANKS ALSO GO TO
HENRY S. MCNEIL AND MARION SWINGLE

Ursula von Rydingsvard's primary material—used in constructing both *Luba* and *For Paul*—is four-by-four lengths of cedar wood, a material that, as the artist has said, "it seems to be I'm able to speak through." Von Rydingsvard stacks, glues, and cuts into these beams freehand with a circular saw—an intuitive process that the artist has likened to the freedom and creativity that many artists associate with the process of drawing. *Luba* is the first work on a large scale that von Rydingsvard created in solid cedar. *For Paul*, made nearly twenty years prior, is composed of an internal honeycomb pattern and sited so that its repeated openings can be seen from a landing above. *For Paul* is dedicated to von Rydingsvard's husband.

Von Rydingsvard's sculptures are large, but retain a sense of human scale. On one side of the main form of *Luba*, a delicate appendage extends down to the ground; von Rydingsvard has said that it is intended to resemble the arm of a mother cradling a baby. The lower portion of this arm, supporting its spindly reach, is made of bronze and marks the first time von Rydingsvard has combined bronze and cedar into a single work. Highlighting the handiwork and a physical, tangible connection to her sculpture, von Rydingsvard then rubbed graphite into areas of the surface of *Luba*, emphasizing the shadow and depth of the circular saw's cuts.

Von Rydingsvard has described her background as influential within her practice. Born to Polish and Ukrainian peasant farmers, her early childhood was marked by the strain of living in eight different refugee camps over the course of five years in postwar Germany. She immigrated with her family to the United States when she was still a small child. In form, process, and meaning, she sees her work as responsive to eastern European peasant traditions.

R

VON RYDINGSVARD, URSULA

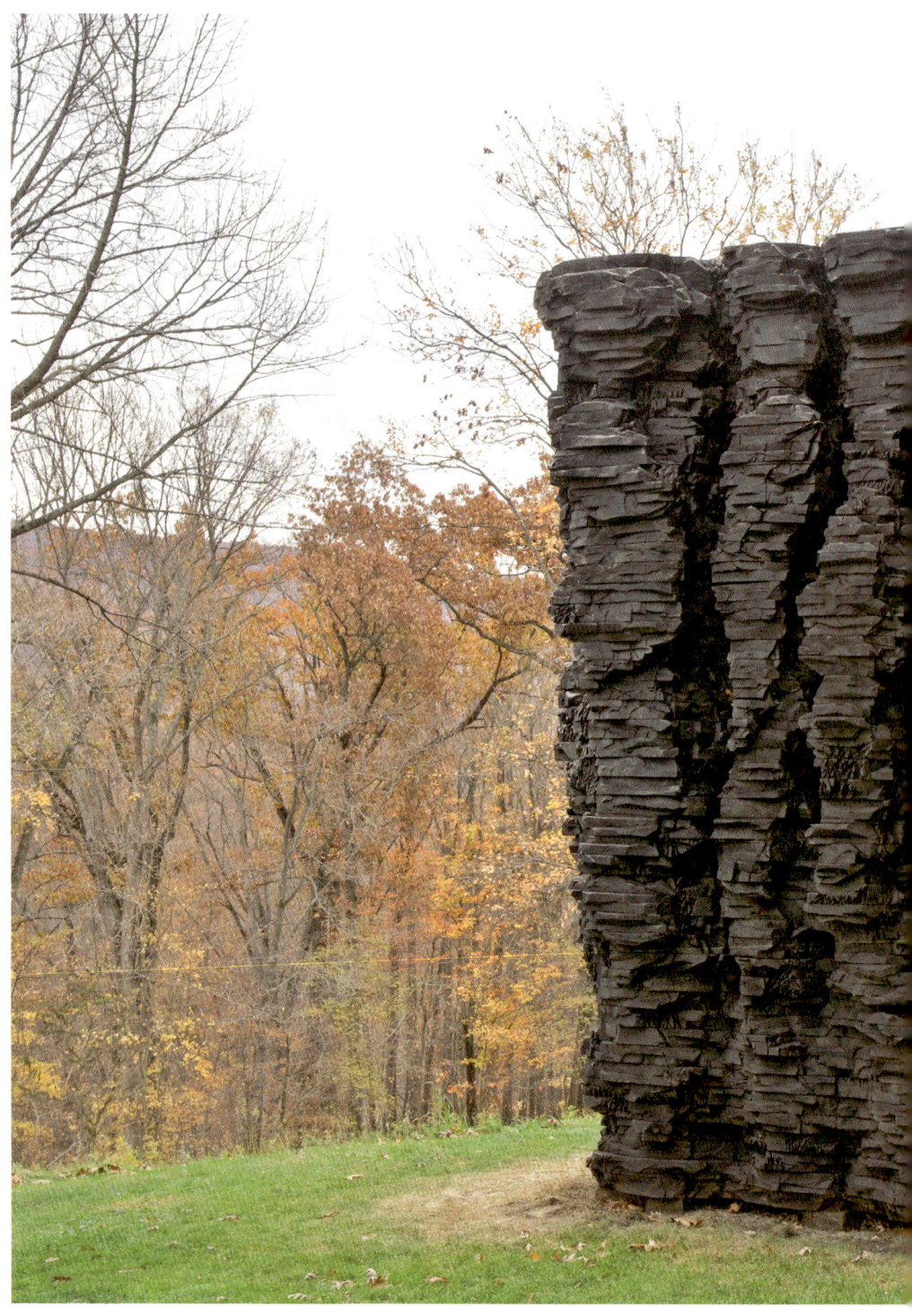

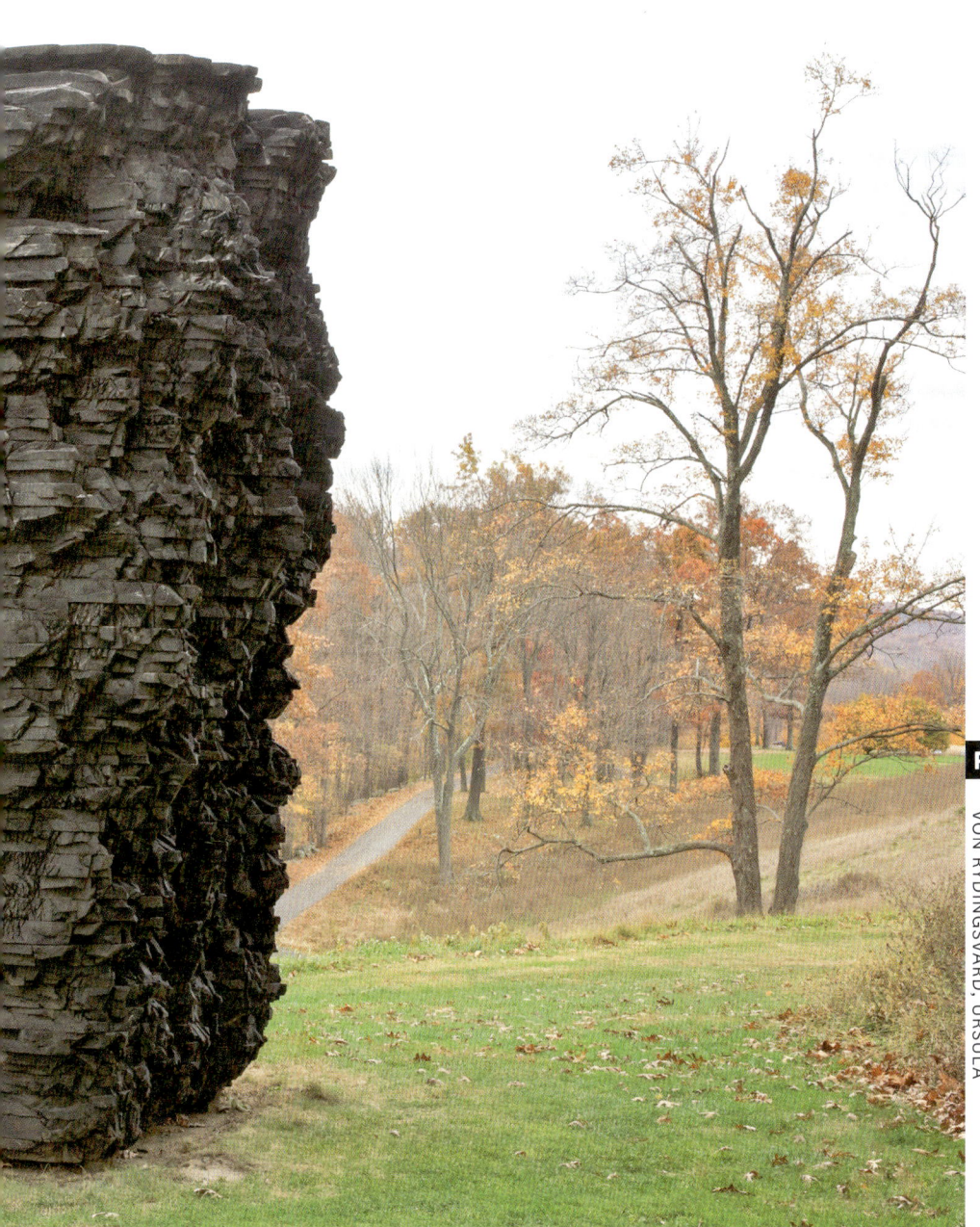

DAVID VON SCHLEGELL

AMERICAN, 1920–1992

SELECTED WORK:
UNTITLED, 1972
ALUMINUM AND STAINLESS STEEL
20 x 304 x 16'
PURCHASED WITH THE AID OF FUNDS FROM THE NATIONAL ENDOWMENT
FOR THE ARTS AND GIFT OF THE RALPH E. OGDEN FOUNDATION

David von Schlegell's three-part work at the base of Museum Hill is one of
the first sculptures that Storm King's founders commissioned. Designed
specifically for its current site, it is comprised of a series of delicate, open
cubes and reaches twenty feet into the air. From a ground-level view, the
thin metallic legs are barely perceptible, so that the squares seem to hover
in space; seen from the hill above, the cubes appear to rest on the ground.
Von Schlegell intended the work to be contingent on its natural setting,
elemental phenomena, and the viewer's perspective. As he noted, "These

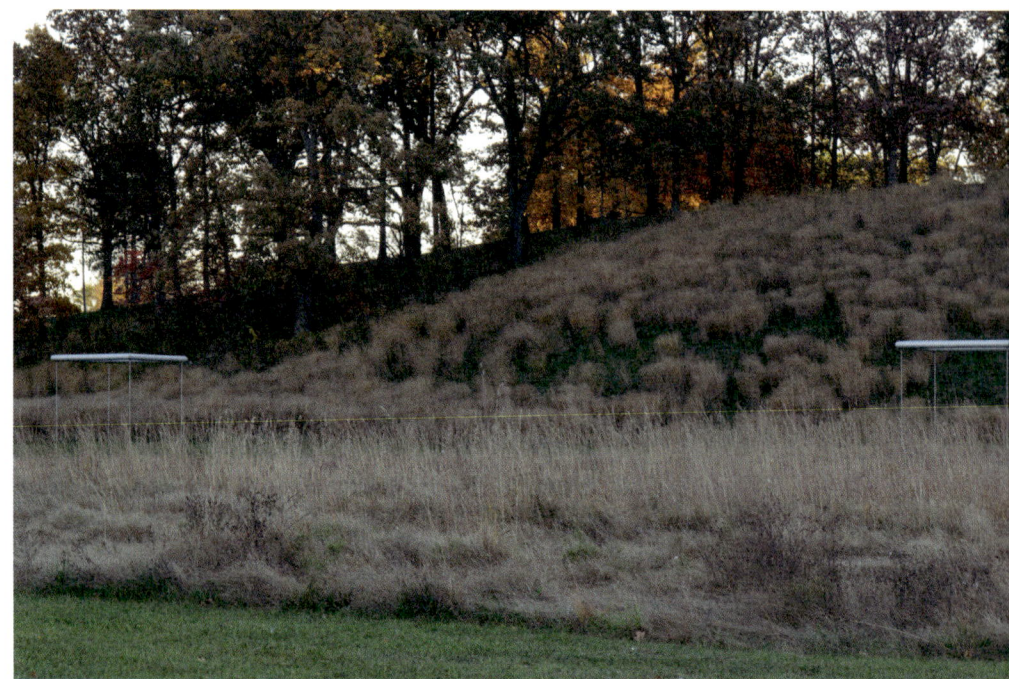

pieces have a specific alignment relative to the earth. Reflecting light, they change with the earth's time and with the flux of its weather. They force a particular awareness of the most basic element of nature, the sun."

Von Schlegell was an engineer before he became an artist, working for Douglas Aircraft in the 1940s. He brought his engineering expertise to bear on his sculptural production, employing industrial materials— aluminum, stainless steel, and wood—and construction methods in the creation of his streamlined, abstract works. As he observed, "All the years of my youth I was obsessed with the lucid structures of boats and airplanes.... They had a clarity and an economy.... I find myself still obsessed by mechanical structures. They possess a kinesthetic resonance, also a resonance with geometric frameworks of the mind."

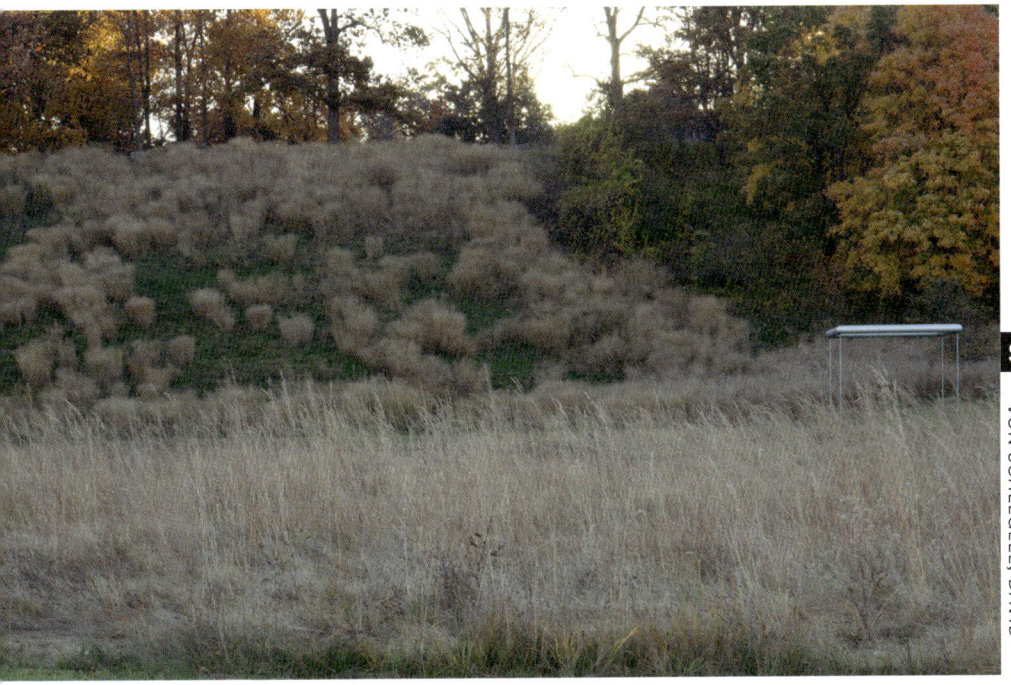

RICHARD SERRA

AMERICAN, BORN 1939

SCHUNNEMUNK FORK, 1990–91
WEATHERING STEEL
A) 8' x 49'1" x 2½"
B) 8' x 35'1" x 2½"
C) 8' x 38'4" x 2½"
D) 8' x 54'4" x 2½"
GIFT OF THE RALPH E. OGDEN FOUNDATION, BY EXCHANGE,
THE BROWN FOUNDATION, INC., AND AN ANONYMOUS FOUNDATION

Schunnemunk Fork, a site-specific commission, is installed in a ten-acre rolling field with a natural border of nearby woods, which, at the time of the work's construction, was the southern edge of the Storm King property. When Richard Serra surveyed Storm King's grounds and chose the site, it had never before been considered for its artistic potential. He arrived at his final composition through a complex process that involved consulting both topographical maps and a surveyor, as well as walking the grounds with his wife, Clara Weyergraf-Serra. The work consists of four weathering steel plates set lengthwise and inserted into the ground at designated intervals. Each plate is eight feet high and two and a half inches thick; lengths vary from thirty-five to almost fifty-five feet. Roughly a third of the length of each rectangular plate is visible; the remainder is buried in the earth. The visible angles correspond to eight-foot drops in the terrain. The title refers to the four-pronged scheme of the piece and references nearby Schunnemunk Mountain.

Schunnemunk Fork does not impose the artist's order on the land, but rather reveals the complexities and nuances of the site, drawing attention to the land more than to the sculpture itself. The four steel plates both divide and unify the space, acting as a foil for the topographical ebb and flow and amplifying changes in the land underfoot. Inscribed into the land, the long, horizontal lines of the steel plates each function as a separate horizon or measuring stick. The various horizons recall the fifteenth-century Zen gardens that Serra first saw in Kyoto in 1970. While walking through those gardens, elements appear and disappear. The whole cannot be apprehended at a glance; instead one comes to understand the arrangement over time, by walking through the space. Likewise, *Schunnemunk Fork* can be enjoyed from a number of vantage points, perhaps most powerfully by visitors who walk to it, navigate the spatial divisions created by the steel plates, and take in the sculpture's visual connection with Schunnemunk Mountain in the distance.

Schunnemunk Fork's site has undergone a series of subtle modifications that reflect broader landscaping developments at Storm King. Hay bales harvested by a local farmer periodically punctuate the landscape, linking the property's agrarian past with the present. New plantings of native grasses and wildflowers have further varied this evolving landscape. When the work was first installed, it seemed to be very far from the Museum Building, which was then Storm King's primary focus. With the passage of time, newly developed walking paths and additional sculptures were installed in adjoining areas, drawing increasing numbers of visitors to the area Serra pioneered. With deceptively simple means, Serra brought a previously unnoticed area of the Storm King property into sharp focus.

Serra's reputation was initially established with urban site-specific sculptures as well as various indoor structures. Perhaps his most well-known works are massive plates of hot-rolled steel shaped into complex curves. These sculptures, made on an architectural scale, enclose and activate space, inviting viewers to navigate spaces transformed by the imposition of these huge steel plates. Serra's outdoor landscape sculptures comprise a less well-known aspect of his work but similarly engage the viewer. Many are comprised of steel plates, but others are marked by low, dense, rectangular or circular solid steel elements or stone shapes. The sites differ, as do the modules, but the approach remains constant, for the subject of Serra's landscape works is always the site itself.

S

SERRA, RICHARD

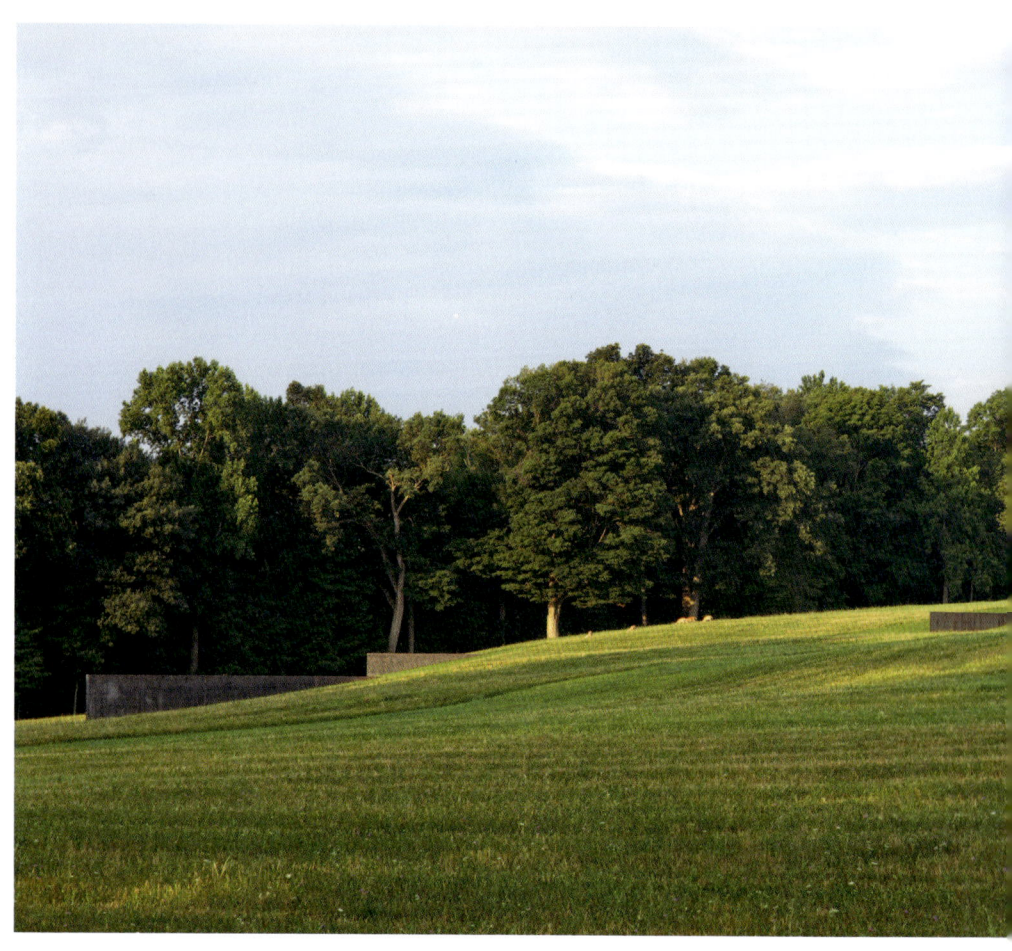

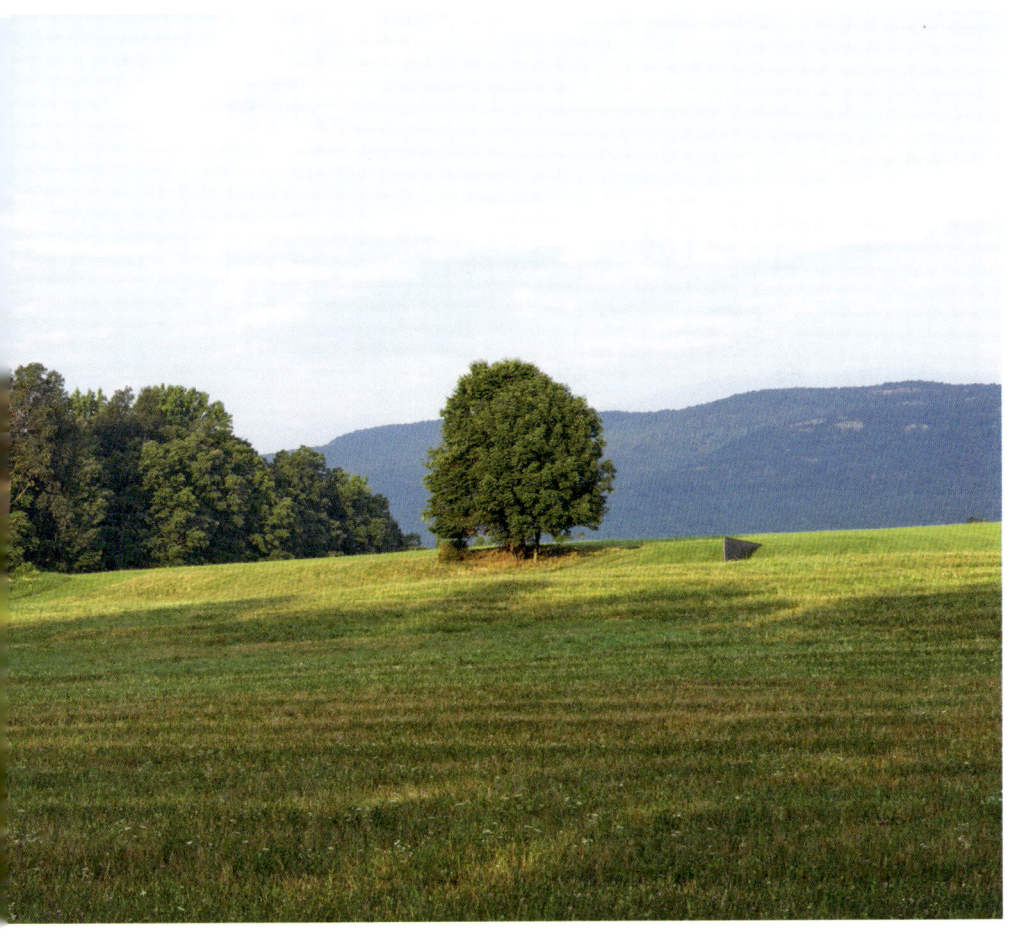

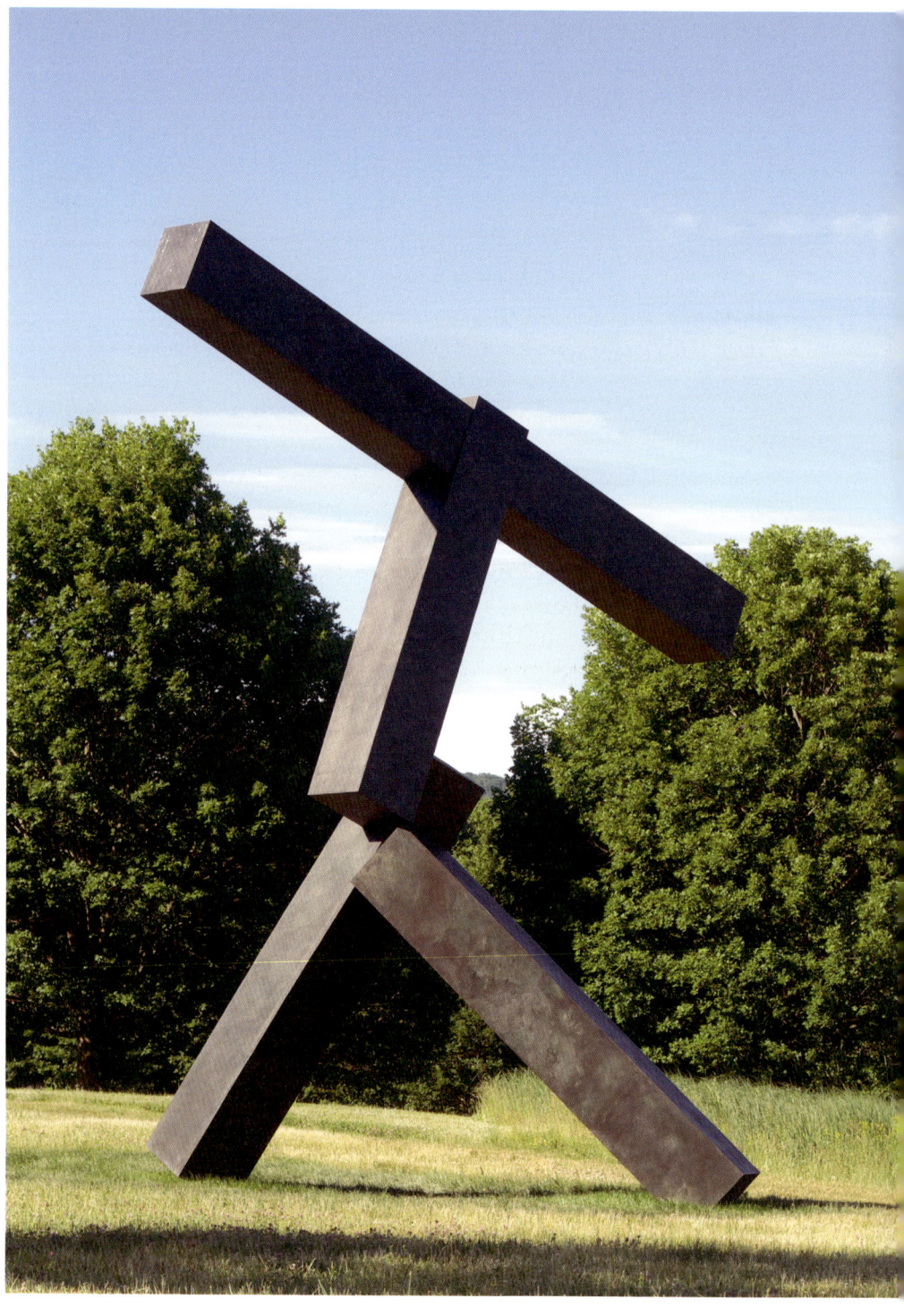

JOEL SHAPIRO

AMERICAN, BORN 1941

UNTITLED, 1994
BRONZE
21 x 19 x 14'
GIFT OF SONY CORPORATION OF AMERICA

Joel Shapiro's untitled sculpture, composed of five diagonal bronze
beams and inspired by the form of a walking man, activates the space
it inhabits and encourages viewers to experience it from all angles.
At the time of its creation, the twenty-one-foot-tall sculpture was the
largest work the artist had ever created.

The sculpture takes its form from a model that Shapiro first created
out of wood; such light, small-scale models allow the artist a greater
freedom and fluidity to experiment with sculptural form. Working
with an industrial fabricator, Shapiro then translated his model into this
large bronze sculpture that still bears clues of its origins in wood. The
work was originally commissioned by the Sony Corporation of America
for the lobby of their former headquarters on Madison Avenue in
Manhattan, and was installed there in 1995. It was sited at Storm King,
in collaboration with the artist, in 2016.

Many examples of Shapiro's work derive from the abstract, geometric
style of Minimalist sculpture while also explicitly referencing the
human figure—a subject almost entirely absent from the Minimalist
generation that preceded him. Since the early 1980s, the figure has
been a primary focus for the artist; even so, he views his subjects as instru-
ments to aid his and his viewers' contemplation of abstract or perceptual
space. "The object in and of itself is totally boring," Shapiro has noted.
"The only interesting sculpture is sculpture that deals with spatial issues
of perception."

S

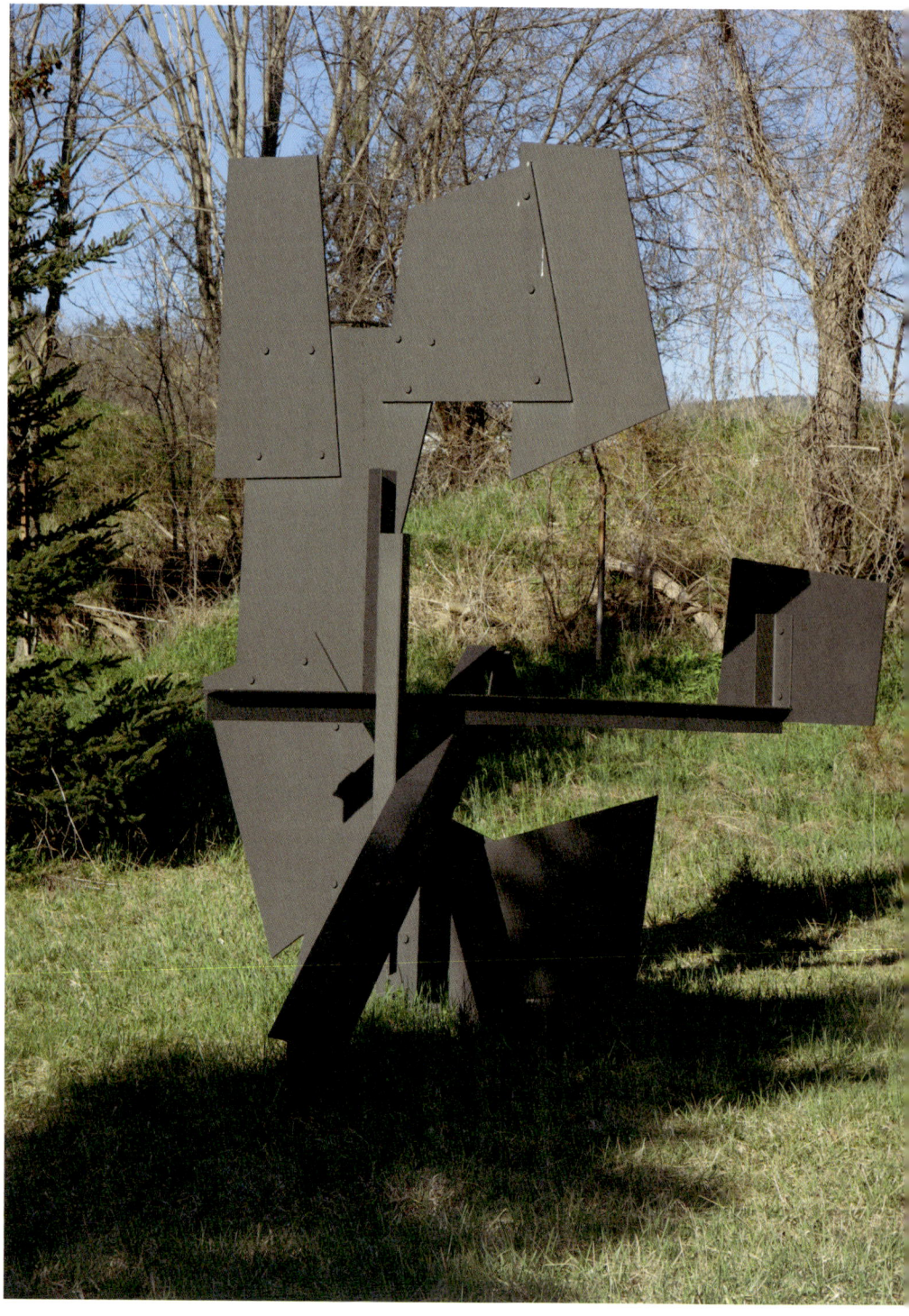

YEHIEL SHEMI

ISRAELI, 1922–2003

COLLAGE SCULPTURE, 1973
PAINTED STEEL
9'10" x 7'4" x 10'8"
GIFT OF ELAINE AND HYMAN G. WEITZEN

The term *collage* is typically applied only to two-dimensional works. Its title connects *Collage Sculpture* to Yehiel Shemi's smaller-scale experiments with paper and perhaps influences the way in which the viewer perceives the work. Shemi claimed that he wanted his work to "bring out only the essential, the inner energy that is the result of a few acts," and indeed *Collage Sculpture*, a reductive, planar abstraction, suggests a kind of simplicity. It was influenced, as were many of Shemi's works, by the frontal and often stylized forms of Assyrian and ancient Egyptian sculpture.

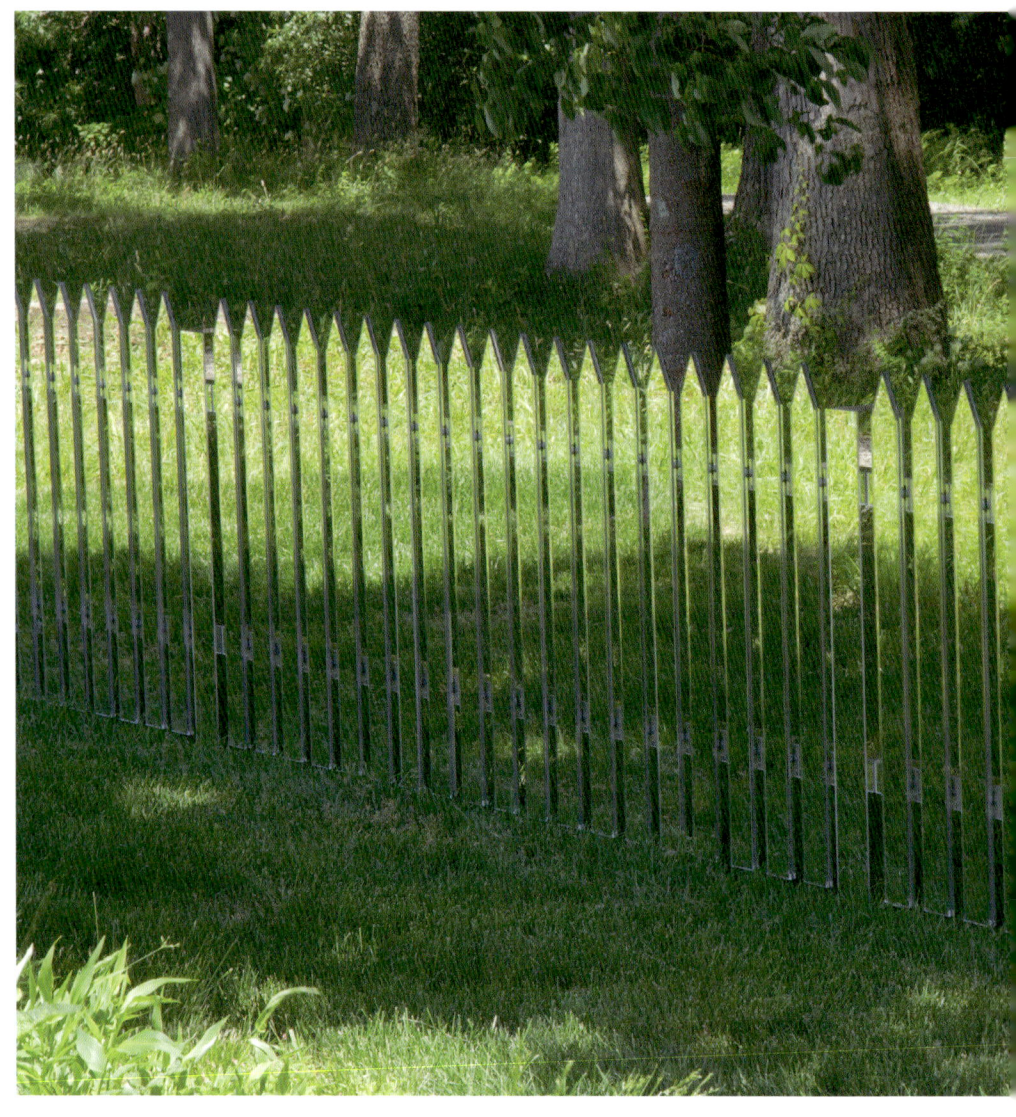

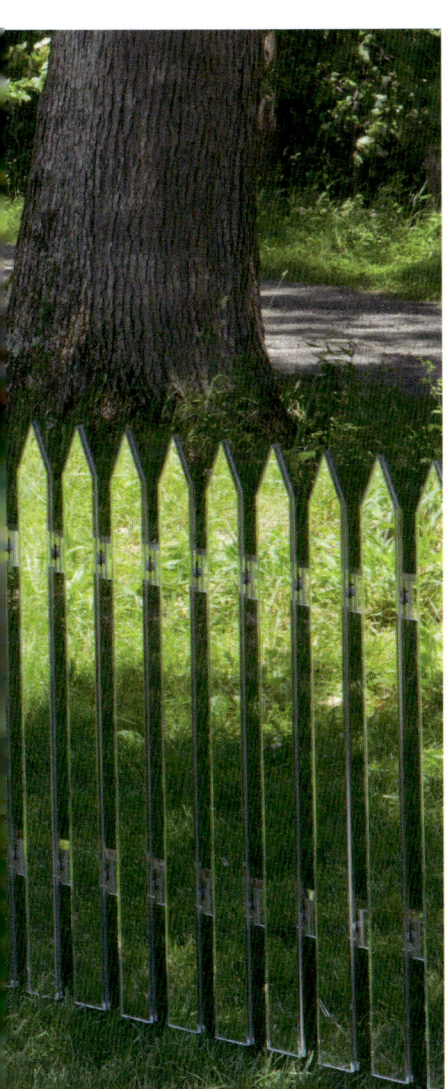

ALYSON SHOTZ

AMERICAN, BORN 1964

MIRROR FENCE, 2003 (REFABRICATED 2014)
STARPHIRE MIRROR AND ALUMINUM
138' x 36" x 4"
GIFT OF THE ARTIST AND DEREK ELLER GALLERY,
WITH GENEROUS LEAD SUPPORT FROM
ROBERTA AND STEVEN DENNING; ADDITIONAL
SUPPORT PROVIDED BY THE DONALD R. MULLEN
FAMILY FOUNDATION AND MR. AND MRS.
RICHARD J. SCHWARTZ

The individual pickets of Alyson Shotz's *Mirror Fence* share their shape and height with picket fences enclosing front and back yards all across the United States, but Shotz's fence is reflective and extends in a straight line, enclosing nothing. Shotz has commented on the irony of the acceptance of the picket fence—it is an innocuous, everyday element in American life, but it serves a protective purpose: each picket is topped with a spike.

Shotz, who studied Geology before becoming an artist, engages in the fleeting realities and subtleties of vision and perception in her work. "I'm interested in making objects that change infinitely, depending on their surroundings," she has noted. "The light at different times of day, the weather, the seasons… all these are just some of the variables that will make the piece different every time one comes in contact with it. For me an ideal work of art is one that is ultimately unknowable in some way."

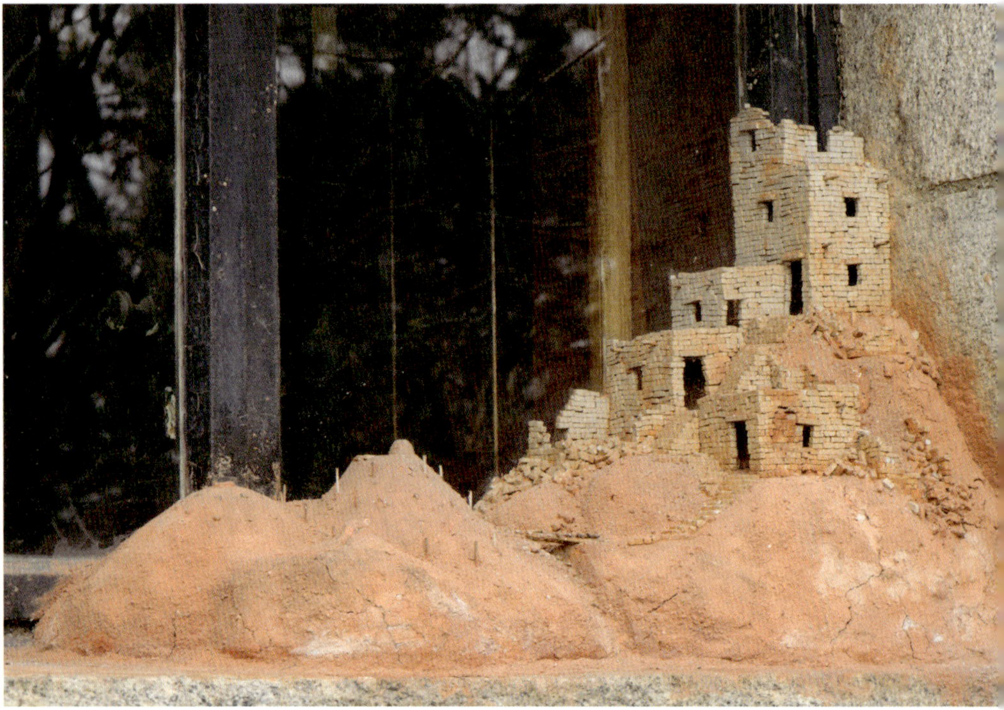

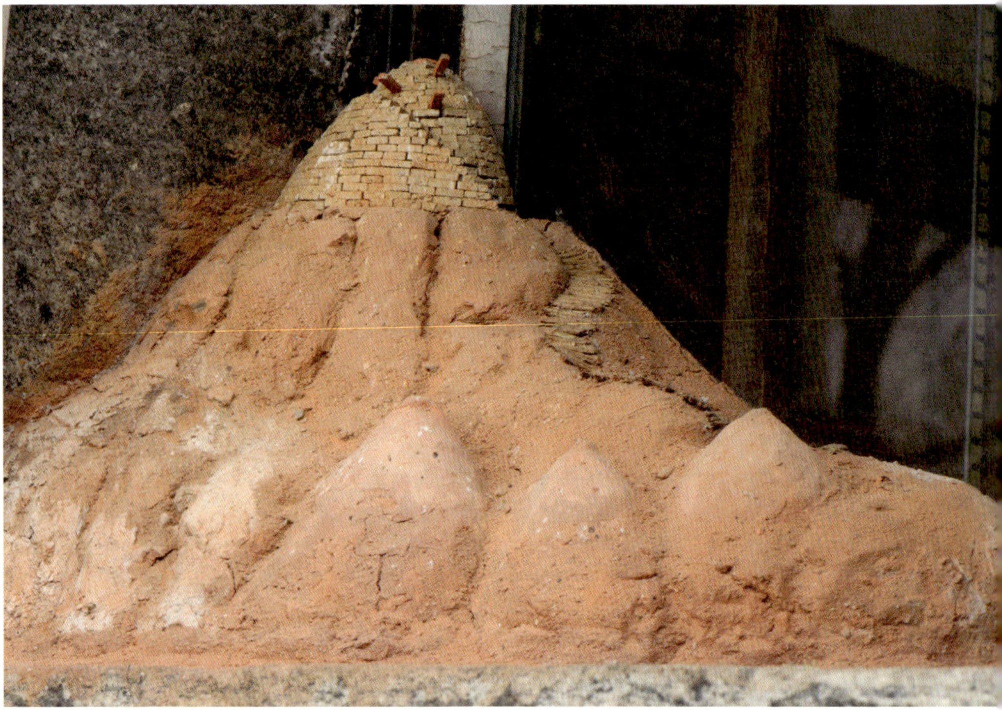

CHARLES SIMONDS

AMERICAN, BORN 1945

DWELLINGS, 1981
CLAY, SAND, CERAMIC BRICKS, AND STICKS
13 x 22½ x 10"
PURCHASED WITH THE AID OF FUNDS FROM THE NATIONAL ENDOWMENT
FOR THE ARTS AND GIFT OF THE RALPH E. OGDEN FOUNDATION

DWELLINGS, 1981
CLAY, SAND, CERAMIC BRICKS, AND STICKS
9½ x 13 x 10"
PURCHASED WITH THE AID OF FUNDS FROM THE NATIONAL ENDOWMENT
FOR THE ARTS AND GIFT OF THE RALPH E. OGDEN FOUNDATION

Storm King's two works by Charles Simonds, each entitled *Dwellings*, are small, detailed installations resembling miniature civilizations. Simonds cut his miniature bricks from flat sheets of clay with a knife, then laid them in place with tweezers. Installed in consecutive window bays of the Museum Building, the installations resemble archaeological remains of the Native American cave dwellings Simonds saw on visits to the southwest United States as a child. Simonds began his series of *Dwellings* in building crevices and vacant lots near his New York City home in the early 1970s. He reflected, "Working in the street revealed extraordinary possibilities to me that threw into relief the limitations of timeless white spaces and their inhabitants." At the time, he was surprised and excited by how much local "truckers and workers...jumped in and loved [the projects], it lightened their day." He was happy, he noted, to have created an art form that was appreciated outside the art world.

S

SIMONDS, CHARLES

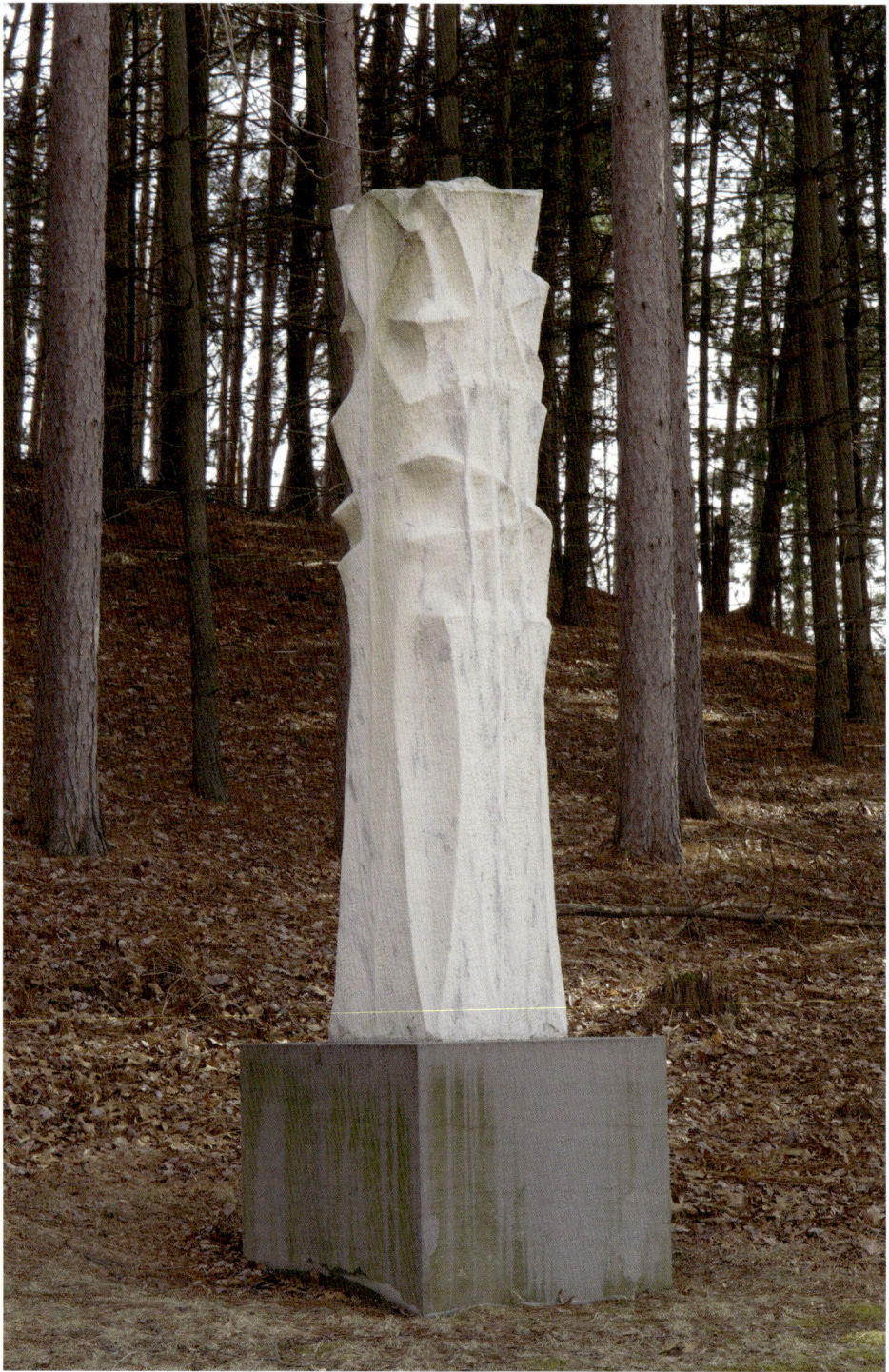

YERASSIMOS SKLAVOS

GREEK, 1927–1967

LES YEUX DU CIEL (EYES OF THE SKY), 1964
MARBLE
8′ 4 ¾″ x 20 ½″ x 21″
GIFT OF THE RALPH E. OGDEN FOUNDATION

After six years of training in the Fine Arts Academy of Athens, Yerassimos Sklavos won first prize in a national sculpture competition, enabling him to study in the École supérieure des Beaux-Arts, Paris. In 1960 he invented a technique of carving stone with a blowtorch, calling it *télésculpture* and patenting it with the French government. This method reveals a stone's grain and core and allows for quick carving of hard stones such as rose porphyry and grey granite.

Upon meeting Sklavos at a sculpture symposium in Montreal, Ralph E. Ogden, Storm King co-founder, commissioned the Greek sculptor to produce a work for the collection. Sklavos was on site at Storm King, at work on a marble block, by October 1964. The resulting sculpture is a roughly rectangular-shaped column of marble, carved in irregular, stepped, angular wedges, with a linear design incised at the center of the front side. Sklavos was known for two abstract sculptural styles: one heavily carved, sometimes with a webbed or network effect; the other a more delicate low relief, which characterizes *Eyes of the Sky*.

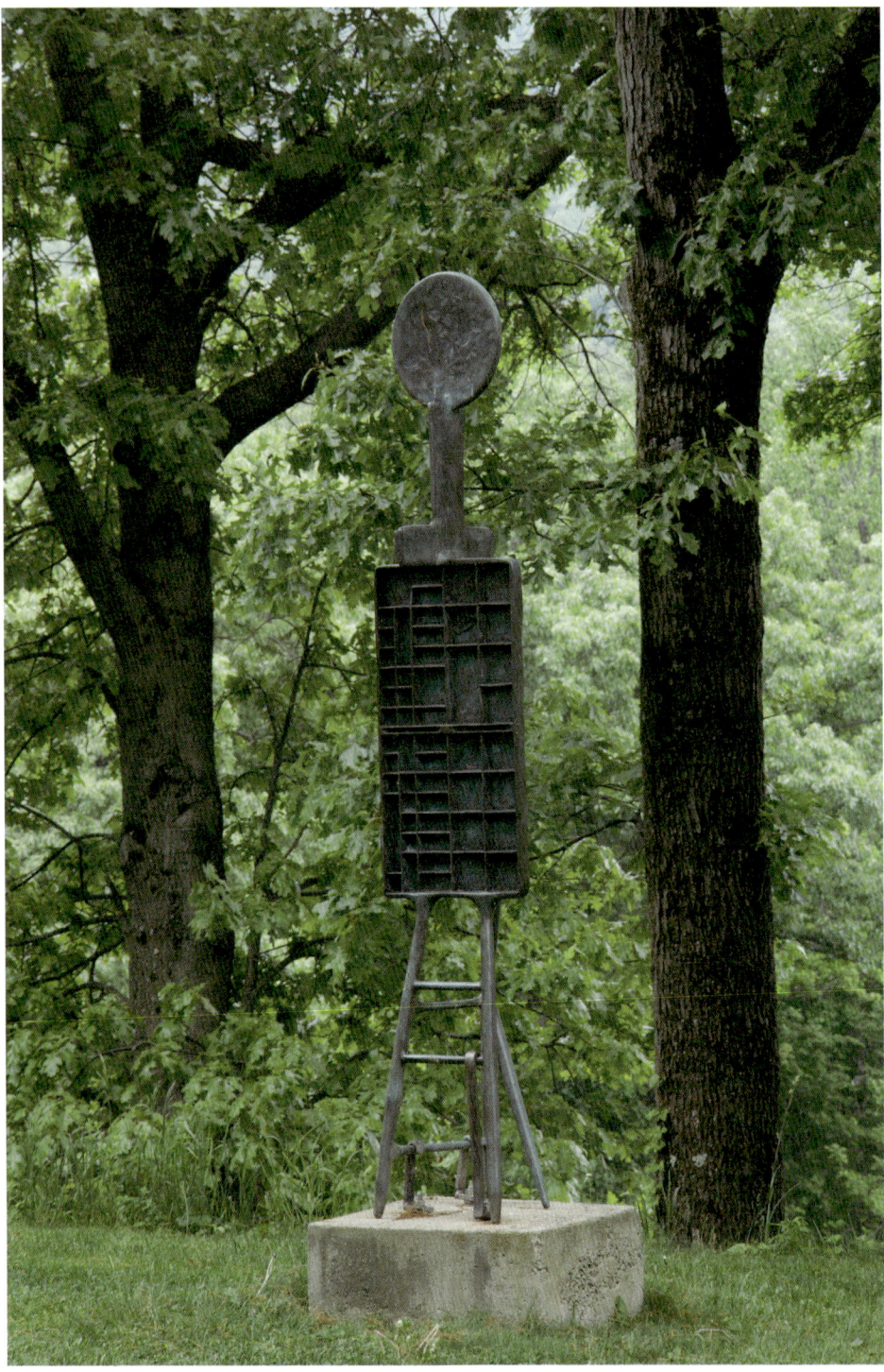

DAVID SMITH

AMERICAN, 1906–1965

SELECTED WORKS:
THE SITTING PRINTER, 1954–55
BRONZE
7' 3" x 15 ¾" x 17"

STUDY IN ARCS, 1957
PAINTED STEEL
11' x 9' 6 ½" x 3' ½"

PERSONAGE OF MAY, 1957
BRONZE
71 ⅝ x 31 ½ x 18 ½"

BECCA, 1964
STEEL
6' 6" x 47 ½" x 23 ½"

XI BOOKS III APPLES, 1959
STAINLESS STEEL
7' 10" x 35" x 16 ¼"

ALL WORKS GIFT OF THE RALPH E. OGDEN FOUNDATION

Storm King has one of the most significant institutional holdings of David Smith's works. Of the fourteen important sculptures among the holdings, all but one entered the collection soon after Storm King's co-founder Ralph E. Ogden visited Smith's home and studio at Bolton Landing, New York, in 1967, two years after the artist's death. Ogden was struck by the outdoor installation of sculpture, which Smith had devised during his lifetime, and acquired thirteen works. Several are on permanent display just outside the Museum Building, while five, too fragile for the outdoors, are on view inside. The acquisition of Smith's works was instrumental in shifting Storm King's primary mission, leading Ogden to focus his collecting efforts specifically on outdoor sculpture.

The Sitting Printer, one of the earliest sculptures by Smith in Storm King's collection, is assembled from cast-bronze elements, including an old printer's box and a stool. Smith found these objects in another artist's studio that he used while teaching at Indiana University, Bloomington, in the fall of 1954. As Smith later recounted the experience: "I had to take another sculptor's studio.... It was a hell of a mess when I walked in there, and I didn't know what to do, so I started picking up things that he had left behind. This is the top of a broken stool...this is the center part of a chair.... The first thing I did was to make a sculpture out of them." The sculpture forms a human-like figure, its elements suggesting body parts.

Inspired by a drawing of a mother and child, *Study in Arcs* metamorphosed into a less specific image as it took form. Comprised of nine long and two short arcs of steel gathered from Smith's stockpile and welded together, the sculpture resembles a drawing in space, its sweeping lines analogous to dance or flight. *Study in Arcs* was composed on the artist's studio floor, then raised up, its flat arrangement projected into three dimensions with the addition of extending arcs. The sculpture's pale pink color contrasts boldly with its natural surroundings, while simultaneously its ample negative space integrates the outside world into the work, making it vital to the whole.

The witty *Personage of May* originated with a hoe and part of a truck fender, which Smith coated with plaster, subtly modifying the original objects' found forms. The "spine" of *Personage of May* is a shovel that Smith also covered with plaster, accentuating its long handle, making it longer and thicker. Impressed "eyebrows" on the spade make it look like a face, and the smoothed truck fenders resemble a cape. Casting the assemblage in bronze unified the surface. Smith characterized this work as "sweet," fondly referring to it as "shovel head."

Becca is simultaneously abstract and an embodiment of its subject. It creatively depicts the buoyant energy of Smith's daughter Rebecca, who was ten years old at the time it was made. *Becca*'s elements

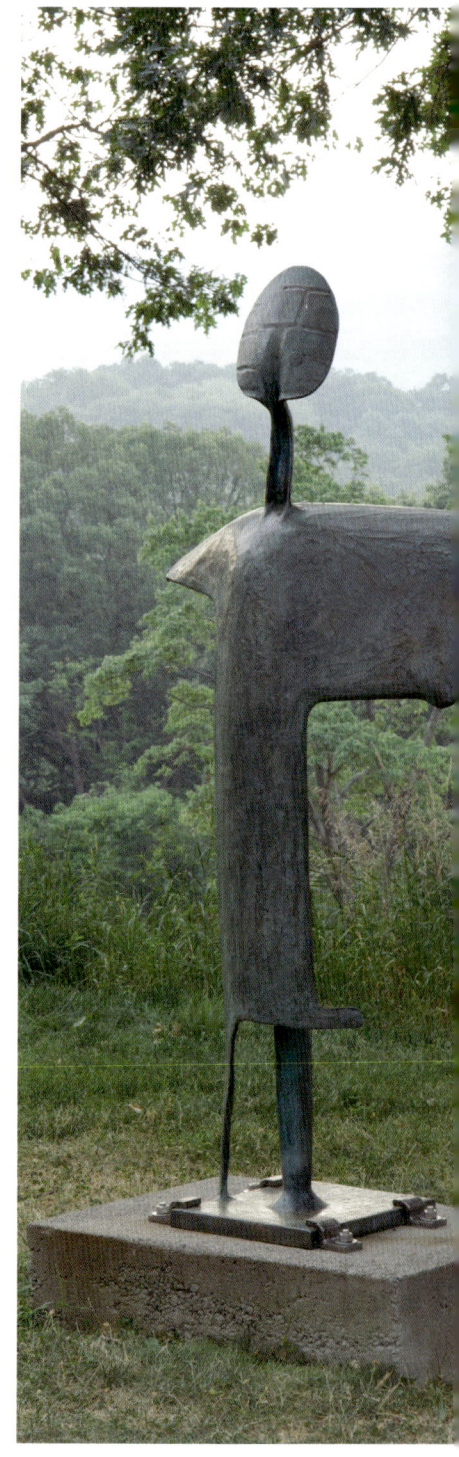

FROM LEFT: *Personage of May*, 1957; *Study in Arcs*, 1957

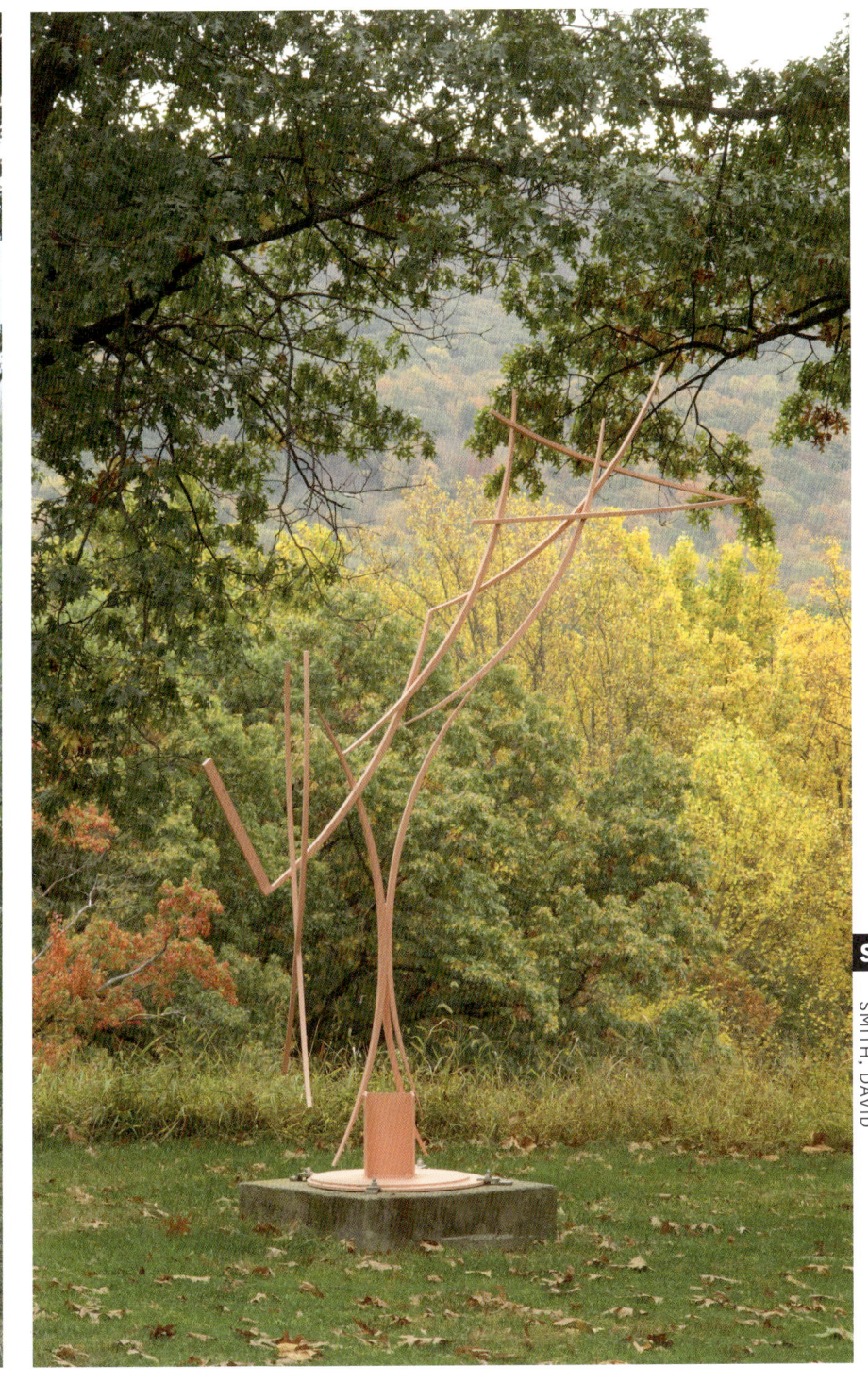

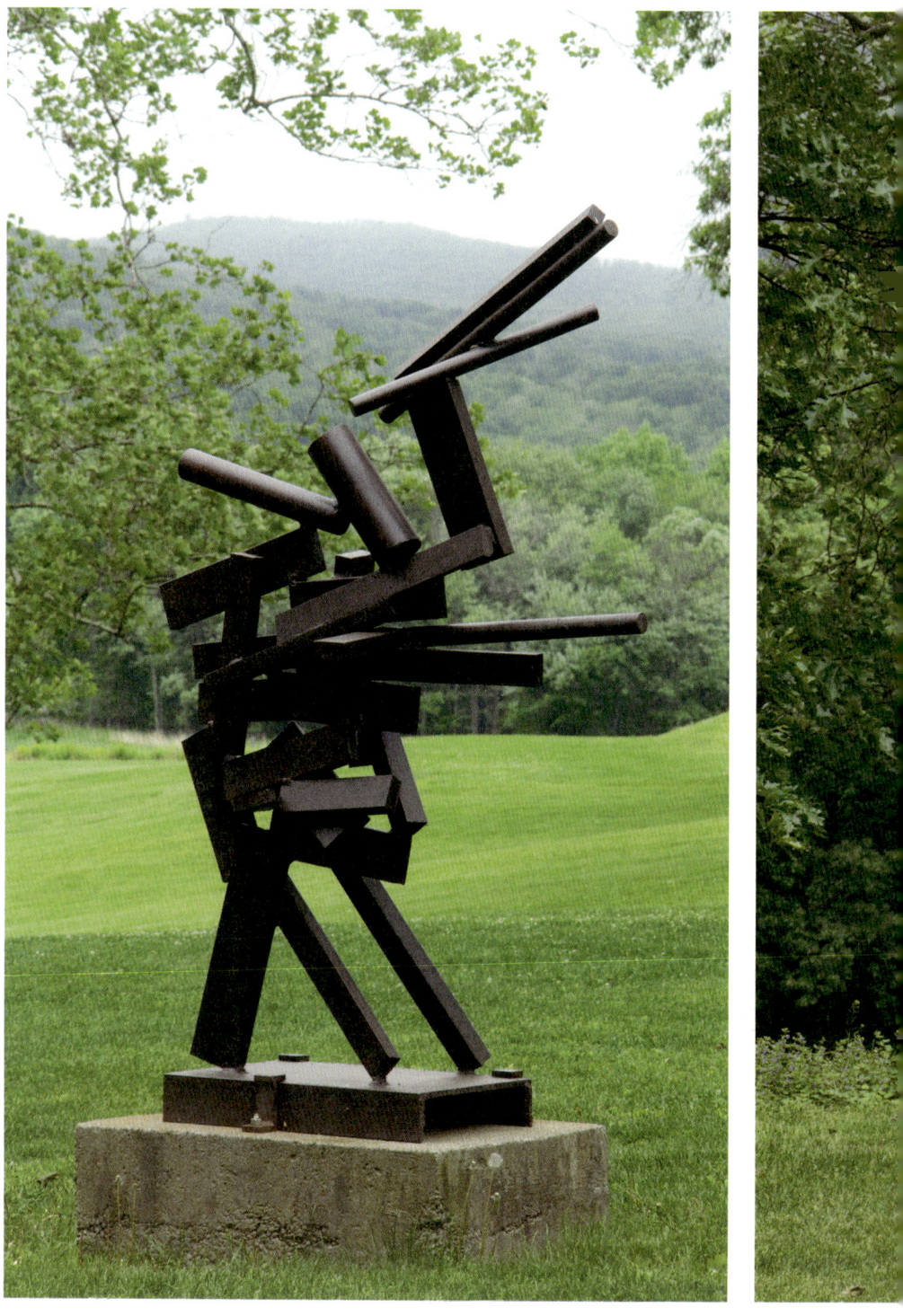

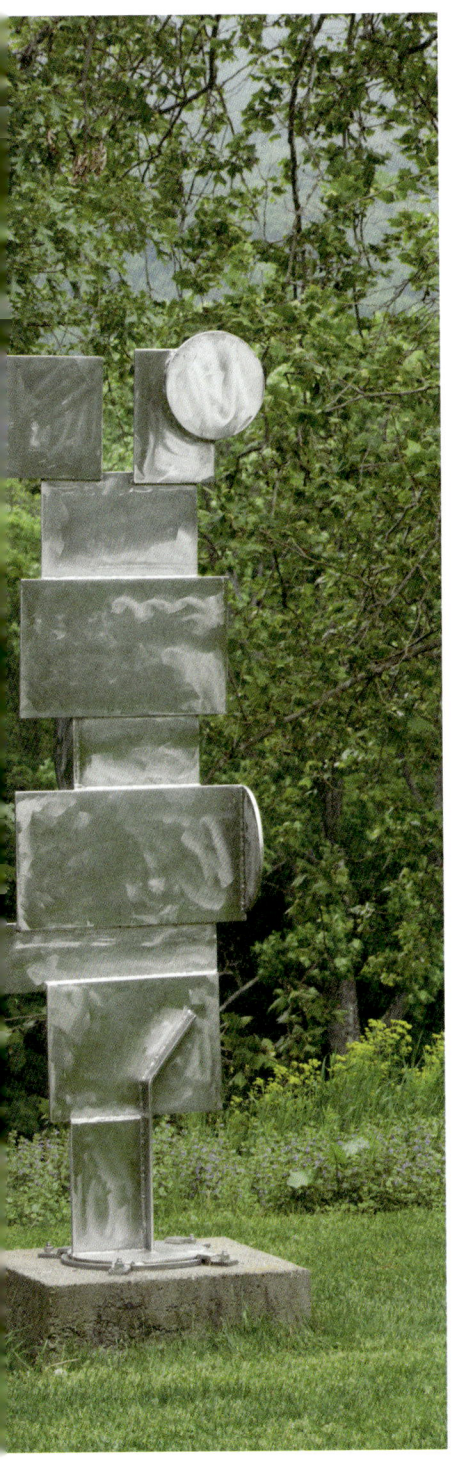

are welded together, a process in which pieces of steel are fused by being pressed together and heated with a blowtorch or other tool until reaching a melting temperature. Smith was considered a master of fine-art welding, and legions of artists have cited his influence on their work. The steel rods that compose this work are analogous to the thick brushstrokes of Abstract Expressionist paintings that other artists were creating in this era.

XI Books III Apples is constructed largely of pre-cut stainless steel pieces that Smith ordered from a Ryerson Steel mail-order catalogue then welded together. Its surface is etched into with a circular sander, which creates a brushstrokes effect—a series of arcs reflecting light to form a visual "painting" without applied color. Smith anticipated that the piece, when set outdoors, would reflect the world around it and change with the light and seasons.

In 1960, Smith noted that he preferred all of his stainless steel pieces to be viewed outdoors: "They are conceived for bright light, preferably the sun, to develop the illusion of surface and depth.... Stainless steel seems dead without light." Smith also recognized the extraordinary physical challenge of working with steel, whose "physical laws...do not permit the flow of realization as easily as most painting materials." Sculpture, he observed, "demand[s] more premeditation and conviction, [more] assurance...than when the same form is indicated by paint or line on the plane surface."

FROM LEFT: *Becca*, 1964; *XI Books III Apples*, 1959

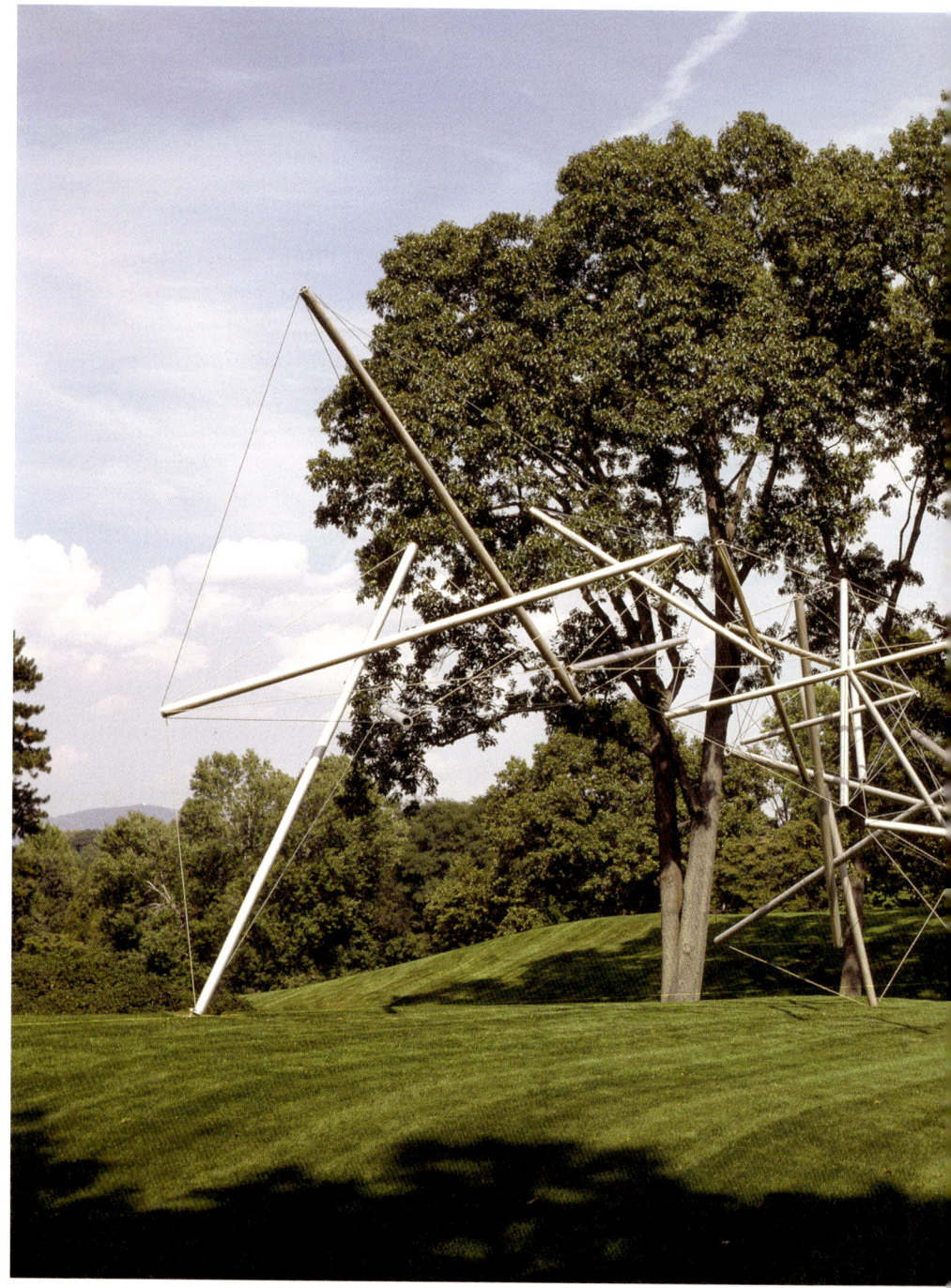

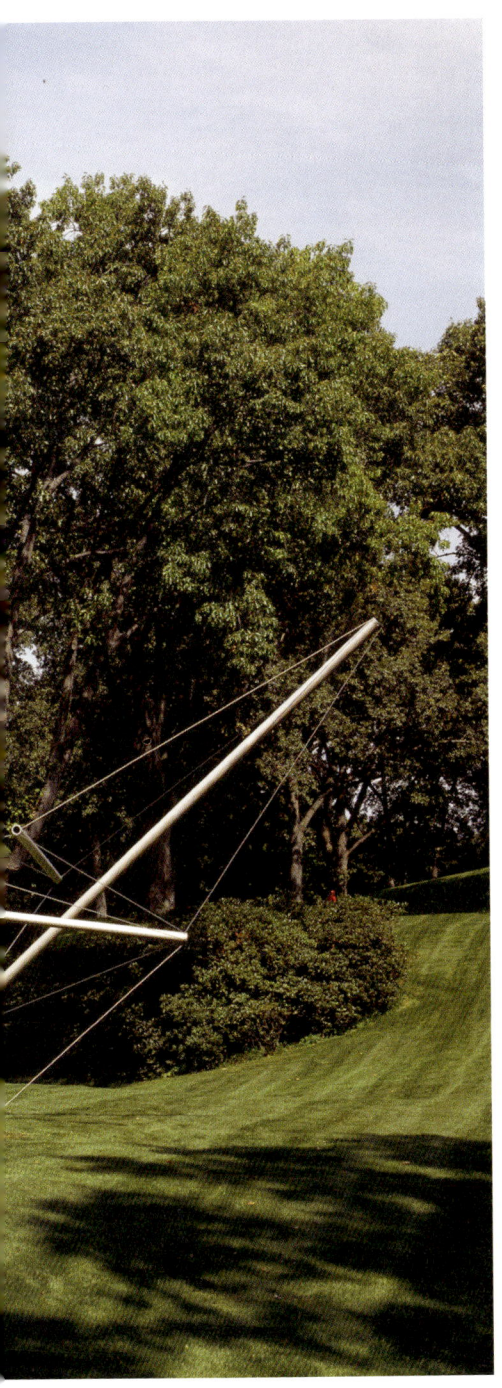

KENNETH SNELSON

AMERICAN, 1927–2016

FREE RIDE HOME, 1974
ALUMINUM AND STAINLESS STEEL
30 x 60 x 60'
GIFT OF THE RALPH E. OGDEN FOUNDATION

When conceiving of *Free Ride Home*, Kenneth Snelson first created a small maquette of metal tubes and knotted strings, envisioning what it would be like to walk under and through its silvery linear forms. "I began by thinking of a sculpture that would soar overhead," Snelson noted. "I started with a central core and then developed it in three directions with three arches. One of the arches began to take on a descending fast plunge. It reminded me of the shape of a bucking horse. So, *Free Ride Home*, the name of a race horse, became the name of the sculpture."

Touching the ground at just three points, the creatively engineered sculpture is fashioned from a network of stainless steel cables knotted to aluminum tubes. Installing at Storm King in the spring of 1975, a crew of just four raised the entire structure in under an hour. *Free Ride Home* is a prime example of Snelson's play with organic forms constrained by internal structural tension, a push-pull system he invented in 1948. In this system, inspired by anatomy, cables function like muscles and the aluminum tubes like bones.

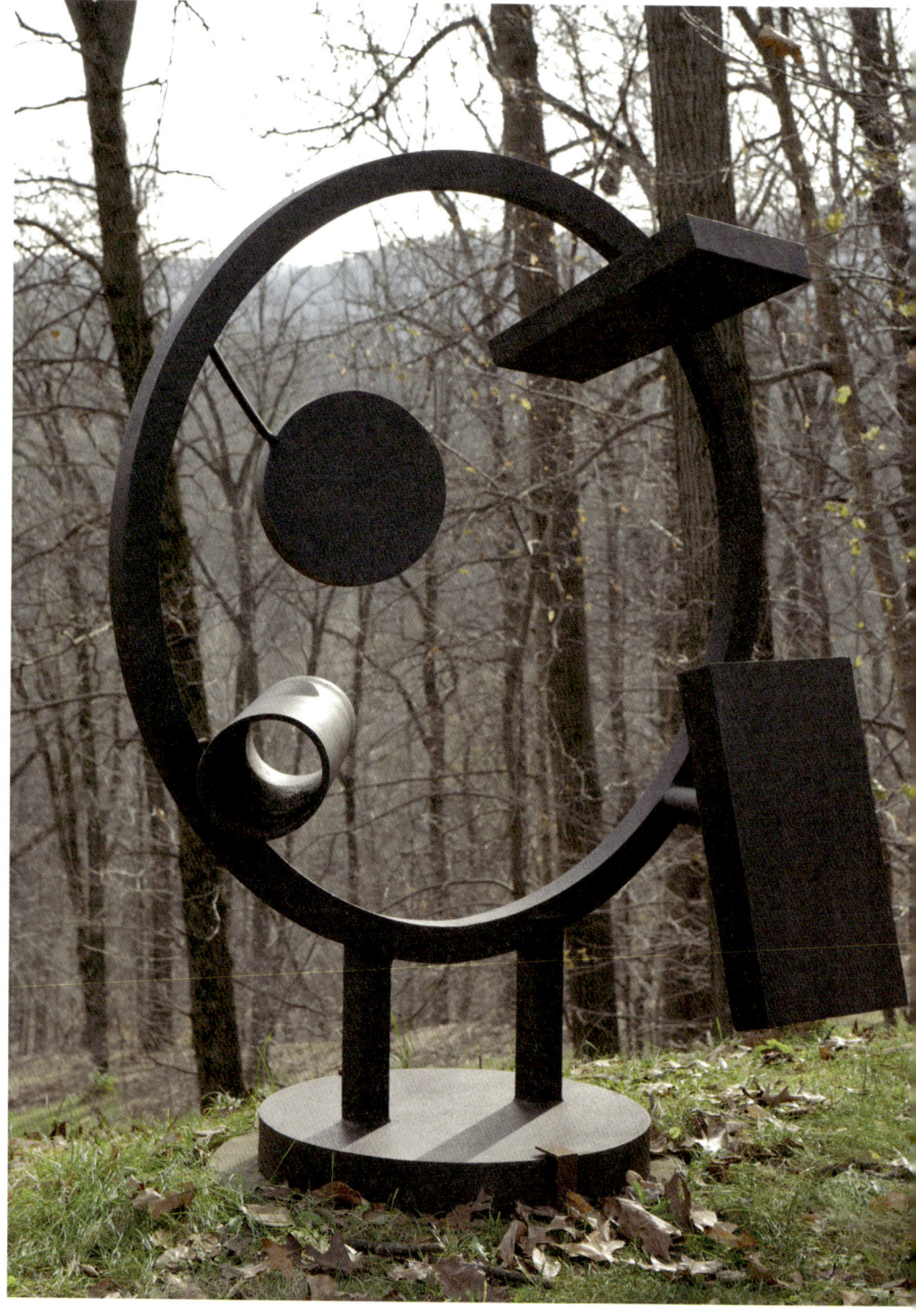

RICHARD STANKIEWICZ

AMERICAN, 1922–1983

SELECTED WORK:
1979-4, 1979
STEEL
60 x 46 x 36"
GIFT OF H. PETER STERN

The spare, round frame of 1979-4, with a few objects affixed to it, typifies late work by Richard Stankiewicz. Originally trained in engineering, Stankiewicz established his reputation in the 1950s as a master of witty junk assemblages. By 1969, however, he was using newly fabricated industrial elements such as cylinders and I-beams to fashion comparatively restrained abstractions. *Australia No. 9,* 1969, another work by Stankiewicz in Storm King's collection, marks this turning point in his career. The sculpture is a result of a three-month visit to Australia, during which he had an opportunity to create work in a steel plant in Sydney. The experience provided Stankiewicz with an understanding of industrial steel manufacturing and new welding techniques, which profoundly impacted his practice. The artistic process was paramount for Stankiewicz, who once commented, "It isn't the thing; it's making the thing. Because in making the thing you are making yourself, and after you have made it you are a little bit changed and that's the product, and the thing, it can go into the world."

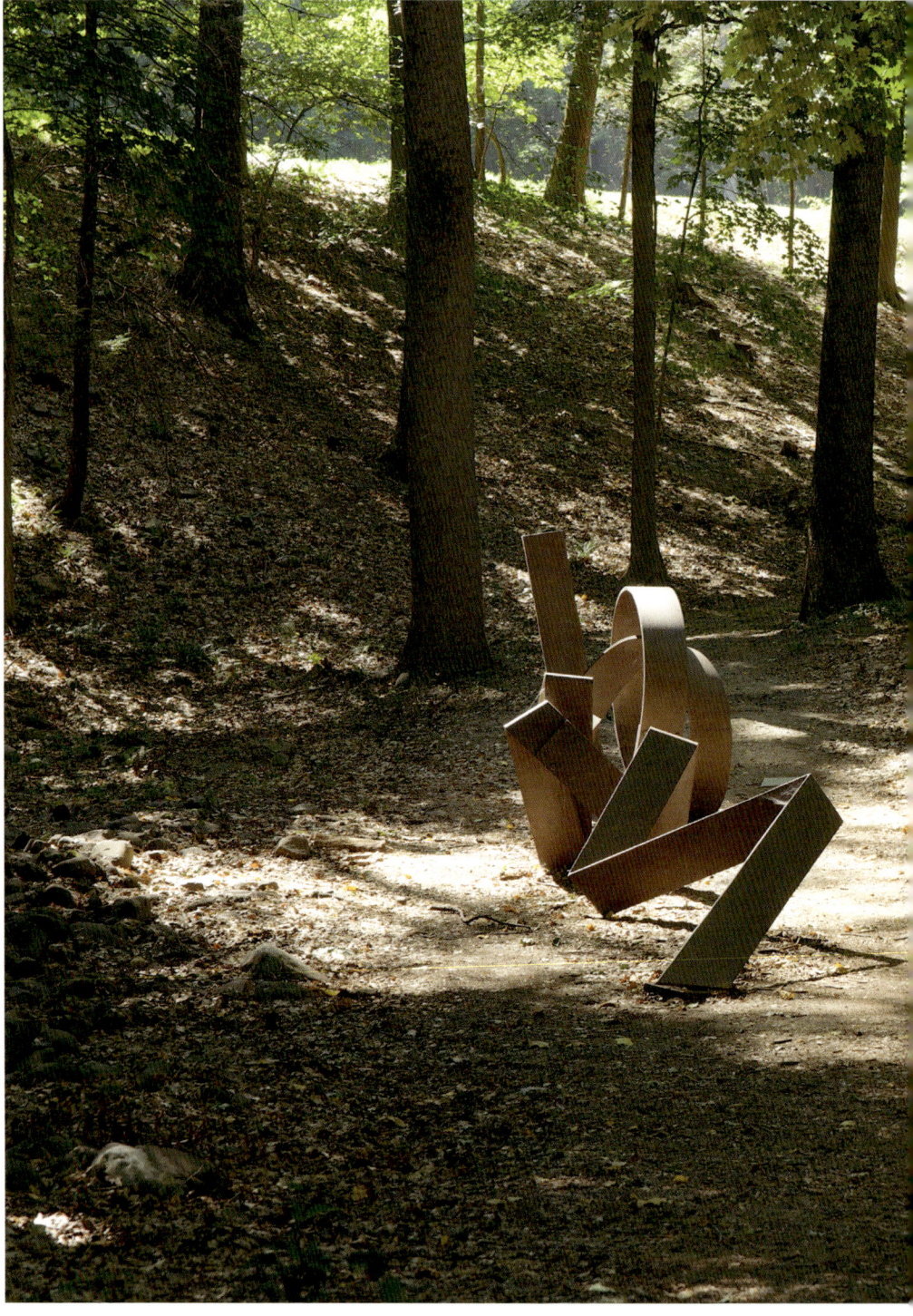

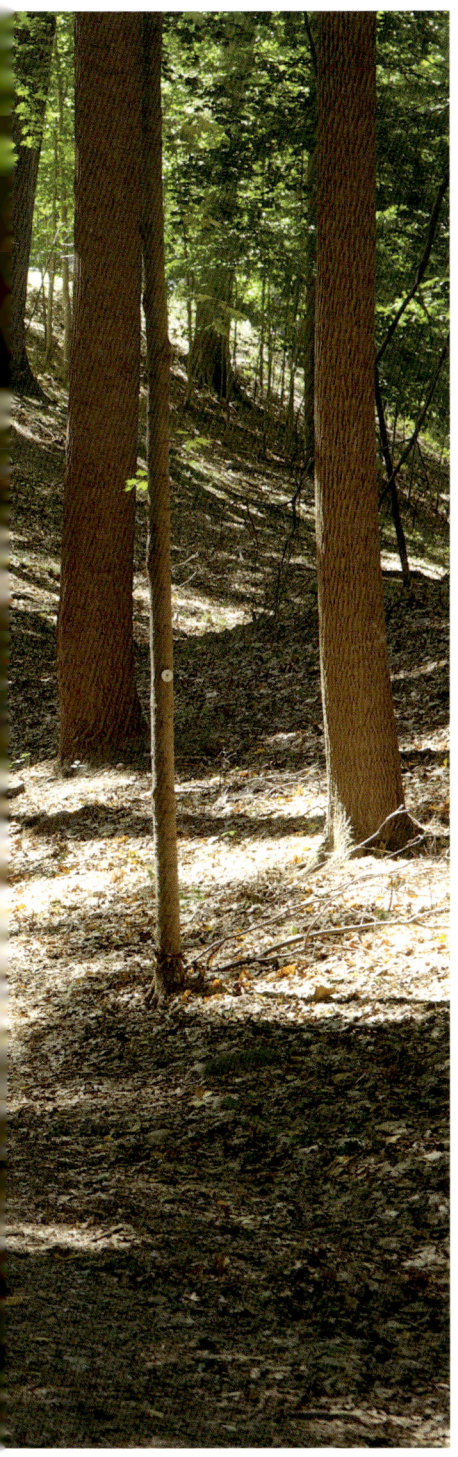

DAVID STOLTZ

AMERICAN, BORN 1943

SELECTED WORK:
DAY GAME, 1972
STEEL
6' 7" x 28' 3½" x 69½"
GIFT OF THE RALPH E. OGDEN FOUNDATION

Day Game, one in a series of similar works by David Stoltz, slithers, loops, and rises from the ground, its form suggesting an animated quality, as if the steel were electrified by a charge of dynamic energy. Its calligraphic qualities reflect Stoltz's training as a graphic artist. Stoltz worked in Bennington, Vermont, where a younger generation of sculptors had gravitated in the late 1960s and early 1970s. During this period Stoltz produced large steel sculptures, three of which are in Storm King's collection: *Day Game*, *River Run*, 1972, and the more ponderous *Owo*, 1972, which is composed of large rolled and bent steel plates. *Day Game* was loosely inspired by Anthony Caro's curvilinear works, such as *Reel*, 1964, which is also at Storm King.

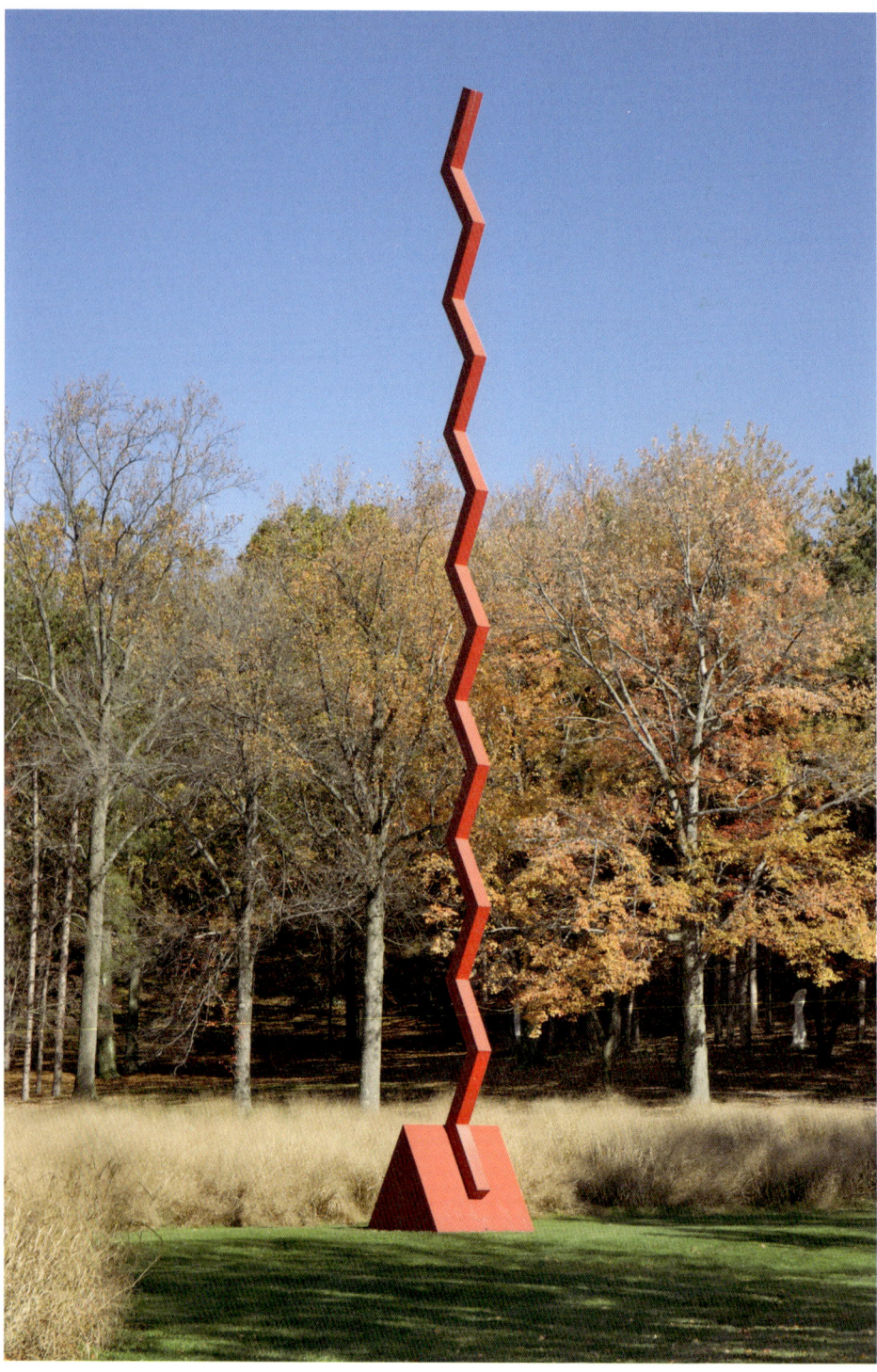

TAL STREETER

AMERICAN, 1934–2014

ENDLESS COLUMN, 1968
PAINTED STEEL
69' 4" x 7' 10" x 7' 6"
PURCHASED WITH THE AID OF FUNDS FROM THE NATIONAL ENDOWMENT
FOR THE ARTS AND GIFT OF THE RALPH E. OGDEN FOUNDATION

Reaching a height of nearly seventy feet, *Endless Column* is taller than any other work at Storm King. Tal Streeter called it "a kind of drawing in space which will take your eyes in a staccato movement to the top and on into the sky." Two maquettes helped him to work out its engineering. He accentuated the linear, lightning-like form with a coating of bright red paint. *Endless Column* marks a pivotal moment in Streeter's career, as his intense interest in the act of looking upward led him to Japan to study kite making. His travels soon extended throughout Asia, followed by publications and teaching on the creation and significance of kites. The title is a direct homage to Constantin Brancusi's *Endless Column*, 1937, installed in Târgu Jiu, Romania.

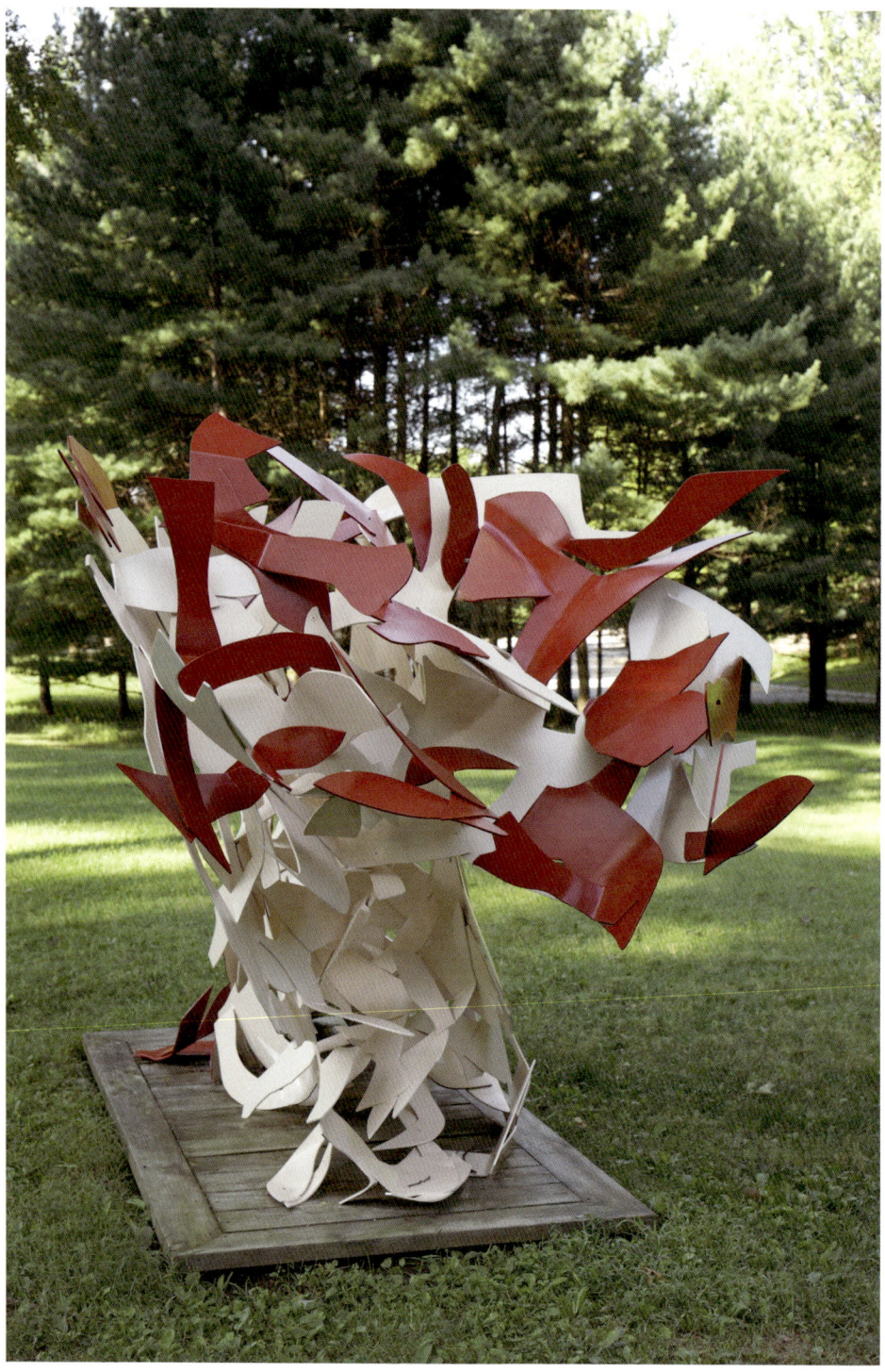

GEORGE SUGARMAN

AMERICAN, 1912–1999

ONE, 1975–77
PAINTED ALUMINUM
6'6" x 8'8" x 6'
PURCHASED WITH THE AID OF FUNDS FROM THE NATIONAL ENDOWMENT
FOR THE ARTS AND GIFT OF THE RALPH E. OGDEN FOUNDATION

Undulating, curling, and twisting, the paper-thin forms of *One* enact a gravity-defying dance in aluminum. The elaborate shapes, both delicate and dense, recall the Baroque art that impressed George Sugarman during his first travels in Europe. Later, reflecting on the period during which he made *One*, Sugarman noted, "All through the '60s and '70s I had no label. I wasn't Pop. I wasn't Minimal. And 'Maximal' was a word that wasn't used. Yet I *was* a Maximalist. I wanted to put *everything* in my work, even the kitchen sink."

Inspired in part by the flat, unmodulated color used by Henri Matisse and Stuart Davis, Sugarman often painted his cut-out forms in bright colors. In *One*, a dark red infiltrates the lace-like white. "In my sculpture, the color is as important as form and space. It is used to articulate the sculpture as much as form articulates the sculpture in space." Like many of his contemporaries, Sugarman also appreciated jazz, which taught him about rhythm, pacing, and form.

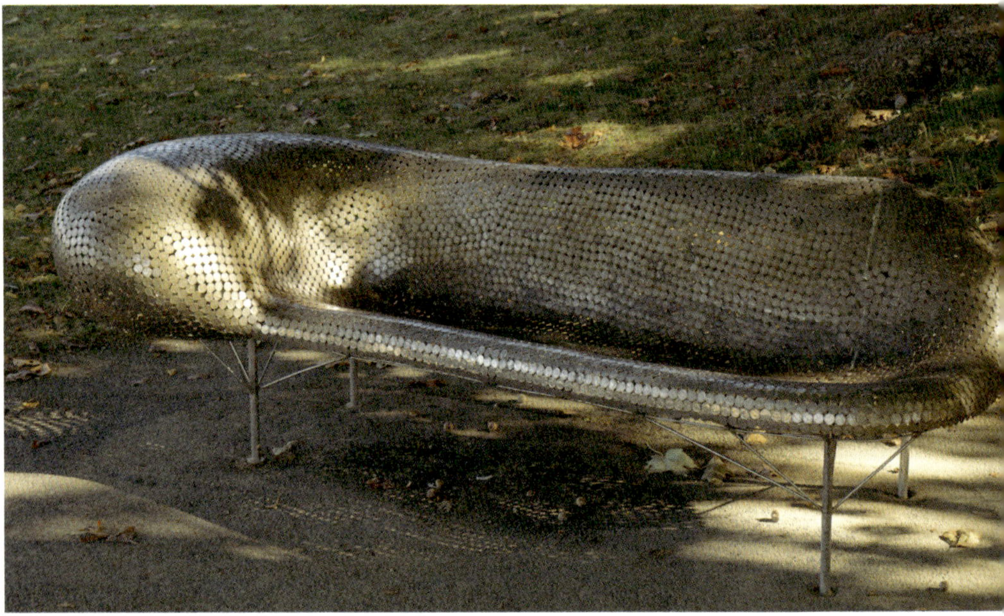

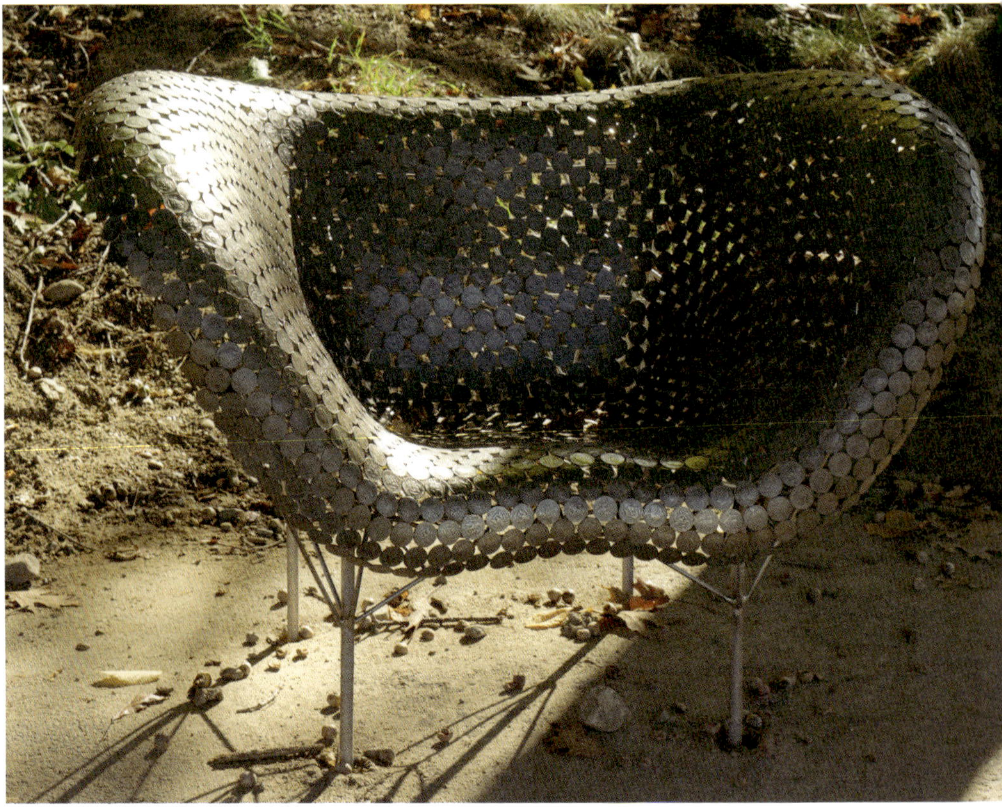

JOHNNY SWING

AMERICAN, BORN 1961

NICKEL COUCH, 2001
WELDED NICKEL COINS
30" x 7' 6" x 42"
GIFT OF THE RALPH E. OGDEN FOUNDATION AND
MARGARET T. MORRIS FOUNDATION

BUTTERFLY CHAIR, 2002
WELDED HALF-DOLLAR COINS
33 x 48 x 34"
GIFT OF THE RALPH E. OGDEN FOUNDATION AND
MARGARET T. MORRIS FOUNDATION

Johnny Swing's *Butterfly Chair* and *Nickel Couch* straddle the ever-changing boundaries that separate art from everyday life. *Butterfly Chair*, named for its symmetrical spread-wing form, envelops the sitter and recalls a traditional wing chair. The sinuous form, made with 1,500 half-dollar coins, is supported by a stainless steel tubular frame. Before a single coin was welded, Swing spent months crafting the biomorphic shapes in polyester resin to ensure that people could sit comfortably in these unconventional seats. It took him more than two hundred hours to weld the *Nickel Couch*'s 6,400 nickels. As part of the design process, sections of welded nickels were draped on top of the mold and pulled off when the metal cooled.

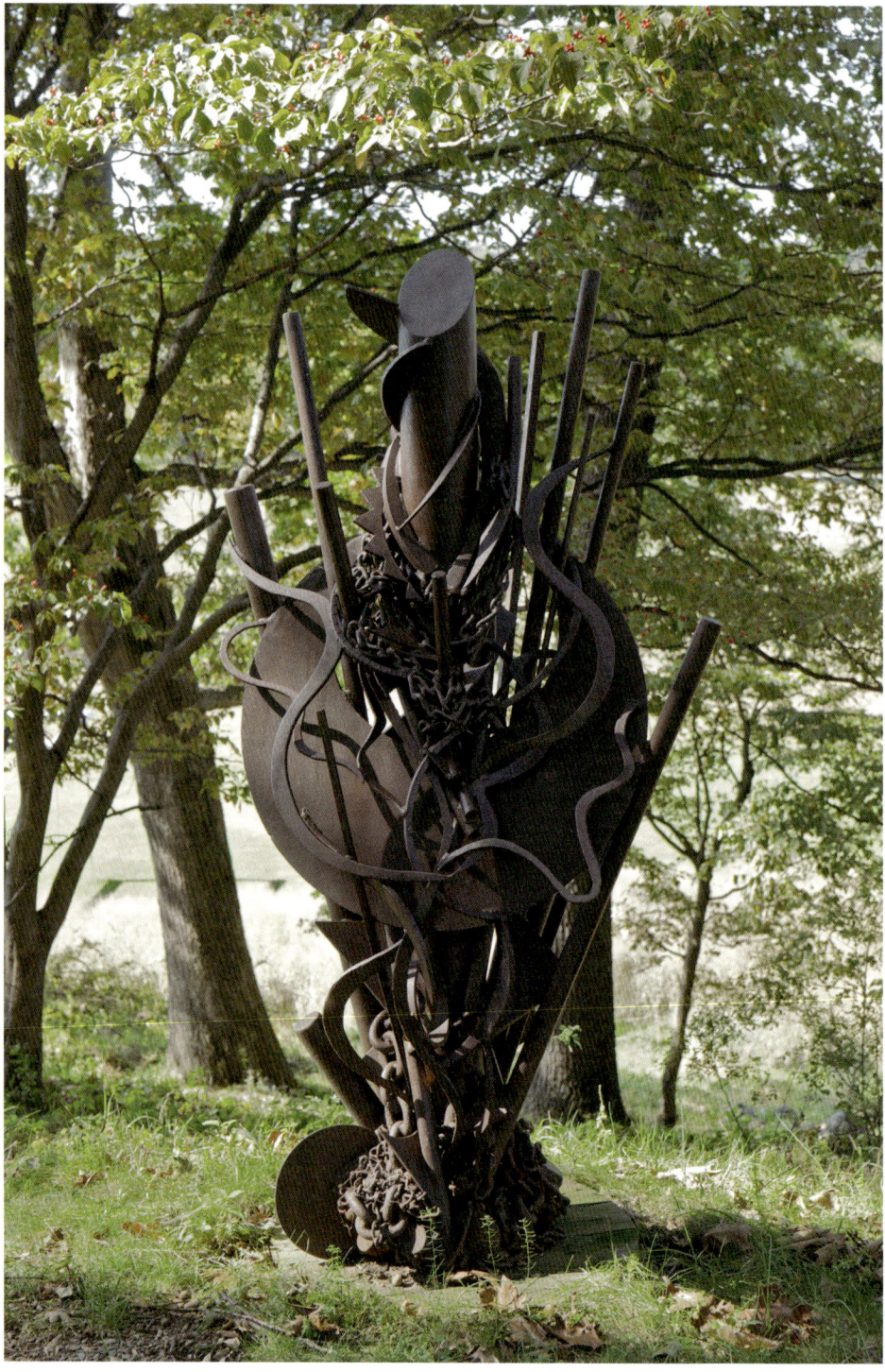

LEE TRIBE

BRITISH, BORN 1945

KING, 1986
STEEL
6' x 37" x 23"
JOSEPH H. HAZEN FOUNDATION PURCHASE FUND

Lee Tribe constructed *King*—a human-scale welded steel assemblage—
without referring to drawings or preconceived ideas for the sculpture,
but rather by working directly and spontaneously with the materials available in his studio. He began with the central vertical form, which struck
him, he noted, as suggesting the "presence of a figure rising up, standing
proud." This evocation persisted, he added, as "the sculpture took on a
regal feeling which grew stronger and stronger, hence the name *King*."
Referring to the effect of his dense layering of lines, shapes, and chains
onto the central core form, Tribe further remarked, "The process of
making exists clearly and is at one with the image of the completed sculpture." Steel has been integral to his life since his teenage years as a steel-
worker on the London docks. His early work was highly influenced
by this industrial experience and helped him to explore the language and
possibilities of non-representational sculpture.

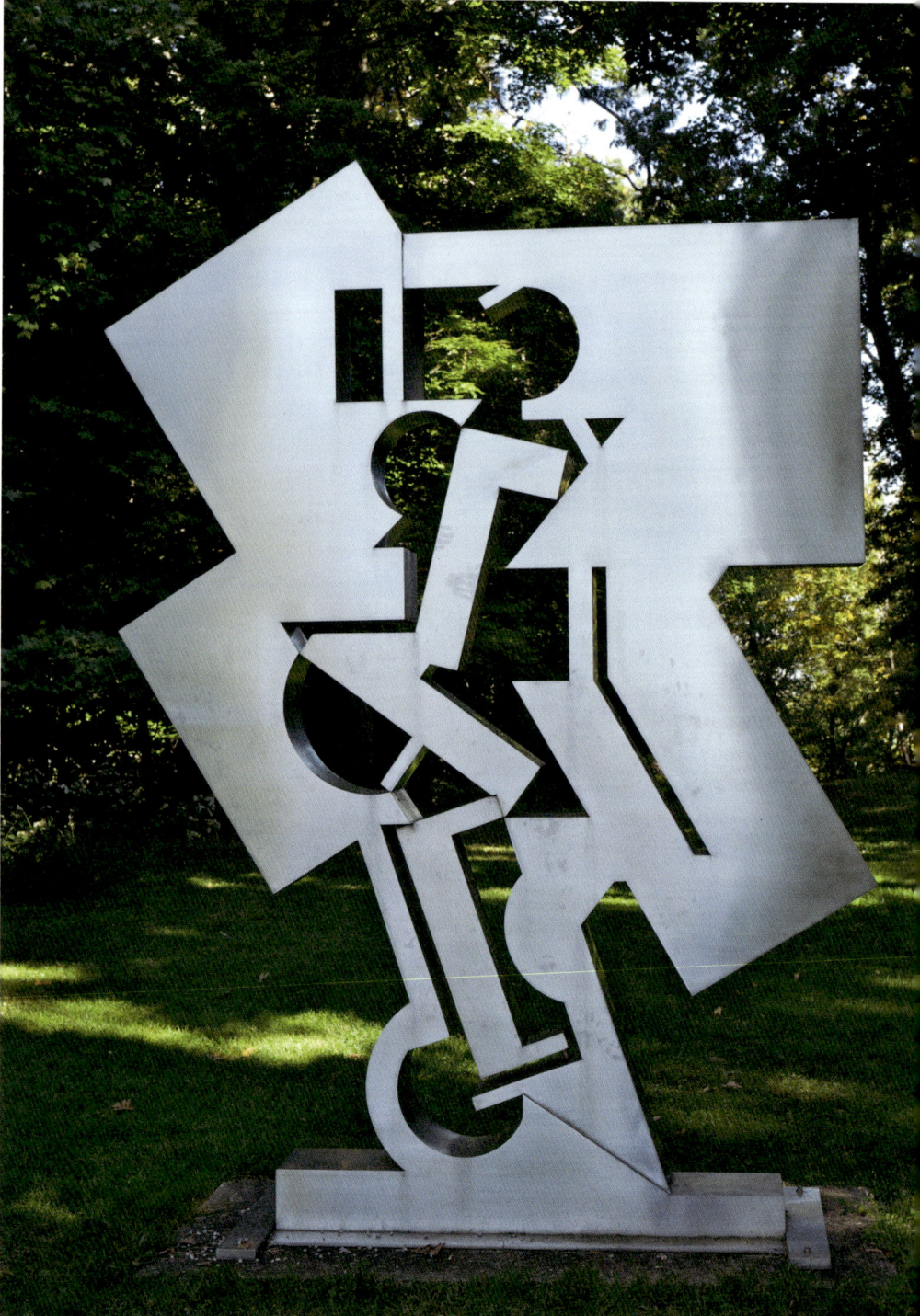

ERNEST TROVA

AMERICAN, 1927–2009

GOX #4, 1975
STAINLESS STEEL
9' x 6' 6" x 28"
PURCHASED WITH THE AID OF FUNDS FROM THE NATIONAL ENDOWMENT
FOR THE ARTS AND GIFT OF THE RALPH E. OGDEN FOUNDATION

The brushed stainless steel surface of Ernest Trova's *Gox #4* shines on a bright day. Upon closer viewing, the negative space in the large cutout abstraction seems to hint at the shape of a figure. A self-taught artist, Trova started his career as a window designer at the age of seventeen. His earliest paintings were inspired by Willem de Kooning and the poet Ezra Pound, and were followed by collages and junk assemblages. *Gox #4* is one in a series of works whose titles stand for "GeOmetric eXercise." Trova is best known for his iconic 1960s *Falling Man* series, featuring anti-heroic figures presented in a variety of media.

T

TROVA, ERNEST

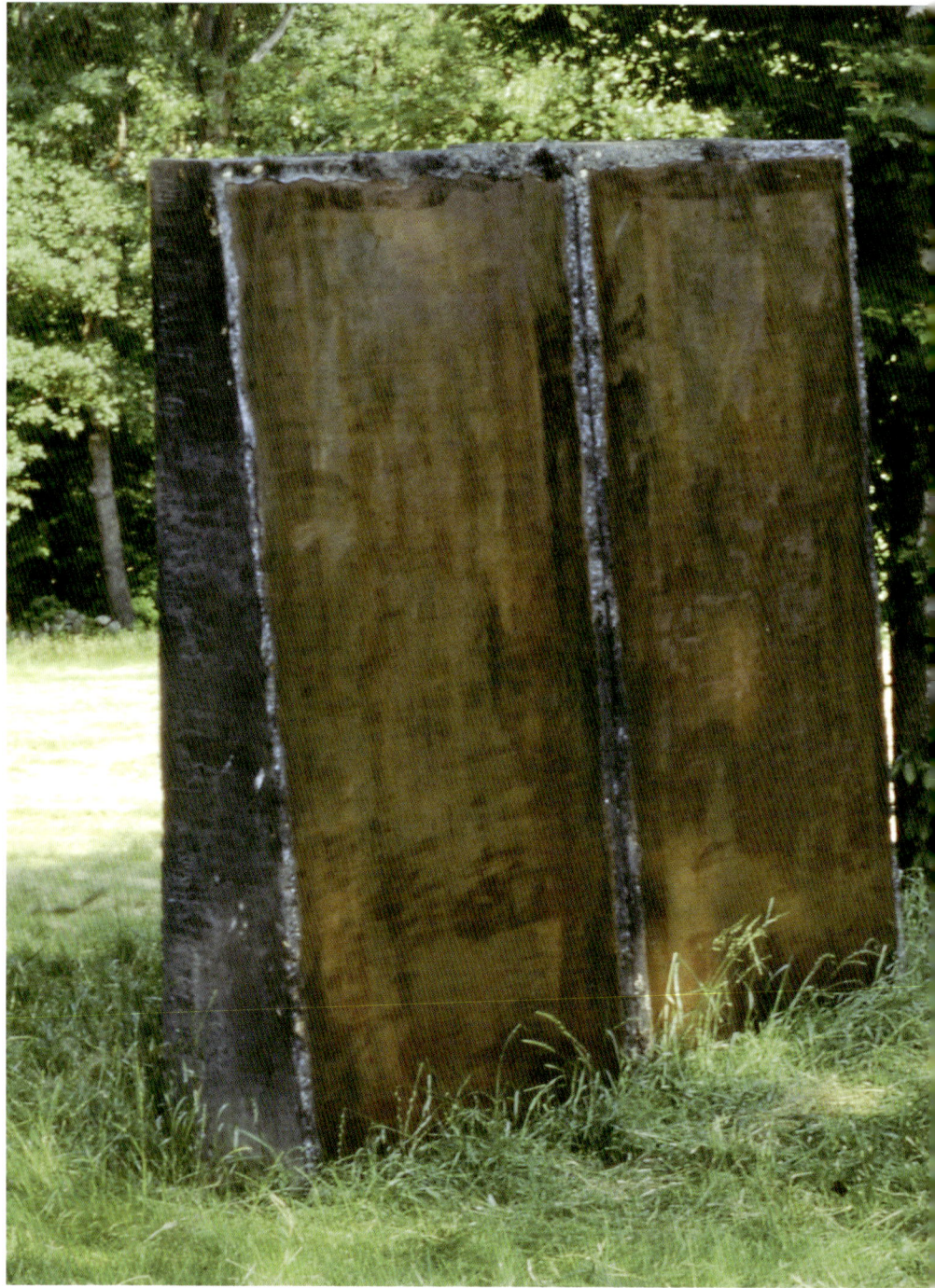

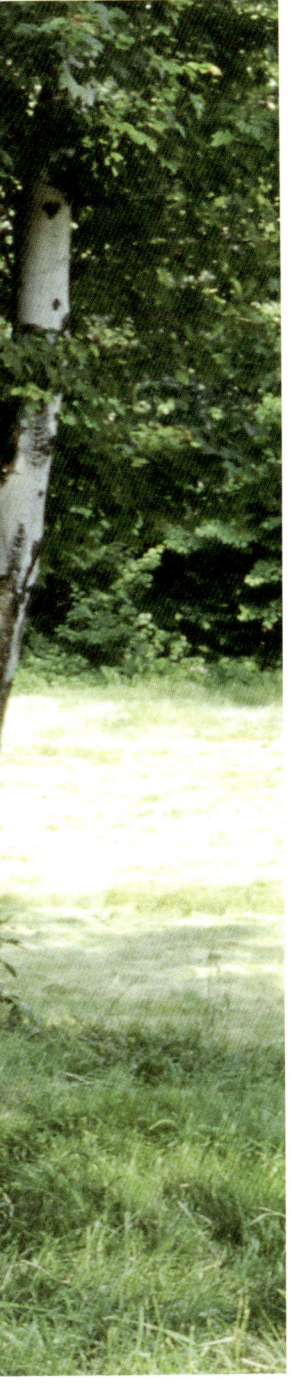

MIA WESTERLUND ROOSEN

AMERICAN, BORN 1942

SELECTED WORK:
MURO SERIES X, 1979
PIGMENTED CONCRETE AND STEEL
10'1" x 10'2" x 48½"
PURCHASED WITH THE AID OF FUNDS FROM
THE NATIONAL ENDOWMENT FOR THE ARTS AND
GIFT OF THE RALPH E. OGDEN FOUNDATION

Muro Series X, commissioned by and created at Storm King, is one in a series of Mia Westerlund Roosen's monumental wall-like pieces from the 1970s. The striking works were made by pouring concrete (and sometimes asphalt) to form thin horizontal slabs that when stood up become monolithic vertical surfaces. Trowel marks preserved in the concrete provide variation, and Storm King's example incorporates an oxidized steel plate at the center that enhances the rough, weathered look.

Westerlund Roosen often employs simple geometric shapes. Working against trends toward strict geometry in the art of the 1970s, however, she imbued her works with an irregular sensuality and suggestive biomorphic power. "[Minimalists] weren't interested in giving life to an object; I am," she noted. "They did not want to show the artist's hand. ... I felt perfectly free to take one of their hard-edged steel plates and fuzz up all the edges in my own feminine way to see what would happen."

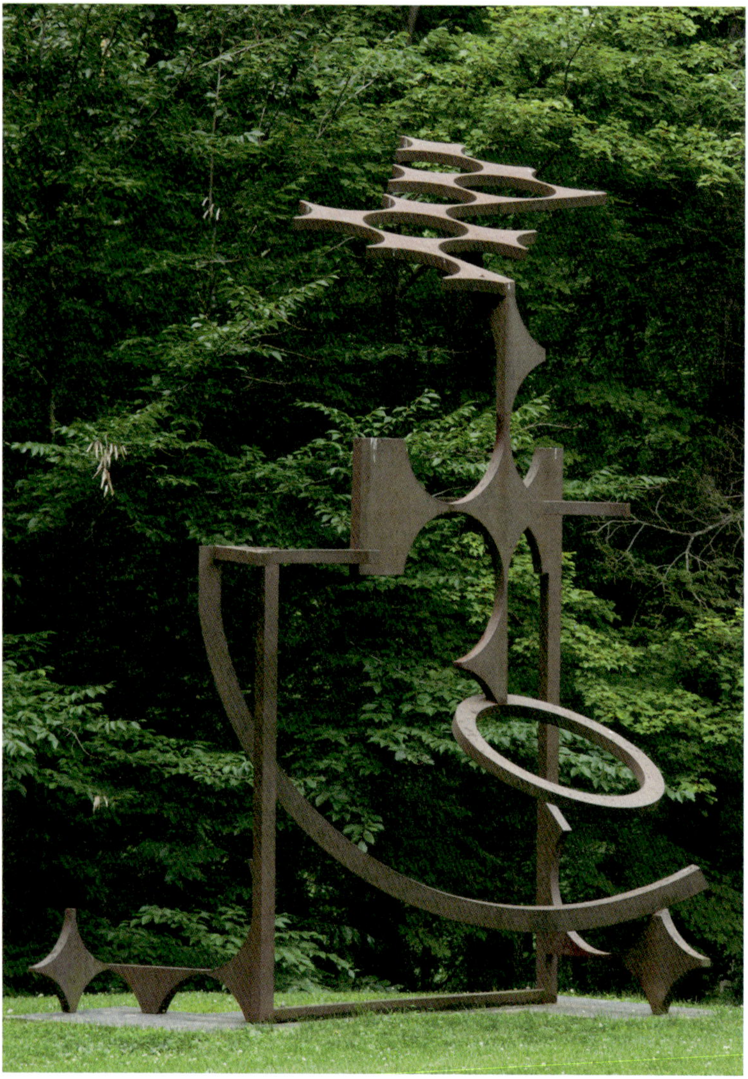

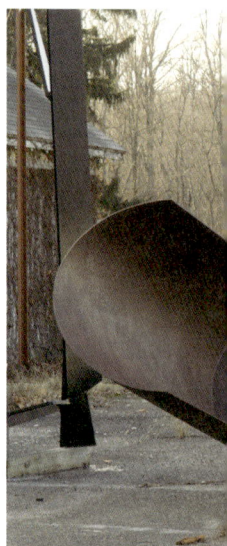

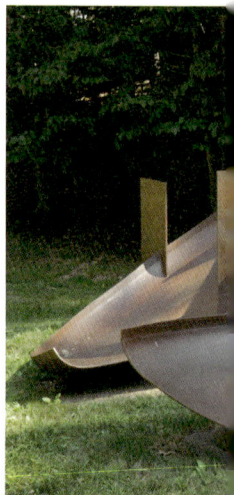

CLOCKWISE FROM LEFT: *Kumo*, 1971; *Shogun*, 1968; *Birth of Aphrodite*, 1977–78

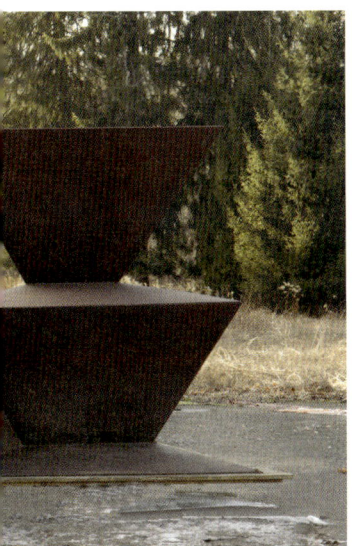

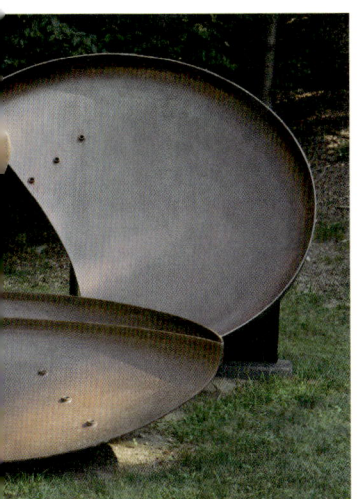

ISAAC WITKIN

AMERICAN, BORN SOUTH AFRICA, 1936–2006

SHOGUN, 1968
WEATHERING STEEL
6' 3" x 11' x 9' 5"
GIFT OF THE RALPH E. OGDEN FOUNDATION

KUMO, 1971
WEATHERING STEEL
16' 4" x 13' 4" x 12' 2"
GIFT OF THE RALPH E. OGDEN FOUNDATION

BIRTH OF APHRODITE, 1977–78
STEEL
6' 10" x 15" x 12"
PURCHASED WITH THE AID OF FUNDS FROM THE
NATIONAL ENDOWMENT FOR THE ARTS AND GIFT OF
THE RALPH E. OGDEN FOUNDATION

Isaac Witkin's energetic, complex works demand to be seen from every angle if the viewer is to grasp the relationship between their parts. As the artist once commented, "I am basically a Baroque sculptor, in the sense that I avoid any strict adherence to the plane and to symmetrical layout. I aim to establish a freedom to move in multiaxial space in a way that will draw the spectator in and around the sculpture to experience different aspects of an evolving dynamic." Material choice is essential to achieving this effect; as Witkin observed, "Steel was the key to spatial freedom. It helped me to get away from the monolith and from making sculpture with a spine."

The open, linear design of *Kumo*, Japanese for "cloud," exemplifies this freedom in its graceful, floating curved forms. *Birth of Aphrodite* evokes mythic and poetic associations. Composed of pan-like forms cut from acid tanks, its watery trails of rust allude to the goddess's origins in the sea. The changing perspectives encountered in viewing *Shogun*—so named, Witkin said, for "its seated, brooding, warrior-like confrontation, while the zigzag shapes resemble a samurai helmet"—exemplify his multiaxial orientation.

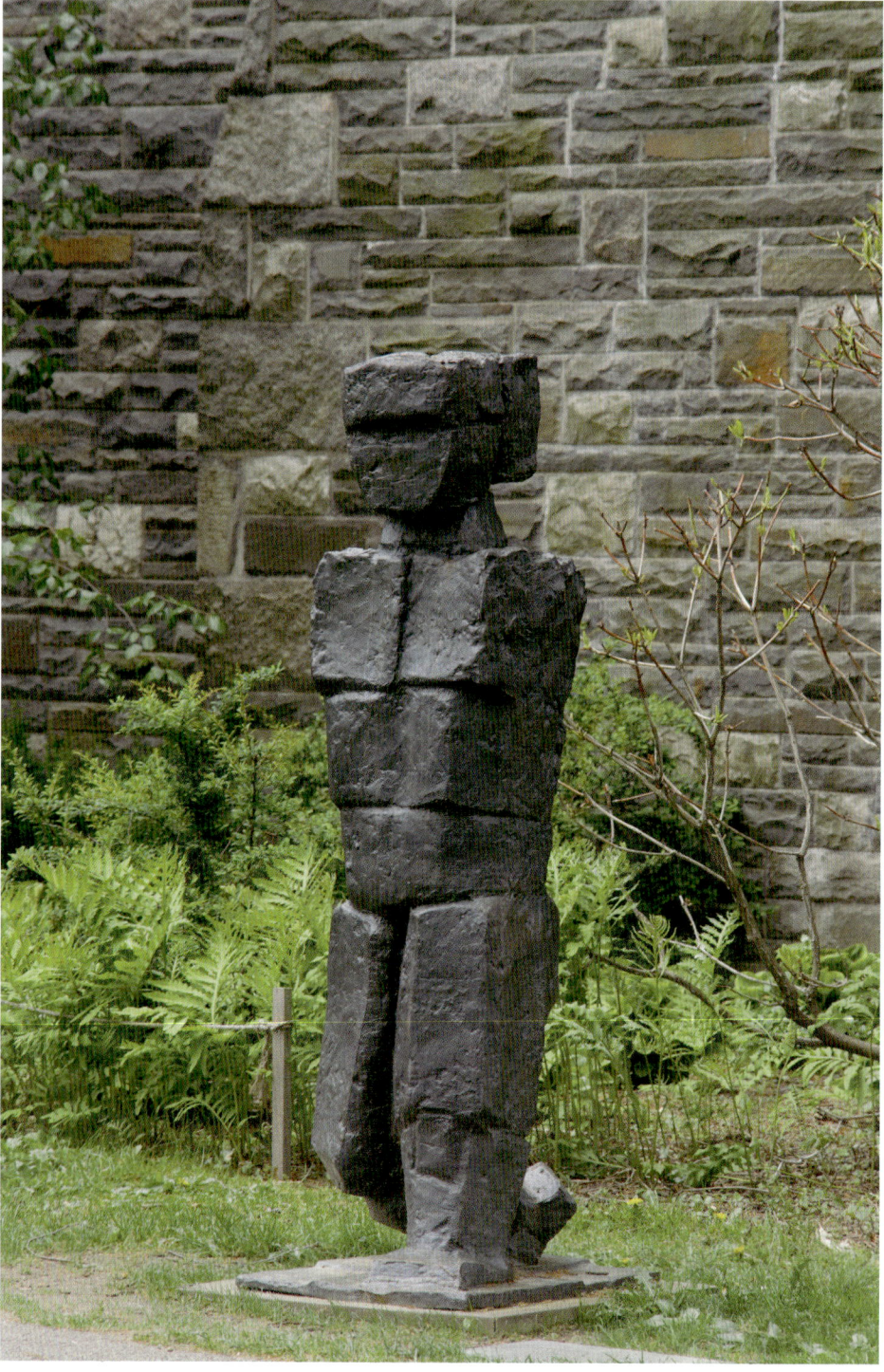

FRITZ WOTRUBA

AUSTRIAN, 1907–1975

MAN WALKING, 1952
BRONZE
59 1/8 x 17 3/4 x 24"
GIFT OF THE RALPH E. OGDEN FOUNDATION

In 1945 Fritz Wotruba returned to his war-ravished native city of Vienna, having fled to Switzerland during World War II. Countering the uncertainty of the time, he emphasized clarity and uncompromising rigor, the need for increasing concentration, radicalization, and avoidance of beauty. He also worked to reclaim the figure for art, following more than two decades when figurative realism was manipulated to support fascist and Nazi ideals. "The human figure, now as much as ever," he stated in 1959, "remains for me the starting point of my work; it stands at the beginning and will stand at the end." Wotruba progressed from figurative cubic structures, such as *Man Walking*, which strides confidently despite the blocky mass in which it is encased, to slender columnar figures and, by the 1960s, to vertical constructions. Throughout his career Wotruba maintained deep ties with artists, architects, composers, and philosophers—often acting as a nexus for artistic and intellectual communities. Among his pupils was Josef Pillhofer. Works by both artists were acquired by co-founder Ralph E. Ogden early on in Storm King's history.

WOTRUBA, FRITZ

W

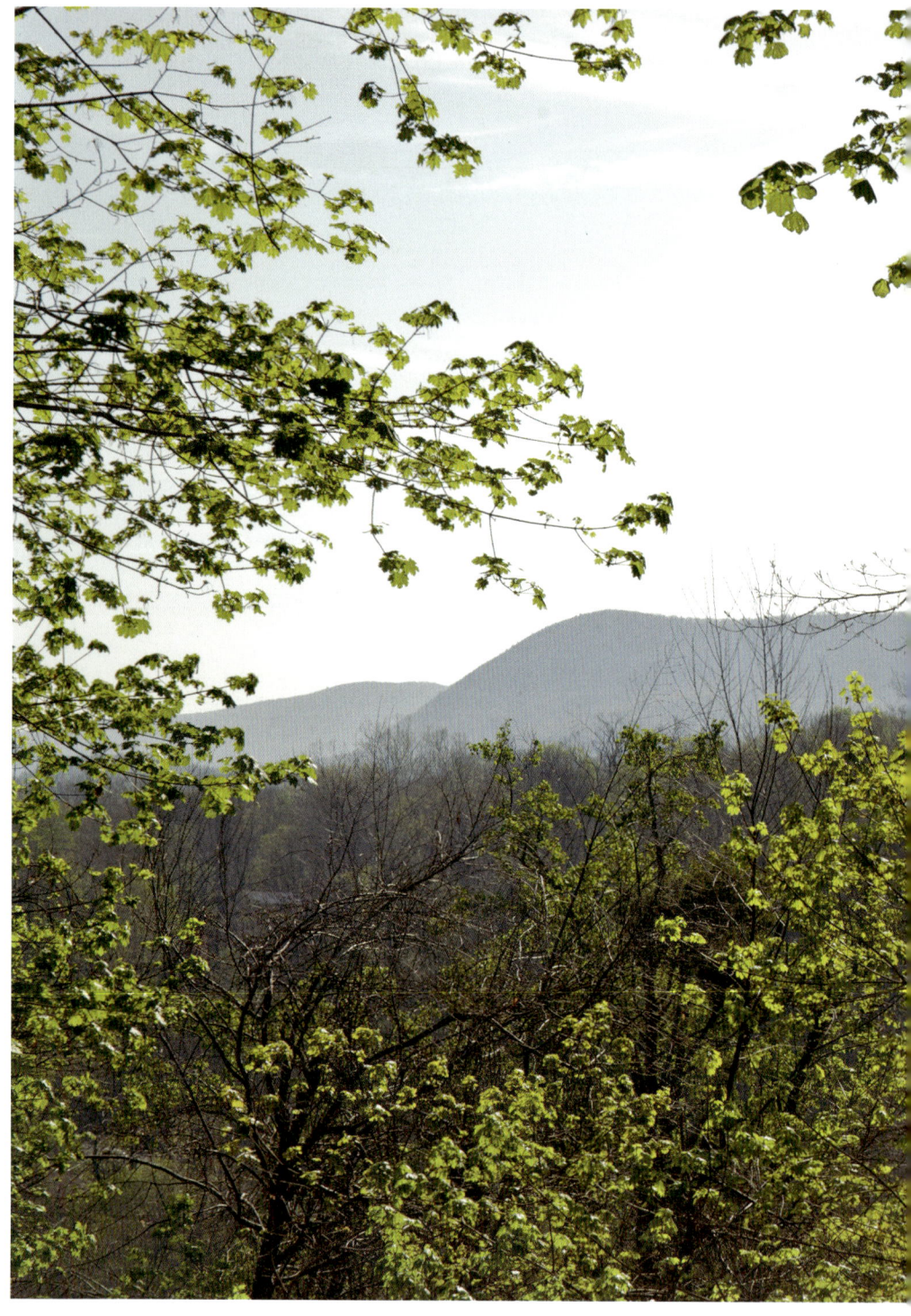

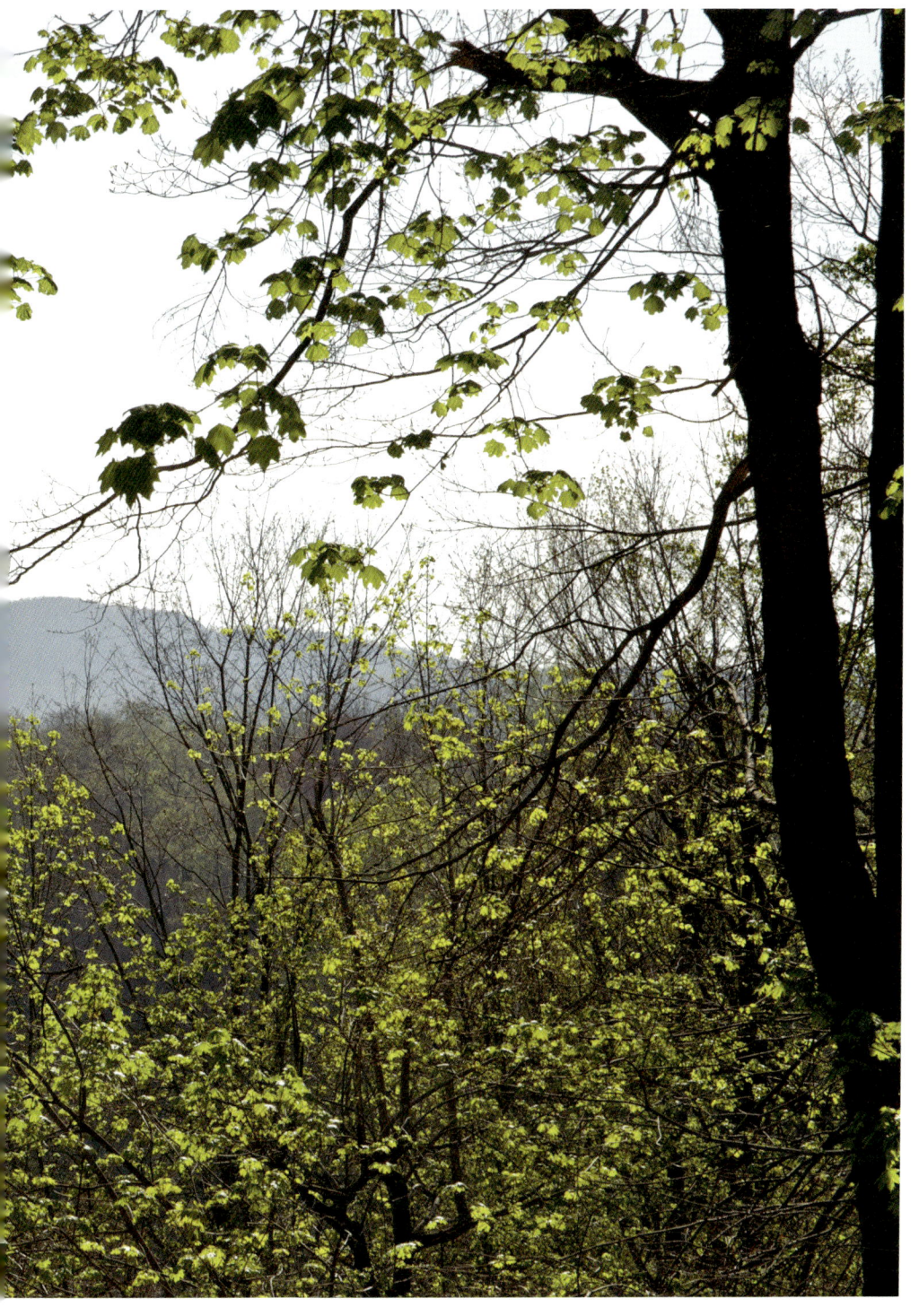